A VISUAL HISTORY OF COOKERY

black dog
publishing
london uk

• INTRODUCTION •

• FRANCE •

• ENGLAND •

• ITALY •

• SPAIN •

• AMERICA •

• INDEX, CREDITS AND ACKNOWLEDGEMENTS •

· INTRODUCTION ·

Opposite: A detail of an illustration of a Medieval French banquet.

Right: An early twentieth century Italian food advertisement.

A *Visual History of Cookery* seeks to draw together the seemingly disparate, but often subtly connected, gastronomic histories of five major epicurean cultures: the richly historical developments and traditions of French eating; the globally influenced but locally peculiar tastes of England and the United States; and the regional delectations of Spain and Italy. Foregoing attempts at encyclopaedic content *à la* the scholarly and thorough *Oxford Companions* or the seminal *Larousse Gastronomic*, interest here is found in a particular compilation of material, with *A Visual History of Cookery* being assembled to allow the reader to view these culinary histories in conjunction with, rather than as wholly distinct from, each other. Trans-border themes are found within these narratives, whether those be in the embracing of Italian and French cuisine in New York and New Orleans—not to mention the significant pan-Asian "fusion" influence now so ubiquitous in American and English cooking, the animal rights movements of the European Union which keep traditional *gavage* derived *foie gras* a particularly Gallic institution, or the current trends in cutting-edge gastronomic science, as popularised through Ferran Adrià's El Bulli restaurant near Barcelona and Heston Blumenthal's Fat Duck in Bray, England.

A *Visual History of Cookery*'s key focus is on the aesthetic aspect of food and its preparation. Whilst contextualising detail is essential—this is reflected in the informed and diverse content—the story here is really being told by the vivid, exuberant and sometimes peculiar images featured. From the antiquated frontispieces of historical cookbooks, through rich Renaissance representations of royal banquets, to contemporary food photography and celebrity chef profiles, it is clear that the history of cookery holds a rich aesthetic tapestry, and is an aspect essential to understanding the developments in the socio-cultural significance of an art which can be found in all aspects of life around the world.

The chapters are structured with a chronological overview observing the historical developments of each respective country's gastronomic traditions. Points of interest are drawn out in further detail, be they historically significant

Right: A mid-twentieth century Chicago restaurant.

Opposite: Regional varieties of American hot dogs.

or peculiarly fascinating: from the development of French *nouvelle cuisine*, the introduction of New World ingredients to Europe, and the influences of religion on cooking, to the impacting of fringe groups such as the American Hot Dog Association, the early influence of the cult of celebrity on the cooking world, and the regional peculiarities of each country's cuisine.

Reprinted texts are interleaved throughout the sections, providing an authentic voice from experts and notable individuals selected from different historical points of the transatlantic epicurean tradition. The texts included—written by minds as diverse as Elizabeth David, the Marquis de Sade, AA Gill, MFK Fisher, Anthony Bourdain, and the Slow Food Movement's Carlo Petrini—exemplify myriad topics, from the subversive to the mainstream, taking in literature, history, cultural foibles, and personal enthusiasms.

Finally, each country has a culminating section exemplifying dishes and recipes both commonplace and atypical to their cultures, revealing further how different meals and ways of eating are understood. Each country's dishes are set out in accordance with recognisable, traditional methods of differentiation in each area: the inland, coastal, and cultural regions of Spain; the traditional *charcuteries*, *boulangeries* and *pâtisseries* of France; the range of traditional daily meals in England; the extensive course-structure of Italian eating; and through America's myriad global influences.

And while *A Visual History of Cookery* is aimed at the reader with a casual interest in food, its preparation and presentation, it makes no claims to comprehensive expertise, but is also intended to provide pleasure to those with a greater knowledge of the subject, through the rich, visual imagery and fascinating variety of sources, histories, and, of course, foods celebrated.

· FRANCE ·

Previous pages: Le Restaurant Bouillon Chartier was founded in 1896 and initially known for its reasonably priced *bouillon*. It is now a fashionable Parisian landmark noted for its food, service and *décor*.

Opposite: An illustration depicting an elaborate royal Medieval feast, with the abundance of serving staff in comparison to diners necessary to the period serving style of *en confusion*. From *The Story of Alexander the Great*.

Right: Frontispiece from *Le Viandier de Taillevent*. This edition was printed in the fifteenth century by Barnabus Chaussard in Lyon.

The first French cookbooks—dating from circa 1400—took considerable influence from Moorish cookery, utilising sugar, saffron, almonds, and rose water amongst other key ingredients. Despite this, the heritage of modern French cuisine can be traced back to the eating habits of the country's later Medieval aristocracy and upper classes. The recorded roots of current-day Gallic eating stem largely from Guillaume Tirel's (circa 1310-1395) seminal fourteenth century tome *Le Viandier de Taillevent*. Though it was largely believed that the recipes in the book were purely historical, only 80 of the 230 entries were from antiquated Medieval texts; Tirel invented the rest, perhaps further cementing his personal influence, as derived from the publication's popularity. Tirel was chef to several French kings, including Philip V and Charles V, and his collection, the first printed title of its kind in France, is an essential resource for information on contemporary Medieval cooking. Its popularity and influence was such that it was still ubiquitous, essentially in its original text, in households well into the sixteenth century. Indeed, between 1486 and 1615, *Le Viandier* was reprinted 23 times by 13 different publishers.

Tirel was popularly known as "Taillevent", a nickname allegedly earned in the royal kitchens in which he worked. Beginning as a mere kitchen boy, he rose through the ranks to the august service of the royalty, becoming personal chef to Charles V in 1370. He was so loved by the king that he was eventually ennobled; his tombstone depicts, as well as Tirel in his knights armour and effigies of his two wives, three cooking pots strung together to signify his trade. The notable influence of French aristocratic cuisine at the time meant that Tirel's cooking came to represent the finest in European gastronomy.

Right: This painting is derived from an early fifteenth century manuscript of Gaston Phebus' *Livre de la Chasse* and depicts a pre-hunt feast. The lord and two of his huntsmen discuss the day's report with the lymerer, shown with his hunting horn.

Opposite: "January" from the *Très Riches Heures du Duc de Berry*. Painted by the Limbourg brothers, the image depicts the many simultaneous dishes of a contemporary royal feast, which is being blessed by a priest on the far side of the table.

The book's opening passage succinctly exemplifies the chef's extensive influence: "Here begins the Viandier of Taillevent, master chef of our Lord the King of France, by means of which can be prepared all manner of foods worthy to be served before kings, dukes, counts, lords, prelates, bourgeois, and others."

French food at this time was typified by elaborate banquets amongst the aristocracy, with dishes commonly being particularly heavy on meats, spices, and rich sauces. Items were usually heavily seasoned, and often preserved with honey or salt. A common misconception of the era is that cheap meats were preserved in spices to disguise poor taste. In reality, spices were expensive luxuries and only commonly used by those in the aristocracy and upper classes; ingredients such as cinnamon, cloves, and nutmeg were highly prized. Thus, those that could afford such exotic additions to their supplies would not typically need to purchase low quality or dubious meat to start with.

Though Medieval European cookery was largely based around the three fundamental flavours of pungent, sour, and sweet, French cuisine almost entirely abandoned the latter element. France's attitude to sugar would change from the fifteenth century—largely with the influence of countries such as England and Belgium—but its consumption at this time was hugely limited. A taste for sharp acidity was especially prevalent in Gallic cuisine; indeed, Tirel's book required sour ingredients for around 70 per cent of the recipes. These acidic elements were often combined with the pungent.

A particularly common combination was that of mixing cider or white wine vinegar with ginger. Chefs very rarely used bitter ingredients.

Opposite: An orchard harvest scene from *Croissens* manual of agriculture, a manuscript dating from the late fifteenth century.

Left: This fifteenth century painting depicts an *etrement* of a stuffed peacock, as mentioned in *Le Viandier*.

Typical ingredients largely depended on the seasons, the church calendar, and the medical recommendations of physicians. Subsequently, particularly with reference to the latter, foodstuffs considered "gross" or overly robust such as pork, beef, and most vegetables, were left to the more 'hardy' stomachs of the poor. The upper classes tended to eat more delicate meats such as fowl, light fish, and soft breads. The medical profession recommended against cooking anything to the point that it would be either too moist or dry, and more hard to digest meats were highly spiced. Game, though highly praised, was not as commonly eaten as one might expect, and was largely consumed by the upper classes. Kitchen and medicinal gardens and orchards were common and hugely popular at the time. Many grew plants now rarely used, such as tansy and pennyroyal. The interest in growing was heightened by titles such as Nicolas de Bonnefon's *Le jardinier français*, and was such that fresh fruit began to be available all year round, as more and more individuals perfected the skills necessary to successful yields.

Dishes were created as much for their colour and aesthetic as for their gastronomic verve. Colouration was supplied through the use of various products, like spinach juice (green), saffron (yellow), and sunflower (red). Swan and peacock were commonly eaten, and a noted dish was a whole roast bird, sewn back into its skin and given a gilded beak. Tirel's book, appropriately, contained the first example of an *etrement*, a visual culinary display of which the peacock or swan would be a fine example.

Meals were often served *à la française*, or *en confusion*— with all fare being presented to the table at once—and usually included an *issue de table*, a precursor to the modern dessert course.

CATHERINE DE MEDICI

In 1533, Catherine de Medici relocated from Italy to France to marry the future King Henry II, bringing many of the culinary traditions of her home country with her. Her arrival was considered something of a turning point in the history of French gastronomy; she is popularly seen as having revolutionised French food, whilst also initiating a widespread interest in the arts and literature of Renaissance Italy. Catherine brought with her an entourage of chefs; they were experts in the subtleties of Italian Renaissance cooking, introducing dishes and ingredients as varied as aspics, sweetbreads, artichoke hearts, truffles, *liver crépinettes*, *quenelles* of poultry, macaroon, ice cream and *zabagliones*.

LADURÉE

Ladurée, a Parisian bakery most famous for its double-decker macaroon, was founded in 1862 by Louis-Ernest Ladurée. Within a decade, it had been burnt down during the Paris Commune uprising and was subsequently reopened as a pastry shop. But it did not gain true fame until 1930, when Ladurée's grandson decided to stick two macaroon shells together using a flavoured *ganache*. The double-decker macaroon is now a widely available, and much imitated, speciality.

Opposite: This illustration by Le Sier Berthod, derived from *La Ville Paris*, 1655, depicts a chaotic Parisian market scene from the mid-seventeenth century.

THE ANCIEN RÉGIME

The guild system was a notable feature of the *Ancien Régime* era, the term referring to the period between the fourteenth and eighteenth centuries under the Valois and Bourbon dynasties, and later removed by the French Revolution in 1789. The system restricted those within particular branches of the culinary industry to their fields—bakers, pastry chefs, or poulterers, for example. The rules of how a guild could operate within its field were incredibly stringent and infringement on the functions of another could lead to legal action. Located particularly around the contemporary Parisian markets of Les Halles and La Mégisserie, these guilds acted as efficient training grounds for young chefs. Levels of expertise became explicit within these confraternities of workers; the positions of assistant-cook, cook proper, and masterchef were recognised.

The Italian Catherine de Medici has been credited with introducing *haute cuisine*—or "high cooking"—proper to France through the lavish preparations of her Florentine chefs. Historians, explaining that the food served in the royal courts during her marriage to French King Henry II was markedly similar to that derived from the Medieval period under the kings Philip V and Charles V, have, however, subsequently dismissed this theory. The fifteenth and sixteenth centuries saw the rapid introduction of many New World foodstuffs, such as haricot beans—now an integral ingredient to the classic French dish *cassoulet*, potatoes, and turkey. The latter replaced the relatively inedible favourites of swan and peacock, which had, in the royal courts and work of Taillevent of the previous period been fairly ubiquitous.

LA TOUR D'ARGENT

La Tour d'Argent first opened its doors in 1582 as a retreat for aristocrats tired with the lowly eating afforded in the Parisian taverns. The name was derived from the shiny kind of Champagne stone used in its construction. Its popularity quickly grew: infamously, the 1600s saw duels over table reservations.

Frédéric Delair, the restaurant's owner in the nineteenth century, was responsible for the creation of the ritualistic *Canard au Sang*, or "pressed duck", a dish which encompasses the crushing of the animal's carcass to extract the juices and blood to be used in the sauce, and which is still served today. Delair also invented the novelty

of numbering every duck and presenting each diner with a corresponding postcard. André Terrail purchased the institution in 1910, updating the facade of the building but keeping its gastronomic traditions alive. In 1936, he added an upper sixth floor, affording amazing views of the Seine and the Bateaux-Mouches. André's son Claude Terrail took the helm in 1947, and opened a gastronomic museum in the building six years later. The restaurant's international name continued to rise, and La Tour d'Argent Tokyo opened in 1984. Though Claude Terrail died in 2006, his son André took over its running, and La Tour has taken its place as a loved monument to Parisian epicurean tradition.

Top: Panoramic view of Paris, seen from the restaurant at La Tour d'Argent.

Bottom: Frédéric Delair prepares *Canard au Sang*—pressed duck—circa 1890. The silver duck press is seen on the right.

LOUIS XIV

Louis XIV ascended to the French throne a century after the arrival of Catherine de Medici. During the King's reign, the style of cooking—also known as *grande cuisine*—was incredibly rich and tended towards the spectacular rather than the refined and the elegant, as exemplified in the Medieval style meats shown in the illustration to the left. The King's kitchen employed 324 people, all of which were set into procession to bring the food, cutlery and other accoutrements into the kitchen at mealtimes. Once prepared, the food was tasted to ensure that the king would not be poisoned.

During the sixteenth century, the first cookery book addressed to ladies—*Excellent et moult utile opuscule*, by Nostradamus—appeared in France. The recipes in his book concerned sweets and syrups. This was a popular subject matter in the century's culinary literature, and indicative of France's growing fondness for sugar, particularly in contrast to the staunchly savoury tastes of the Medieval period. *Excellent et moult utile opuscule* was seen as a feminine speciality, and cookbooks proper continued to be written by men, for male cooks.

An increase in the recognition of regionalism in cooking grew significantly during the time of the *Ancien Régime*. To the centralised government, France was a composite mass of distinct territories, known as *pays* or *provinces*; the term "region" was not officially recognised at this point. Whilst Parisian cooking at this time was mostly concerned with the notion of *haute* or *grande cuisine* dedicated to the king, regional food still depended on the basic availability of produce and the social status of local communities. Medieval cookbooks bore some reference to regional dishes, but examples from the *Ancien Régime* and later noted the diversity of country-wide eating more explicitly, and began to add regional prefixes and epithets to recipes in order to specifically include certain ingredients; for instance, the cheeses of Brie, the apples of Normandy, and the Breton delectation of oats all began to be mentioned.

Left: A spread of seventeenth century meats. To the left of the suckling pig is a *pâté*, or "raised pie".

"The Pastry Cook", from *The Trades*
by Abraham Bosse, 1633.

The stringent andrigid guild system was largely swept away in the cultural restructuring of the French Revolution, but the Boulanger affair was an ominous event in the lead up to their dissipation. In 1765, a tradesman named Boulanger, also known as *Champ d'Oiseaux*, opened a store near the Louvre in Paris where he sold so-called *restaurants* or *bouillons restaurants*; these were meat based *consommés* meant to 'restore' a persons vitality. Patrons were enticed in with the Gospel-derived legend "*Venite ad me omnes qui stomacho laboratis et ego vos restaurabo*"–"Come to me, all of those who's stomachs are in distress, and I will restore you". Boulanger's clash with the guilds began when they realised he was selling leg of lamb with white sauce as well as *consommés*, thus infringing on the business of the caterers guild. Though they filed suit, claiming Boulanger was selling unauthorised ragouts, the judgement surprisingly ended in favour of the small shopkeeper, marking the first stages of the downfall of the guild's influence within the French gastronomic sphere.

LE GRAND VEFOUR

Le Grand Véfour was opened in 1784, by Antoine Aubertot. Aside from 40 years when it was closed in the early twentieth century, the restaurant has consistently been a Parisian institution. It was originally named the Café de Chartres; in 1820, Jean Véfour bought it and changed its name to his own due to the number of cafes closing at the time, as well as to give the appearance that it was a high-end luxury establishment. Véfour sold it a few years later, but the new owner kept the name. By this point, the restaurant was firmly renowned as a place for the wealthy to visit. It is the birthplace of the sauce *mornay*, which reveals the level of impact the restaurant's cooking has had on French cuisine. The *décor* is neoclassical and the cuisine reflects this as it has retained the same traditions in the handling and production of food.

The surreal illustration to the right shows an 1844 dinner at Le Grand Véfour in dedication to Saint-Hubert, the patron saint of hunters.

Right: *Ravioles de foie gras* from Le Grand Véfour.

Right: *Coq au vin*; a literal interpretation of "chicken in the pot".

Opposite: This painting depicts a late *Ancien Régime*-era supper, with a lesser number of dishes and less opulent banquet-style setting informing the era's move towards lighter eating.

The eating habits of the aristocracy became even more extravagant during the 1600s. The banquets of Louis XIII and Louis XIV were notably indulgent. The latter's sister-in-law is recorded as having observed the king consume, in a single sitting, "four soups, a pheasant, a partridge, a plate of salad, sliced mutton with garlic, two lumps of ham, a plate of pastries, fruits and preserves". The contemporary royal patronage of hearty eating around the country—the Louis' predecessor Henry IV called for a "chicken in the pot" of every member of the lower classes—seems to have allowed for such excesses. François Massialot's 1691 publication *Cuisinier royal et bourgeois* reprints a number of royal menus from this period, exemplifying the decadent epicureanism enjoyed by the aristocracy of the era.

• THE MARQUIS DE SADE'S SWEET TOOTH •

MEDLAR LUCAN AND DURIAN GRAY, *THE DECADENT COOKBOOK*

It is impossible to talk about Decadence and food without touching on the greatest Decadent of them all—Donatien-Alphonse-François de Sade. Eating was a matter of great importance to the Divine Marquis. His correspondence with his wife is crammed full of requests for food, which is hardly surprising when you consider that he spent most of his adult life—27 out of his 64 years—behind bars. A letter written from his cell at Vincennes in July 1783 asks Mme de Sade for "... four dozen meringues; two dozen sponge cakes (large); four dozen chocolate pastille candies—with vanilla—and not that infamous rubbish you sent me in the way of sweets last time". The odd delicacy was all he had to look forward to much of the time.

Food played a central role in his fiction too. *Les 120 Journées de Sodome* was described by de Sade as *L'histoire d'un magnifique repas*. And the feast laid on by the Comte de Gernande in *La Nouvelle Justine* was typical. It consisted of 89 dishes.

"They were served two soups: one Italian pasta with saffron, the other a *bisque au coulis de jambon*, and between them a sirloin of beef *à l'anglaise*. There were 12 *hors d'œuvre*, six cooked and six raw.

Then 12 *entrées*—four of meat, four of game and four of *pâtisseries*. A boar's head was served in the middle of 12 dishes of roast meat, which were accompanied by two courses of side dishes, 12 of vegetables, six of different creams, and six of *pâtisseries*. There followed 20 fruit dishes or *compotes*, an assortment of six ice creams, eight different wines, six liqueurs, rum, punch, cinnamon liqueur, chocolate and coffee. Gernande got stuck into all of them. Some of them he polished off on his own. He drank 12 bottles of wine, starting with four Volneys, before moving on to four Ais with the roast meat. He downed a Tokay, a Paphos, a Madeira and a Falernian with the fruit and finished off with two bottles of *liqueurs des Hes*, a pint of rum, two bowls of punch and ten cups of coffee."

The libertine uses these banquets to stoke up the furnaces of his lust. His ability to eat huge meals is a sign of his sexual prowess. One appetite is connected to the other—and the pleasures of satisfying them are closely allied: *Après les plaisirs de la luxure*, says Gernande, *il n'en est pas de plus divins que ceux de la table*. (After the pleasures of lust... there is none more divine than those of the table.)

But there's also a link between food and cruelty. Gernande again:

J'ai desiré souvent, je l'avoue, d'imiter les débauches d'Apicius, ce gourmand si célèbre de Rome, qui faisait jeter des esclaves vivants dans ses viviers pour rendre la chair de ses poissons plus délicate: cruel dans mes luxures, je le serais tout de même dans ces débauches-là, et je sacrifierais mille individus, si celà était nécessaire, pour manger un plat plus appétisant ou plus recherché.

("I admit that I have often wanted to imitate the debauchery of Apicius, that most famous of Roman gourmets. He had slaves thrown live into his fish ponds so that the flesh of his fish would achieve a greater delicacy. I am cruel in my lusts and would be even more so when it came to such acts of debauchery. I would sacrifice a thousand if necessary, just to eat a dish which was more tempting or *recherché*.")

The Count's banquet is a prelude to numerous acts of depravity and cruelty, which end with another meal. This is described as *Le plus magnifique souper* the centre-piece of the table being the body of Gernande's wife, the Comtesse, whom he has bled to death. This doesn't seem to worry his guests unduly, or spoil their appetite.

Although he doesn't actually eat his wife—the Count is more of a vampire than a cannibal—there are, as you might expect, several cannibalistic episodes in the writings of De Sade.

In *Aline et Valcour*, Sainville, in search of his beloved Léonore, arrives in the kingdom of Butua, ruled over by Ben Mâacoro. In this society, captive Jaga tribesmen are eaten piecemeal, sometimes cooked, sometimes raw. When Sainville expresses his moral outrage, Sarmiento, the prime minister, is surprised. *l'anthropophagie n'est certainement pas un crime*, he says and justifies the practice in various ways. To begin with, in Butua, young men are simply more tasty than tough old monkey meat. Then, whether a man is buried in the bowels of the earth or the bowels of another man makes no difference. But also, as man forms part of *le système de la nature* there is no reason not to eat him just like any other animal. (This brings to mind the story of the Reverend Thomas Baker who took part in an expedition into the interior of Fiji in 1867. He was proudly showing his comb to a local chief, who thought it was a gift and stuck it in his hair as an ornament. Baker brusquely took it back, not realising that touching a Fijian leader's head was a mortal insult. The chief demanded vengeance. He sent a messenger ahead of Baker on his travels, announcing that a whale's tooth would be the reward for whoever killed him. The mountain tribe at Navatusila took up the offer, killed the Reverend, and cooked him. (Unfortunately the recipe is lost.) Most of the tribe enjoyed eating their exotic meal, but those who had been given a leg found that even after lengthy cooking it remained extremely tough. It took some of the more sophisticated islanders to point out that the Wellington boot it wore was not part of the European's skin.)

The argument about the 'naturalness' of cannibalism occurs again in the *Histoire de Juliette* when Juliette and her companions are waylaid by the Russian ogre, Minski. He lives in fabulous wealth in a castle hidden away among the Apennines, not far from the volcanic region of Pietra-Mala. Juliette and the others are invited to dine with him in a room where the tables and chairs are formed by *des groupes de filles artistiquement arrangées*. Seated at this strange furniture the guests are served *plus de vingt entrées ou plats de rôti*. Minski then informs his guests that all the dishes served arc human flesh. They overcome any repugnance with phrases like *il n'est pas plus extraordinaire de manger un homme qu'un poulet* and tuck in. In true Sadean form, Minski not only eats vast quantities but drinks copiously too; 30 bottles of Burgundy, Champagne with the *entremets*, Aleatico and Falemian with the dessert. By the end of the meal, more than 60 bottles of wine *étaient entrées dans les entrailles de notre anthropophage*. Again the meal acts as an overture to the most grotesque scenes as the protagonists hurl themselves into the abyss of depravity.

The other cannibal in the *Histoire de Juliette* is Pope Pius VI. Having performed a black mass—itself a form of meal—on the steps of the altar in St Peter's, the Pope "drunk with lust" tortures and kills an adolescent boy, before tearing out his heart and eating it.

But to return to the man himself, behind bars at Charenton. Or more precisely, to his wife. Given that she needed to cater for the Marquis' sweet tooth, and wary of providing any more "infamous rubbish in the way of sweets" Mme de Sade could do no better than turn for help to the sisters of the Santa Trinita del Cancelliere in Sicily. The aristocratic nuns of this Cistercian convent were famous for their *fedde* (sweet cakes, literally "slices"). These were made in oval-shaped moulds hinged rather like a mussel shell. They were lined with marzipan (*pasta reale*) and filled with apricot jam and egg custard. When one half of the mould was folded over on the other, the filling oozed out and the result looked amazingly like female pudenda.

Another form of *fedde* produced by the nuns were called *Fedde del Cancelliere*. The Chancellor referred to was the twelfth century founder of the convent and here *fedde* can mean not only "slices" but also "buttocks".

Reprinted from Medlar Lucan and Durian Gray's The Decadent Cookbook, 1995, courtesy Dedalus.

LE
CVISINIER
FRANÇOIS,

ENSEIGNANT LA MANIERE
de bien apprester & assaisonner
toutes sortes de Viandes grasses
& maigres, Legumes, Patisseries,
& autres mets qui se seruent tant
sur les Tables des Grands que des
particuliers.

Par le Sieur de LA VARENNE
Escuyer de Cuisine de Monsieur le
*Marquis d'*VXELLES.

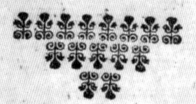

A PARIS,
Chez PIERRE DAVID, au Palais,
à l'entrée de la Gallerie des Prisonniers.

M. DC. LI.
Auec Priuilege du Roy.

FRANÇOIS PIERRE DE LA VARENNE

Seventeenth century chef François Pierre de la Varenne's (1618–1678) practices exemplified a turning point in the history of French cooking. Strong spices were eschewed in favour of milder herbs—such as tarragon, chervil, sage, and parsley—and a renewed emphasis was placed on the natural flavour of foods. This led to a focus on the preparation and quality of the ingredients as opposed to simply relying on dishes as vessels for spices. The cooking of meats and fish became a new art in itself defined by its own rules and codes of practice; no longer did the Medieval style rules of physicians have to be so stringently abided by when cooking, which allowed for a greater variety and level of expertise in the preparations of meats. La Varenne identified these in his seminal text *Le cuisiner françois*, which articulated this new cuisine. He followed his era-defining work with the first authoritative guide on pastry-making, *Le pastissier françois*.

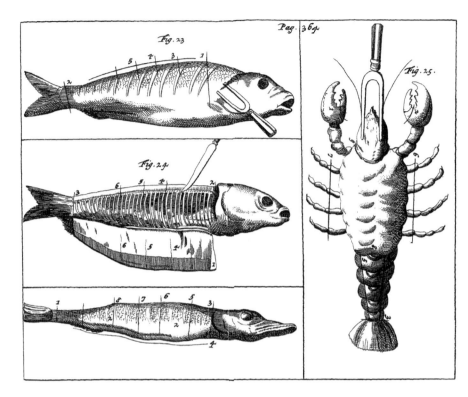

An illustration of different cuts of fish and lobster, from François Pierre de la Varenne's *Le cuisinier François*, 1651.

THE MODERN PERIOD

Changes to the elaborate preparations of *haute cuisine* began with the seventeenth century chef François Pierre de La Varenne and his hugely influential book *Le cuisinier françois*, considered by many to be the founding text of the modern French culinary tradition. This period saw the exotically spiced foods of Medieval cuisine rejected, and replaced by the lighter, subtler flavours of seasonal herbs and local spices. More detail began to be paid to the freshness of ingredients, as the key flavours of the food—rather than previously heavy seasoning and spicing elements—became more important. La Varenne also introduced many basic recipes and techniques still prevalent today, such as those for *béchamel* and *bouquet garni*.

Vincent La Chapelle and his book *Le cuisinier moderne*, the second edition of a multi-volume treatise, afforded the full hypothetical transition to the more simplified form of *nouvelle cuisine* in 1742. The style of cooking would become ubiquitous with French gastronomy, being developed and reinvented throughout the nineteenth and twentieth centuries.

The years immediately following the French Revolution saw the birth of one of France's most well-known chefs, Marie-Antoine Carême. Famous for expanding French *haute cuisine*, Carême was known in his early years for his *pièces montées*, elaborate architectural pastry-and-sugar constructions. Carême went on to play an important part in the refinement of French cuisine, emphasising the use of 'foundation' sauces such as *béchamel* and *espagnole*, and recording the first recipe for a *soufllé*. His book, *L'art de la cuisine française* was beautifully illustrated and encyclopaedic in its content.

Opposite: A 1651 edition of *Le cuisinier françois*.

ANTONIN CARÊME

Often considered to be the first true cooking star, Marie-Antoine 'Antonin' Carême (8 June 1784–12 January 1833) gained fame by publishing his recipes in cookery books—still a relatively novel concept at the time—and in doing so, codified the classic French recipes that are still used to this day by chefs all over the world. Renowned for the complexity of his dishes, the quality and luxury of the ingredients used, and the attention paid to the marriage of different flavours, Carême was also a master of presentation,

spending considerable time studying architectural designs for inspiration. He would often model his extraordinary and spectacular sugar sculptures on temples, pyramids and ancient ruins. Carême was passionate about writing and his published output includes such seminal and groundbreaking books as *Le pâtissier pittoresque*, *Le Maître d'Hôtel français* and *Le Cuisinier parisien*. Carême worked for such esteemed individuals as Alexander I, the Prince of Galles, the Princess Bagration, Napoléon Bonaparte, Louis XVIII,

and the Baron Rothschild. His influence was vast, from inventing the *toque*—the classic chef's hat, to his, perhaps, most significant contribution to French gastronomy, the distinguishing of what he deemed the four 'mother' sauces, from which a much wider repertoire could be made. The sauce 'families' are: *béchamel*, *espagnole*, *velouté*, and *allemande*. Auguste Escoffier would later update and expand this list to include such ubiquitous examples as mayonnaise and tomato sauces.

Top: An illustration by Carême of a tiered buffet published in *Maître d'hôtel*, 1822.

Opposite: An illustration of desserts atypical of those served by Antonin Carême to the aristocracy in early nineteenth century Vienna.

• APHORISMS OF THE PROFESSOR •

JEAN ANTHELME BRILLAT-SAVARIN, APHORISMS OF THE PROFESSOR
THE PHYSIOLOGY OF TASTE, 1825

I. The universe would be nothing were it not for life and all that lives must be fed.

II. Animals fill themselves; man eats. The man of mind alone knows how to eat.

III. The destiny of nations depends on the manner in which they are fed.

IV. Tell me what kind of food you eat, and I will tell you what kind of man you are.

V. The Creator, when he obliges man to eat, invites him to do so by appetite, and rewards him by pleasure.

VI. Gourmandise is an act of our judgment, in obedience to which, we grant a preference to things which are agreeable, over those which have not that quality.

VII. The pleasure of the table belongs to all ages, to all conditions, to all countries, and to all areas; it mingles with all other pleasures, and remains at last to console us for their departure.

VIII. The table is the only place where one does not suffer from *ennui* during the first hour.

IX. The discovery of a new dish confers more happiness on humanity, than the discovery of a new star.

X. Those persons who suffer from indigestion, or who become drunk, are utterly ignorant of the true principles of eating and drinking.

XI. The order of food is from the most substantial to the lightest.

XII. The order of drinking is from the mildest to the most foamy and perfumed.

XIII. To say that we should not change our drinks is a heresy; the tongue becomes saturated, and after the third glass yields but an obtuse sensation.

XIV. A dessert without cheese is like a beautiful woman who has lost an eye.

XV. A cook may be taught, but a man who can roast, is born with the faculty.

XVI. The most indispensable quality of a good cook is promptness. It should also be that of the guests.

XVII. To wait too long for a dilatory guest, shows disrespect to those who are punctual.

XVIII. He who receives friends and pays no attention to the repast prepared for them, is not fit to have friends.

XIX. The mistress of the house should always be certain that the coffee be excellent; the master that his liquors be of the first quality.

XX. To invite a person to your house is to take charge of his happiness as long as he be beneath your roof.

AUGUSTE ESCOFFIER

Georges-Auguste Escoffier (28 October 1846-12 February 1935) was a chef, culinary writer and restaurateur, responsible for updating and popularising French cookery methods for the twentieth century. Originally a disciple of Antonin Carême, Escoffier is credited with taking on the chef's ornate style and simplifying it for the contemporary tastes of the era. Operating in the nineteenth century, Escoffier led many other changes alongside the modernisation of French cuisine, in particular the introduction of organised discipline to the kitchen. He instituted a hierarchy to the kitchen that became known as the "brigade system", and replaced the old style of serving—*service à la française*—with the new course-based *service à la russe*.

Escoffier's hugely influential book, *Le Guide Culinaire*, was published in 1903 and is regarded as a pivotal text in the history of French *haute cuisine*. Translated into English in 1907, the text contained 5,000 recipes and aimed to define and streamline the French cuisine of the time. The book turned out to be a phenomenal success and is today considered the definitive reference for the traditional French *cuisine classique*.

Escoffier is well known for his roles in the establishment of several world-renowned hotels, such as the Grand Hotel in Rome and the many Ritz hotels around the world. Initially opening his restaurant, *Le Faisan d'Or* —The Golden Pheasant—in Cannes in 1878, his first foray into hotels came with the running of the kitchen at the Hotel National in Lucerne. There he met César Ritz, his future business partner, and in 1890 they moved to the Savoy Hotel in London. From their newly appointed base, the two went on to establish several famous hotels around the world. After Escoffier had left the Savoy, he and Ritz went on to open the Hotel Ritz in Paris in 1898. The following year, the pair opened The Carlton in London, with Escoffier introducing the original *à la carte* menu. Ritz had a nervous breakdown in 1901, leaving Escoffier to run the latter establishment until after his partner's death in 1919. That same year, Escoffier was awarded the cross of the *Légion d'honneur*, the first chef to receive such a decoration.

Opposite: A 1930s illustration of peaches *à la Melba*. *Pêche Melba* is, perhaps, the most well-known dish devised by Escoffier, consisting of peaches, ice cream, and a reduced raspberry sauce.

Georges-Auguste Escoffier—"the chef of emperors and the emperor of chefs"— popularised and modernised French cooking during the late nineteenth and early twentieth centuries. Active in the years following Carême's death, Escoffier worked in his tradition but simplified the chef's elaborate style, emphasising nutritional value and refined simplicity. Escoffier was also crucial in elevating the status of chef to a respected profession. His most important work was performed at the London Savoy and Ritz Carlton restaurants in partnership with César Ritz, where he famously invented *pêche melba*, *crêpes suzette*, *cuisses de nymphe*—a meal of frogs legs created for the Prince of Wales—and introduced the *à la carte* menu. His book *Le Guide Culinaire*, published in 1903, is one of the most important in French culinary history, and is still hugely influential today.

Illustration depicting a *boucherie* specialising in the sale of cat and dog meat during the Siege of Paris.

THE SIEGE OF PARIS

During the Franco-Prussian War of 1870-1871, Parisians were held under siege by the Prussian army for 135 days, forcing the population to disregard prejudices on what could and could not be eaten as food supplies for the city were cut short. In December 1870, it became increasingly difficult to get hold of "suitable" meat such as beef, veal and mutton. Instead, Parisian citizens, and chefs of the restaurants that still remained open, had to venture into cooking dog, cat, rabbit, and rat. To later keep the Parisians from starvation, even the animals of the Paris Zoo were to be found on restaurant menus around the city. The most famous of these creatures were probably the two elephants Castor and Pollux, who ended up on a Christmas menu of 1870, along with kangaroo, camel, bear, wolf, deer, and antelope.

• FRENCH CULINARY AND TABLE SLANG •
ARGOT DE CUISINE ET DE TABLE

SLANG USED BY RESTAURANT CHEFS CIRCA 1910, FROM GASTON ESNAULT'S *DICTIONNAIRE HISTORIQUE DES ARGOTS FRANÇAIS (HISTORICAL DICTIONARY OF FRENCH SLANG)*, 1965

Slang, wrote Gaston Esnault in his *Dictionnaire historique des argots français* (Larousse) is "a collection of non-technical spoken words that appeal to a social group". The group—corporative, schoolboy, fashionable society—is, he specifies, a more or less coherent one, adding, "Slang varies from profession to profession."

It is therefore only right and fitting that the culinary profession should have its own brand of slang.

The table is *la carante*. Then the food, in other words *la fripe, la croûte, la briffe, la cuistance, la béquetance, la jaffe, la graine, la tortore, la daronge, le frichti arrives*. Everyone has *un estome* (stomach), and one has to eat in other words, *clapper, croquer, tortorer, cacher, grainer, claboter, clapoter, claquer, gousser, morfiler, morfier*, to live. And if *la jaffe* is good then *on se morfale, on fircote, on se beagle* (one enjoys oneself).

Bread and wine are placed on the table first. Bread, or *le gringue, l'artifaille, la brèque, le brigeton, le brignollet*. Wine, or *le sirop, le pivois, le jaja, le pive, le tutu, le busard, le picrate, le pichtegom*. If it is a robust red wine it is *le coaltair*; if it is a fine light wine, it is *le coulange*. It can be *rouquin* (red) or *beaujolpif* and will be in a bottle, that is to say *la betterave, la boutanche, la rouille*. If it is in litres, it is *le kil* or *kilo* and *on le pictera* (it will be quaffed with a right good will).

If it is a bottle of *champ* (Champagne) it becomes a *roteuse*. It is drunk in *un guindal*, *un bennard* or *un glasse*.

The appetite begins with *l'apéro* (the alfa of the good old days has gone—*l'alfa* being the absinth (*la verte*) of *la Belle Époque*). From *la bouillante* (soup) we move on to *la barbaque* or *bidoche*, *le sauciflard* (*saucisson*), also called *du bits*, then came *les navarins* (turnpis), *les loubiats* (haricot beans), then *le calendo* (*Camembert*) which is *un rême*

(cheese), then *le caoua* (coffee) which, being black, can also be called *biffi*. At last it is time for *la consolante*, a bottle of wine drunk before leaving (or after the *coup de feu*).

Prosper Montagné, *New Larousse Gastronomique*, 1960/1977/1986, courtesy Octopus Publishing Group.

An early twentieth century illustration depicting one of the many contemporary *Confréries de guile*—groups of gastronomically-minded devotees of good food.

RESTAURANT LASSERRE

The Parisian Restaurant Lasserre appeared in its first form as the "bistrot hangar" at the Universal Exposition in 1937. When André Lasserre took over operations in 1942 it was in bad condition but under his direction it quickly attracted famous names such as Audrey Hepburn and an artistic following that included Salvador Dalí and Marc Chagall. By 1946, Lasserre had already been awarded his first Michelin star, and had achieved his third by 1962.

The *André Malraux pigeon*—pigeon stuffed with cock's combs, bacon, shallots and mushrooms—named after the author, is a signature dish at the restaurant.

MAXIM'S PARIS

Maxim's is now a famous destination for Hollywood notables, but when it opened it was a small bistro owned by a single waiter. Maxime Gaillard opened the restaurant at 3 rue Royale in 1893, during the *Belle Époque*. Shortly after opening, it became an unlikely hotspot for the fashionable and the fabulous. Financial troubles meant the bistro was soon taken over by Eugène Cornuché, who turned it into a destination for courtesans and the French elite looking for glitzy entertainment. He also hired contemporary artists to decorate the building in the style of the day, giving it its *art nouveau* aesthetic. In 1981, it changed hands again and was bought by Pierre Cardin, who added events and further transformed the bistro into a place of epicurean and celebrity interest.

Below: Example of a *menu du jour* from Restaurant Lasserre.

Opposite: Yul Brynner dining at Maxim's; the restaurant has long been one of Paris' eminent celebrity hotspots.

Clockwise from left: *Asperges vertes de Provence à la menthe, anchois et piment; Banc de sardines in soar, dans un esprit vénitien; Carré-menthe.*

Opposite: The kitchen of La Maison Troisgros, circa 1960s.

LA MAISON TROISGROS

La Maison Troisgros is the culinary concept of Marie-Pierre and Jean-Baptiste Troisgros, who moved from Burgundy to Roanne, just outside Lyon, in 1930, and decided to buy a hotel. The couple established the hotel/ restaurant La Maison Troisgros, with Marie-Pierre in charge of the cooking and Jean-Baptiste overseeing the house. This blueprint has been maintained through three generations of the family. The couple produced two prodigious chefs, Jean and Pierre, who were credited for their part in the development of *nouvelle cuisine* in the second half of the twentieth century.

At present, Michel Troisgros, son of Pierre, and his wife, Marie-Pierre, run the restaurant. However, the roles have been reversed, with Michel running the kitchen and Marie-Pierre taking care of the hotel and shop, as well as the *décor*. Michel's modern take on the culinary legacy of the restaurant takes influence from Japanese cuisine, as well as utilising seasonal produce he adds acidic tones to his dishes. La Maison Troisgros has been awarded three Michelin stars each year for the past 30 years consecutively. In *Restaurant* magazine's 2008 Top 50 poll, Troisgros' restaurant was ranked 25th best globally. Michel Troisgros has gone on to turn the family name into a national and global brand, developing restaurants in Moscow, Tokyo, Paris and Iguerande, France.

PROSPER MONTAGNE AND THE LAROUSSE GASTRONOMIQUE

Larousse Gastronomique, written by French chef Prosper Montagné in 1938, now comes with the tagline "The World's Greatest Cookery Reference Book". Written by a chef with a history of working in the world's greatest restaurants, as well as organising the kitchens of the Allied armies during the First World War, the claim does not come lightly. World-famous chef Auguste Escoffier provided the preface to the first edition. The book was translated into English in 1961 and has been modernised and revised in three editions since its initial publication. Indeed, alongside other leading chefs at the time, Prosper Montagné is credited with revolutionising and simplifying modern French cuisine, and his 'encyclopaedia' is believed by many to remain the finest example of its kind.

Prosper Montagné, a contemporary of Escoffier's, wrote the *Larousse Gastronomique* in collaboration with Alfred Gottschalk in 1938. The cooking encyclopaedia became the first and last word in modern French food books, and the *Larousse* name guaranteed an academic reception to the title on its release, helping push the publications incredible sales.

The term *nouvelle cuisine* became common usage during the 1960s, after two authors, Henry Gault and Christian Millau, used it to describe the work of Paul Bocuse, Jean and Pierre Troisgros, and Raymond Olivier, amongst others. Cooking against the structured orthodoxy of Escoffier's tradition, these chefs delineated a series of characteristics of this "new" food, particularly praising flavour preservation, freshness, lightness and technological innovation. Paul Bocuse is considered one of the finest twentieth century chefs, and famously created his signature dish—a black truffle soup with a pastry crust—for Valery Giscard d'Estaing at the presidential dinner where he received the *Légion d'honneur* for his service to cooking, an award which further exemplifies the importance of gastronomy in French culture even into the twenty-first century. His own cooking award, the *Bocuse d'Or* is regarded as one of the most prestigious in the world of cookery, and is often seen as a kind of unofficial world championship.

Modern French culinary masters such as Joël Robuchon and Pierre Gagnaire are currently flying the flag for French *haute cuisine*, and are internationally regarded for their classic, faultless food, publishing books that serve as personal testimonies, and reference volumes on the subject, without "codifying the cuisine of the late twentieth century". Robuchon currently holds the record for the most Michelin stars awarded, with 25 allocated to his restaurants around the world.

PAUL BOCUSE

Born into a family line of cooks dating back to the seventeenth century, Paul Bocuse took over his father's simple inn in 1960, transforming it into a fine dining restaurant. He initially earned his fame as a leading figure of the 1960s *nouvelle cuisine* movement—it is said that the term *nouvelle cuisine* finally became ubiquitous in mainstream culinary vocabulary following a visit by food critic Henri Gault to Bocuse's restaurant. In 1958, he achieved his first Michelin star, gaining a second in 1960 and a third in 1965. In 1975, he was decorated with the *Légion d'honneur*, and it was for this occasion that he created the infamous *Soupe aux truffes noires Élysée*. Over the years he has received extensive acclaim for his work; in 1989 he was named "Cook of the Century" by the Gault-Millau guide, as well as being proclaimed the "Pope of Cuisine".

Today, Bocuse has numerous restaurants in the Lyon area, as well as the family restaurant L'Auberge du Pont de Collonges in Collonges-au-Mont-d'Or, which has held its three Michelin stars for more than 40 years. He is also president of L'Institut Paul Bocuse, which trains students from all over the world in the culinary arts and hotel and restaurant management.

Top: The cover of the 1986 edition of the *New Larousse Gastronomique*.

Opposite: Paul Bocuse, wearing the medal of the *Légion d'honneur*.

Legendary French chef Paul Bocuse (centre) shares a meal with 12 of France's most prominent and influential chefs of modern times.

From left to right: Alain Dutournier, Gérard Boyer, Jean-André Charial, Jean Delaveyne, Roger Vergé, Gérard Antonin, Paul Bocuse, Michel Guérard, Alain Chapel, André Daguin, Alain Senderens, Jean-Pierre Morot-Gaudry and Gérard Pangaud.

• NOUVELLE CUISINE •

AA GILL

THE CASE FOR...

Sitting around a table last week, someone said: "What is the most depressing thing you can read on a menu?"

"Oh, lightly steamed."

"No, no, nestling in a basket of root vegetable matchsticks."

"A warm salad."

"Wilted mixed leaves."

"A *coulis*!"

"Oh yes, *coulis*, any *coulis*, all *coulis*. The only good *coulis* has a pigtail and humps tea chests on the Shanghai docks."

There was no end to the things we hated on menus. All the twee language: the succulent, moist, drizzle-drenched, delicate vegetable verbiage, and the hot adjectives promising a slow pulse. All the things we hated, all the little terms of chewable endearment could have come under one heading. What we really hated was *nouvelle cuisine*.

These are terms associated with that most despised movement of twentieth century culture, more loathed than 1970s disco dancing, more ridiculed than plywood effect, stack-heeled cowboy boots, responsible for more merciless hilarity than the Turner Prize. *Nouvelle cuisine* is now universally derided. So I'm now about to embark on the most difficult and dangerous paragraph known to restaurant writers. Drum roll, maestro, if you please.

Ladies and gentlemen, a defence of *nouvelle cuisine*.

It wasn't all bad. Some of it was really very good. *Nouvelle cuisine* was like Protestantism. It started in a blaze of righteousness as a reaction to the discredited Catholicism of old, thick, saucy *haute cuisine*. All that flambeed at your table, stuff-a-truffle-up-his-bum cooking. *Nouvelle cuisine* had high ideals of honesty, simplicity and respect but, like Protestantism, it descended into factionalism and fervent absolutist splinter groups such as the rigorous and absurd *cuisine minceur*. The original simplicity was lost in a wave of internecine argument over how many kumquats you could get in a filo pastry basket, and whether *crème fraîche* really transubstantiated or was just a symbol.

And then the health fanatics got hold of it and it became a silly slimming cult—eat out and lose money.

At heart, *nouvelle cuisine* was sound and worthy, and it changed the way we eat. It made French food more Italian in style, it put ingredients above recipes, and it accented harmonised flavours as opposed to big homogenous single tastes.

Now, I'm as glad as the next trencherperson that we've seen the last of huge plates with an infant carrot, Kenyan black bean and asparagus lying in a gob of pimento puree, but I'm equally glad that we've seen the end of scallops floating in a glutinous *mornay* sauce, gratineed with breadcrumbs and cheddar, with piped potato round their shells. There are many roads to foodie heaven, but, as nanny said, they all have to go down the same big red highway. Hideous shoes may come back into fashion, the Turner Prize may still be ridiculous, but the most important bit of our culture, the dining table, is seeing something of a renaissance, and we have, in large part, *nouvelle cuisine* to thank for that.

... AND AGAINST

The room was small and full and had the bustle of serious intent and the smuggery of missionaries. The menu came in doggerel—that is, five verses of three lines each, each line being a list of ingredients and a cookery term. The waitress, who came a couple of feet behind her smile, asked if we'd eaten here before. "Well, then, I'd better explain the menu."

I could feel myself bridle. (Actually, I couldn't—I've no idea what bridling feels like, but I've read that other people do it, so I wanted to have a go.) What's the point of writing a menu and then having to explain it, particularly when it's a clear list? "Our portions aren't very large...." (I gave up trying to bridle and silently screamed: oh my God, I'm falling through a hole in the space-time continuum, and I'm going to meet Antony Worrall Thompson at the other end.) "... so we suggest you choose, say, three dishes each, or have the gastro-digestive people-carrier option." Just give us the whole menu, I offered. There's seven of us. Go for it. The waitress caught up with her smile. "Better not", she said. "Confuses the kitchen."

After much toing and froing we ordered. And then, slowly, like the retreat from Moscow, plates started turning up. Sometimes we'd wait half an hour, sometimes only 28 minutes. For a tiny plate of crisp fillet of red mullet, red mullet soup and red pepper *beignet.* Or rump of lamb, *confit* shoulder, turnip *tatin*, lamb *vinaigrette*, crackling. Or quail, glazed salsify, *sauté* of *foie gras* and hazelnuts.

Now, I'm not going to knock the size, because, as you know, size isn't everything. But what is everything is rhythm and pleasure. And size doesn't matter in the least if it's absent. I started with the soup of mussels, baby fennel, saffron *velouté, crème fraîche*, which was award-winningly excellent, but only three mouthfuls. I wanted a bowl, and if not a bowl, I wanted something else as good immediately. A postage stamp of excellent honey-glazed belly pork an episode of *East Enders* later didn't do it. Dinner was a syncopated tease that just got you going, then buggered off. It was infuriatingly frustrating. For pudding, I ordered the cheeseboard because I was still ravenous.

All the food was fantastically well made and incredibly clever. But instead of loving it, I wanted to punch its taunting little lights out. It reminded me what the insuperable flaw in *nouvelle cuisine* is. A mode of cooking invented in a kitchen, not a dining-room, it's perfectly, gratifyingly revolutionary if you're a chef, but tastes like a sermon with footnotes if you're a customer. Restaurants don't sell emotion—we bring that with us. What they do is lay a table and offer the means to evoke it. And that's an ingredient that's older than fire and one I've mentioned before and no doubt will again.

What this place didn't offer is hospitality. It made the easy mistake of imagining that what restaurants sell is food.

"Nouvelle Cuisine", *Table Talk* by AA Gill and Weidenfeld and Nicolson, an imprint of the Orion Publishing Group, London. Reprinted by kind permission of AA Gill.

Opposite: Veal chop and kidney garnished *à la bourgeoise*, from Paul Bocuse's L'Auberge du Pont de Collonges.

Left: An ice cream dessert from Paul Bocuse's flagship restaurant in Collonges-au-Mont-d'Or, near Lyon.

NOUVELLE CUISINE

Vincent La Chapelle first coined the term *nouvelle cuisine* in the eighteenth century, using it to describe the simplified style of cooking used throughout his 1733 publication, *Cuisine Moderne*. Literally translated as "new cuisine", the term has been applied throughout the centuries to describe contemporary developments in cookery. However, it is more commonly associated with the 1970s discipline described by authors Henri Gault and Christian Millau, who championed the simplification of cookery through steaming and brief cooking times for meat and fish, the use of fresh ingredients and the rejection of heavy sauces. These methods are still ubiquitous in fine dining restaurants today.

Although they are both technically progressive forms of *haute cuisine*, *nouvelle cuisine* is distinguished from *cuisine classique* by its lighter, more delicate dishes, with a greater emphasis placed on presentation. Regional dishes were used for inspiration instead of established *cuisine classique* dishes, with chefs paying greater attention to the dietary needs of their guests. This resulted in simpler dishes being prepared, such as a well-made salad or simply cooked fresh vegetables, with the emphasis on quality rather than invention. Chefs began embracing new technological advances, such as the microwave oven, as well as decreasing their use of refrigeration. In turn, this helped to reduce and refine the choice on menus,

with larger menus previously resulting in huge stock intakes and an over-use of cold storage. Cooking times were also re-thought, with fish, pasta, game meat and some green vegetables being cooked for shorter periods of time.

However, enthusiasm for invention and the rejection of traditional culinary principles meant that chefs began to forget the notable achievements of past epicurean figures, and the importance of appreciating the country's traditional historical cuisine. Many began to follow the new movement without question, attracted to the fact it was without roots and open to all influences. This led to elements of *nouvelle cuisine* being overused and misinterpreted,

such as the excessive decoration of dishes, systematic under-cooking, and miniscule portion sizings.

During the 1980s, several culinary writers claimed that *nouvelle cuisine* had been exhausted, with many chefs returning to the *cuisine classique* method of cooking. But although their methods referred back to traditional cooking styles, many of the new techniques and lighter methods of presentation of the *nouvelle* movement continued to influence their practice.

Top: Sphere of sugar with violet and lychee and milk ice cream, by Joël Robuchon.

Bottom left: Interior of La Table de Joël Robuchon, Paris.

JOËL ROBUCHON

Joël Robuchon is a leading figure in the development of post-*nouvelle cuisine* French gastronomy. With an aim to accentuate the tastes of the basic ingredients, Robuchon's cooking has been seen as a return to the authentic *bourgeois* traditions of French cuisine. This can be witnessed in the simplicity of his signature dishes: mashed potatoes with lashings of butter, and steak *tartare*. Robuchon began his culinary career aged only 15, and in his 20s was awarded the *Meilleur Ouvrier de France*, a prestigious title afforded to excellence in a particular craft. For many years he has had his own eponymous restaurant in Paris, and has been responsible for training such renowned chefs as Gordon Ramsay, Tom Aikens and Michael Caines, who all recall his distinct perfectionism and discipline. In 1992, he closed his restaurant to travel the world, which eventually led to the opening of 15 eponymous sites worldwide, in cities including London, Monaco, New York, and Tokyo. Robuchon is infamous for his fierce criticism of the Michelin rating system, questioning its objectivity, although in 2008 he was awarded 18 Michelin stars, currently making him the most decorated chef in the world.

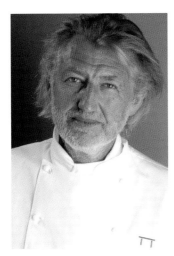

PIERRE GAGNAIRE

Pierre Gagnaire is a world-renowned French chef and owner of the restaurant of the same name on rue Balzac in Paris. Gagnaire is also Head Chef at the cutting-edge restaurant Sketch, in London. A great champion of the fusion movement, he has a number of Michelin stars to his name. His method of cooking distinguishes itself through challenging juxtapositions of flavours and ingredients. His efforts to tear up the rulebook for French cooking have provoked culinary reverberations worldwide. Gagnaire's latest gastronomic concept—Pierre, at the Mandarin Oriental Hotel in Hong Kong—opened in October 2006.

A signature *terrine* from Pierre Gagnaire's eponymous Parisian restaurant.

A selection of regional French cheeses.

FRENCH BREAD AND PASTRY

France is famous for the quality of its breads and pastries, and has a well-established network of *boulangeries* across the country, continuing traditions of local produce, delivering fresh supplies, and keeping modern supermarkets at bay. Interestingly, the origins of the products most popularly associated with France, the *croissant* and the *baguette*, are surrounded by controversy.

The birth of the *croissant*—the ubiquitous breakfast pastry formed of numerous rolled layers of yeast dough and butter, with or without various myriad common fillings—is hotly contested. Theories abound: it was the creation of a Hungarian baker faced with a Turkish invasion in 1686; a celebratory dish devised when the Franks defeated the Turkish forces at the Battle of Tours in 732; or Marie-Antoinette's yearning for fare of Polish origin. Despite the variety of disparate ideas, many are quick to argue that the pastry's provenance was some quite unknown place in France in the nineteenth century.

Meanwhile the *baguette*, a long stick of crispy bread, is considered quintessentially French, but in fact its roots are thought to trace back to nineteenth century Vienna; the *pain viennois* was, and still is, often a long, part steam-cooked, loaf, albeit with a softer crust than is normally found with the *baguette*. The *baguette de tradition française*—the name can also be found as a derivative of this—is an officially stipulated criterion for the production of *baguettes*, following certain rules: —The dough must be mixed, worked, shaped and baked on the premises. The bread must not be frozen at any stage or include any additives—with the exception of miniscule quantities of derivative flours—and should only include bread-specific wheat flours, clean water, and kitchen salt. —Only natural yeasts should be used: *poolish*, a pre-prepared liquid starter; a regular immediate use of baking yeast; or *levain*, a pre-ferment derived from sourdough starters, are all acceptable.

Illustration of a fifteenth century baker's workshop.

A *boulangerie* stall selling traditional French breads.

Cured meats for sale at a *charcuterie* market stall.

· CHARCUTERIE ·

These translations, both courtesy of James Prescott, are derived from Guillaume Tirel's *Le Vandier de Taillevent*. Tirel's recipes assumed the attention of a fully trained cook, hence the relative brevity in his instruction. The majority of entries from the first half of his tome—comprising largely of examples copied from Medieval texts—appeared simply as an ingredient list, or even just a serving suggestion. The later recipes of the latter half of *Le Viandier*—those more likely written by Tirel himself—are more explicit in their details, such as the example of "Soup of red deer testicles" below.

50. SWAN AND PEACOCK (DERIVED FROM THE "MEAT ROASTS" PORTION OF *LE VIANDIER*).

"Kill it like a goose, leave the head and tail, lard or bard it, roast it golden, and eat it with fine salt. It lasts at least a month after it is cooked. If it becomes mouldy on top, remove the mould and you will find it white, good and solid underneath."

67. SUBTLETY OF A SWAN RECLOTHED IN ITS SKIN INCLUDING ITS PLUMAGE (DERIVED FROM THE "MEAT ROASTS" PORTION OF *LE VIANDIER*).

"Take the swan, inflate it between the shoulders, slit it along the belly, and remove the skin (including the neck cut close to the shoulders). Leave the feet attached to the body. Put it on the spit, bard it, and glaze it. When it is cooked, reclothe it in its skin, with the neck very upright on the plate. Eat it with Yellow Pepper [Sauce]."

176. SOUP OF RED DEER TESTICLES IN DEER HUNTING SEASON (DERIVED FROM THE "POTTAGES" PORTION OF *LE VIANDIER*).

"Scald and wash the red deer testicles very well in boiling water, cook them well, cool them, slice them into cubes (neither too large nor too small), and fry them in lard. To the same pan add some beef broth and leafy parsley. Add Fine Powder (in moderation so that it is not too spicy) steeped in one part of wine and two parts of verjuice (or gooseberries instead of verjuice). To give it liquid, you need to have a little Cameline [Sauce]; or take one or two chicken livers and a little white bread, [soak in beef broth], sieve, and add to your pot instead of Cameline [Sauce]. Throw in a bit of vinegar, and salt to taste."

ANDOUILLETTE

One of the more idiosyncratic of French dishes, and certainly one popularly considered unpalatable outside of Gallic gastronomy, *andouillette*—not to be confused with its almost namesake *andouille*—is a coarse tripe sausage made from the pig's colon, also known as chitterlings, and intestinal tract. Often appearing on French menus as AAAAA—or *Association Amicale des Amateurs d'Andouillette Authentiques*, the governing body responsible for the quality of approved examples—the sausage infamously smells strongly of faeces, owing to the provenance of the offal it is made from. Enthusiasts insist that beyond the occasionally overpowering odour, the meat retains an earthy, smoky, sensual flavour.

CASSOULET

"God the father is the *cassoulet* of Castelnaudary, God the Son that of Carcassonne, and the Holy Spirit that of Toulouse." With this, Prosper Montagné attempted to cement the provenance of one of the more historically disputed Gallic dishes, the duck, mutton, sausage and haricot bean stew *cassoulet*. The dish is seen to date back to the fourteenth century siege of the town of Castelnaudary, in which the local citizens invented the dish for defending soldiers, which subsequently proved so satisfyingly rustic that they drove the enemy away because of it.

The term *cassoulet* derives from the large clay pot it was traditionally cooked in, the *cassolle* or *cassolo*. The hearty nature of the dish—an uncomplicated mix of ingredients, very slowly cooked—owe to its peasant origins. The traditional process of deglazing and not cleaning the *cassolle* before making a new *cassoulet* has resulted in tales of single dishes partly lasting for hundreds of years.

Jars of duck *cassoulet*.

CROQUE-MONSIEUR

The *croque-monsieur*—or "crisp mister"—is a fried cheese and ham sandwich, and originated in France in the early twentieth century, a rudimentary prototype for Gallic fast food. The dish first appeared on Parisian café menus in 1910. Its first published appearance, like that of the *madeleine* was in Proust's *Remembrance of Things Past* (*À la recherche du temps perdu*), published in 1918. Though the basic *croque* traditionally consisted of simply the sandwich fried in butter, the recognised 'modern' version usually elaborates on this by including a *béchamel* or *mornay* sauce, as well as a crisp topping of *Gruyère* cheese.

Many other variations on the theme abound, including: *croque-madame*, which has a fried egg on top; the *croque-gagnet*, using *gouda* cheese and *andouille* sausage; and the *croque-provençal*, which utilises tomato.

FOIE GRAS

Foie gras, or "fatty liver", is the name of a *mousse, parfait,* or *pâté* made from the liver of a force-fed goose or duck. Though the *gavage* (the method of force-feeding the bird) production of the dish dates as far back as Ancient Egypt, it has become synonymous with French cuisine. The country has the highest consumption rate in the world; in 2006, 19,552 tons were produced in France alone, with 42 per cent of households purchasing *foie gras* at some point in the year.

The industry is swathed in controversy due to the issues of inhumane treatment and animal cruelty associated with *gavage.* The process consists of force-feeding 24 hours worth of food—around 250 grams of fat soaked grain—in a few seconds, using pump pipes placed down the throats of the bird. This process is carried out twice a day for 12 days before slaughter for ducks, and four times daily for 15 days prior for geese. Despite worldwide vocal criticism of its production—in 1998 the European Union banned farming methods which caused "unnecessary pain" to animals, leading Italy and Germany to cease manufacture, and many Western chain grocers to remove the dish from their shelves—the French government declared *foie gras* a "protected cultural patrimony", meaning it bypasses European animal rights laws.

Foie gras can be prepared hot or cold. Low-heat methods of cooking produce the common *parfaits, pâtés, mousses,* or *terrines,* typically served with fruit or *brioche.* High-heat methods require a short cooking time due to the high fat content, and seared *foie gras* is often served with similarly basic *accoutrements,* though it can also be found in certain gourmet beef burgers, and served alongside other roasted meats in *haute* and *nouvelle* dishes. Consumption of a sweet white wine, such as *Sauternes,* with the *foie gras* is also traditional in France.

An elaborate *foie gras* window display.

Steak tartare, a dish comprised
entirely of raw ingredients.

BLANQUETTE DE VEAU

Blanquette de veau is a creamy veal based stew, and one of France's most recognisable comfort foods. Veal meat, traditionally taken from the belly and breast, is slow simmered until incredibly tender with onions, celery, and root vegetables. The sauce is then reduced and cream is added to enrich.

STEAK TARTARE

The name *tartare* derives from the historic Tartar peoples of Asia Minor, who were alleged to have tenderised raw meat by placing it underneath their horses saddles when they did not have time to cook. The dish is now synonymous with Gallic cuisine.

Usually made from raw minced beef or horse, *steak tartare* is usually served with pickles or capers, onion, peppers, and a raw egg. The meat can also be marinated in wine. The dish is considered *gourmet* and is traditionally prepared in restaurants at the diner's table.

• RECIPE •

500 g fresh lean fillet or sirloin,
minced or finely chopped
1 medium red onion
50 g capers
50 g cornichons
100 g shallots
1/2 tsp mustard
1 small egg yolk, whisked
2 tsp olive oil
salt and black pepper

Ask your butcher to mince your meat if you do not have a home mincer, or chop it very finely with a sharp knife with the grain. Finely chop the onion, capers, cornichons, and shallots.

Mix all the ingredients together in a bowl. Mould the mix into thick patties and serve. Adjust seasoning to taste. Serve with *pommes-frites*.

• STEAK AND CHIPS •

ROLAND BARTHES

Steak is a part of the same sanguine mythology as wine. It is the heart of meat, it is meat in its pure state; and whoever partakes of it assimilates a bull-like strength. The prestige of steak evidently derives from its quasi-rawness. In it, blood is visible, natural, dense, at once compact and sectile. One can well imagine the ambrosia of the Ancients as this kind of heavy substance which dwindles under one's teeth in such a way as to make one keenly aware at the same time of its original strength and of its aptitude to flow into the very blood of man. Full-bloodedness is the *raison d'être* of steak; the degrees to which it is cooked are expressed not in calorific units but in images of blood; rare steak is said to be *saignant* (when it recalls the arterial flow from the cut in the animal's throat), or *bleu* (and it is now the heavy, plethoric, blood of the veins which is suggested by the purplish colour—the superlative of redness). Its cooking, even moderate, cannot openly find expression; for this unnatural state, a euphemism is needed: one says that steak is *à point*, "medium", and this in truth is understood more as a limit than as a perfection.

To eat steak rare therefore represents both a nature and a morality. It is supposed to benefit all the temperaments, the sanguine because it is identical, the nervous and lymphatic because it is complementary to them. And just as wine becomes for a good number of intellectuals a mediumistic substance which leads them towards the original strength of nature, steak is for them a redeeming food, thanks to which they bring their intellectualism to the level of prose and exorcise, through blood and soft pulp, the sterile dryness of which they are constantly accused. The craze for steak tartare, for instance, is a magic spell against the romantic association between sensitiveness and sickliness; there are to be found, in this preparation, all the germinating states of matter: the blood mash and the glair of eggs, a whole harmony of soft and life-giving substances, a sort of meaningful compendium of the images of pre-parturition.

Like wine, steak is in France a basic element, nationalised even more than socialised. It figures in all the surroundings of alimentary life:

flat, edged with yellow, like the sole of a shoe, in cheap restaurants; thick and juicy in the bistros which specialise in it; cubic, with the core all moist throughout beneath a light charred crust, in *haute cuisine*. It is a part of all the rhythms, that of the comfortable bourgeois meal and that of the bachelor's bohemian snack. It is a food at once expeditious and dense, it effects the best possible ratio between economy and efficacy, between mythology and its multifarious ways of being consumed.

Moreover, it is a French possession (circumscribed today, it is true, by the invasion of American steaks). As in the case of wine there is no alimentary constraint which does not make the Frenchman dream of steak. Hardly abroad, he feels nostalgia for it. Steak is here adorned with a supplementary virtue of elegance, for among the apparent complexity of exotic cooking, it is a food which unites, one feels, succulence and simplicity. Being part of the nation, it follows the index of patriotic values: it helps them to rise in wartime, it is the very flesh of the French soldier, the inalienable property which cannot go over to the enemy except by treason. In an old film (*Deuxième Bureau centre Kommandantur*), the maid of the patriotic *curé* gives food to the Boché spy disguised as a French underground fighter: "Ah, it's you, Laurent! I'll give you some steak." And then, when the spy is unmasked: "And when I think I gave him some of my steak!"–the supreme breach of trust.

Commonly associated with chips, steak communicates its national glamour to them: chips are nostalgic and patriotic like steak. *Match* told us that after the armistice in Indo-China "General de Castries, for his first meal, asked for chips." And the President of the Indo-China Veterans, later commenting on this information added: "The gesture of General de Castries asking for chips for his first meal has not always been understood." What we were meant to understand is that the General's request was certainly not a vulgar materialistic reflex, but an episode in the ritual of appropriating the regained French community. The General understood well our national symbolism; he knew that *la frite*, chips, are the alimentary sign of Frenchness.

Roland Barthes, "Steak and Chips", *Mythologies*, published by Jonathan Cape. Reprinted by permission of the Random House Group Ltd., Hill and Wang and Edition du Seuil.

COQ AU VIN

Coq au vin is, historically, a slow-cooked stew consisting of cockerel meat—the eponymous *coq*, bacon, red wine, onions, and garlic. Today, cockerel has generally been substituted for less tough chicken meat, though its original inclusion and the necessity for the casserole-style tenderising cooking of the dish qualified its ubiquity amongst the poorer members of the French population. Traditionally, cockerel would have been included as a use for birds several years old who had outlived their true purpose as practical farmyard breeders. Despite this, the 1999 edition of the *Oxford Companion to Food* declares the dish to be of fairly modern origins, with one of the first recorded "discoveries" of a recipe appearing in Edmond Richardin's *L'Art de Bien Manger* in 1913. Richardin noted that the methods for the dish he had found explicitly required more expensive wine, and he also highlighted the regional differences of wine choices in preparing essentially the same dish, as well as the addition of various extra local and seasonal ingredients at times.

• RECIPE •

30 g butter
150 g shallots, peeled
3 garlic cloves, crushed
150 g lardons or unsmoked bacon
sprig of fresh thyme
200 g button mushrooms
2 sticks of celery
a bottle of good red wine
500 ml of good chicken stock
2 tbsp balsamic vinegar
1 large free range chicken, cut into 8 serving pieces,
on the bone but skin removed
small bunch flat leaf parsley, chopped

—Place the lardons or bacon in a hot casserole dish and cook for two to three minutes, or until browned. When done, remove from the pan, leaving the oil and juices.
—Place the chicken pieces in the hot fat and cook until a pale golden colour, turning so that each side is equal. Remove with the lardons. Place the shallots, garlic, celery, mushrooms, and most of the butter in the hot casserole dish. Cook until browned and the onion is translucent. Add the red wine, chicken stock, and vinegar, and bring to a simmer. When bubbling, return all the pork and chicken to the pan, making sure the liquid covers the chicken. Simmer gently for about 25 minutes or until the chicken is tender and cooked through. If you want a thicker sauce, remove the contents of the pan and boil the liquid over a high heat for a few minutes, stirring regularly, until the consistency required is reached.
—Add the herbs and the small amount of reserved butter. Season with salt and pepper and serve with boiled or roasted potatoes.

The rich, traditionally peasant-derived stew of *coq au vin*.

· FRENCH CHEESE ·

With over a 1,000 different types France holds the record as the country with the most varied cheese production. Traditionally, the number has been said to be around 400, but as private cheese lovers have begun to share their cheese experiences and record the names of the different artisanal varieties encountered on travels in France, the number has risen impressively. Cheese is an integral part of the French dinner table, usually following the main course before dessert. The French population consumes the most cheese of any other in the world, eating an average of 20.4 kg per person annually.

The Appellation d'Origine Contrôlée (AOC) is a seal given to those agricultural products produced following a set of criteria defined by a government bureau that ensures that the special geographical conditions appointed to the different types of foods are fulfilled. In terms of cheese, this certification means that the milk used must originate from livestock from designated areas, and that the maturing must take place in certain places. Earning an AOC seal also entails following centuries-old production methods. The first time a legal decree such as the AOC was used in France was in 1666, when the Parliament of Toulouse voted a decree allowing for the sanction of producers of counterfeit *Roquefort* cheese. The AOC seal is currently only given to 40 cheeses.

Cheese and France have always been closely linked. During the Second World War Winston Churchill proclaimed "a country producing almost 360 different types of cheese cannot die." Based on such a measurement, the French nation should stand even stronger today.

LA VACHE QUI RIT

One of France's first mass-produced cheeses, thanks to the company owner Leon Bel's quick response to new production modes in the early 1920s. Today *La Vache qui Rit* (*The Laughing Cow*) is an internationally known brand sold in 90 countries throughout the world.

BRIE

Brie is a soft cow's cheese with an edible white rind, and is produced from whole or semi-skimmed milk. The geographically eponymous cheese enjoyed a particular heyday in the fifteenth to eighteenth centuries, being variously bought in great numbers for royal presents, and subsequently appearing in popular contemporary literature, notably in the poet Saint Amant's ode to the so-called "gentle jam of Bacchus". *Brie* has successfully retained its popularity through the ages, as artisan producers uniformly began to use approved ferments to standardise the quality of their wares. There are only two officially recognised varieties of the cheese, *Brie de Meaux* and *Brie de Melun*. The former has been produced on the outskirts of Paris for over a thousand years, and was granted Appellation d'Origine Contrôlée status—protecting its 'authentic' recipe and provenance—in 1980. *Brie de Melun* is made in smaller, thicker rounds, and is more pungent, with a higher salt content.

CAMEMBERT

Camembert is a relatively modern development in cheese history, being altered to its recognisable form in the northern Norman city of the same name around 1790 by a farmer's wife named Marie Harel. Production now takes placed in multiple regions in France, though it is stipulated that the exact provenance of each cheese must be recorded. Traditional *Camembert de Normandie* gained AOC status in 1983. The cheese is made from unpasteurised cow's milk, is ripened with two different moulds for around three weeks, and is often served in thin wooden boxes.

ROQUEFORT

Gaining AOC status in 1925–the first French cheese to do so–*Roquefort* is a blue sheep's milk cheese, specifically one aged in the natural Combalou caves of Roquefort-sur-Soulzon from the milk of the Lacaune, Manech and Basco-Béarnaise breeds. Notably tangy, with a fairly strong odour, the cheese is recognisable by its famous green mould, which is found in the caves where it is produced. Bread was traditionally left in the caves, becoming mouldy with spores from the wet floors. The bread was then dried and powdered, and the breadcrumbs mixed with the cheese curds in production. To gain the recognisable strong smell, the cheese is ideally left to ripen for around a year, though it can be sold after 30 days.

The apocryphal origins of *Roquefort* stem from a story stating that a French youth, whilst eating a lunch of bread and ewe's cheese, deposited his food in the caves to pursue a beautiful woman. Returning months later, the cheese had gained the necessary strain of infused mould, becoming *Roquefort*.

MORBIER

A goat's milk cheese from the eastern region of Franche-Comté, *Morbier* is recognisable for the layer of ash, which runs throughout its centre. The ash stems from the tradition of producing the cheese with a layer of "evening" milk and one of "morning" milk, whereby an amount of curd would be pressed before nightfall and covered with a layer of ash to protect it, before the mould was topped up in the morning. *Morbier* gained AOC status in 2000.

TOMME

Tomme, a traditionally low fat hard cow's milk cheese mutually derivative of the Italian *Toma*, is produced in the Alpine region of France. Unlike many prestigious French cheeses, there are many legitimately recognised regional varieties of *Tomme*, such as *Tomme de Savoie*, *Tomme au Fenouil*, and *Tomme d'Aydiu*. Only one, *Tome des Bauges* from the eastern Bauges pre-Alps, has AOC status, which it received in 2002.

COMTÉ

Of all the cheeses sanctioned by Appellation d'Origine Contrôlée standards, *Comté*—a semi-hard and slightly nutty example from the Franche-Comté region—has the highest production rate. Historically, the cheese was made in huge quantities, by shepherds pooling their milk resources and creating rounds that would take many months to mature, before being sold at the end of the seasons. *Comté*'s regulatory heritage and provenance distinctions were made official by the AOC in 1958, and state that the cheese must be made from the milk of the Montbéliarde breed of cow, that cheese production must begin immediately after milking, and that no grated cheese can be sold under the name. Similarly, no cheese awarded a score of 12 or under out of 20 by a number of specialised inspectors can be officially named *Comté*.

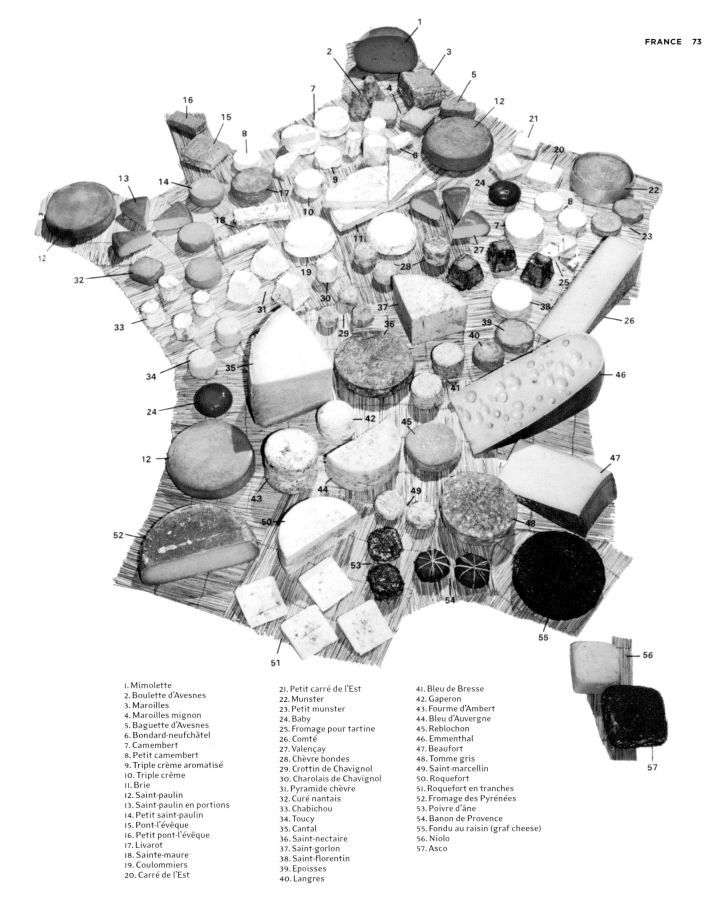

1. Mimolette
2. Boulette d'Avesnes
3. Maroilles
4. Maroilles mignon
5. Baguette d'Avesnes
6. Bondard-neufchâtel
7. Camembert
8. Petit camembert
9. Triple crème aromatisé
10. Triple crème
11. Brie
12. Saint-paulin
13. Saint-paulin en portions
14. Petit saint-paulin
15. Pont-l'évêque
16. Petit pont-l'évêque
17. Livarot
18. Sainte-maure
19. Coulommiers
20. Carré de l'Est

21. Petit carré de l'Est
22. Munster
23. Petit munster
24. Baby
25. Fromage pour tartine
26. Comté
27. Valençay
28. Chèvre bondes
29. Crottin de Chavignol
30. Charolais de Chavignol
31. Pyramide chèvre
32. Curé nantais
33. Chabichou
34. Toucy
35. Cantal
36. Saint-nectaire
37. Saint-gorlon
38. Saint-florentin
39. Epoisses
40. Langres

41. Bleu de Bresse
42. Gaperon
43. Fourme d'Ambert
44. Bleu d'Auvergne
45. Reblochon
46. Emmenthal
47. Beaufort
48. Tomme gris
49. Saint-marcellin
50. Roquefort
51. Roquefort en tranches
52. Fromage des Pyrénées
53. Poivre d'âne
54. Banon de Provence
55. Fondu au raisin (graf cheese)
56. Niolo
57. Asco

· PATISSERIE ·

MADELEINE

The small, scallop-shaped *madeleine* cakes are ubiquitous to French afternoon eating. There are various hypothetical origins for the cakes: from a servant named Madeleine creating the sweet for a deposed Polish king seeking sanctuary in France in the 1800s; to another like-named girl devising the scallop shaped snack as food for pilgrims travelling to the burial site of Saint-Jacques; or by the "master of *choux*" pastry chef Jean Avice, working for Prince Talleyrand, as suggested by the *Larousse Gastronomique*.

Despite hazy initial provenance of the *madeleine*, the town of Commercy, in Lorraine, eastern France, became the commercial centre of production for the cakes, with manufacturers to this day still marking their products "made in Commercy". The late nineteenth and early twentieth centuries saw *madeleine* vendors around the station of the town famously try to out-scream each other in an attempt to sell their goods.

Like the *croque-monsieur*, the formative literary reference to the cake appears in Proust's *A la recherche du temps perdu*, and the term "Proust's *madeleine*" has now come to represent anything that signifies an intense sense of nostalgia, given the event of the author's protagonist being transported into a vivid childhood memory when he eats one.

· RECIPE ·

65 g unsalted butter, melted
1 large egg
50 g caster sugar
50 g plain white flour
finely grated zest of 1 large lemon

—Preheat the oven to 190°C, gas mark 5. Melt the butter in the pan until it gives off a slightly nutty aroma. Remove a little to cool and use to grease the *madeleine* moulds—around 10 if large, 15 if smaller. Set aside the rest of the butter.
—Whisk the caster sugar and the egg together until thick, and the whisk leaves a trail when pulled through the mixture.
—Sift the flour on to the egg mixture and fold in slowly. Stir in the rest of the butter and the lemon zest.
—Fill the moulds with the mixture and bake in the preheated oven for 7-8 minutes. When golden, turn onto a cooling rack.

Scallop-shaped *madeleines de Commercy.*

PARIS-BREST

Invented in 1891 to commemorate the riders of the similarly named Paris to Brest circular cycle race—known as the PBP—the edible *Paris-Brest* is a cycle wheel-shaped ring of *choux* pastry halved and filled with whipped pastry cream, occasionally flavoured with vanilla.

A *Paris-Brest* pastry, in the shape of a cycle wheel and filled with whipped cream.

CRÊPES SUZETTE

Crêpes suzette is a common French desert, comprising a pancake with a sauce of caramelised sugar, orange juice, peel, and liquor, often Grand Marnier. Usually, the dish is *flambée* after the addition of the alcohol, adding an element of pyrotechnic theatrics which partly makes the dish so popular, as it is often constructed in front of diners in restaurants.

The heritage of the dish is alleged to have stemmed from 1895 at the Café de Paris in Monaco. The visiting Prince of Wales is reported to have ordered a course of *crêpes*, with a sauce of sugar, orange, and liqueur. The responsibility of cooking this was left to a 15 year old waiter, Henri Charpentier, who managed to set fire to the dish. Luckily, the King was delighted with the unexpected taste, and asked Charpentier what he intended to call his invention. The waiter suggested *Crêpes Princesse*, but Edward requested that it be named after one of his guest's daughters. Thus, *Crêpe Suzette* was chosen.

TARTE TATIN

Tarte tatin is a caramelised upside down apple tart, first devised in the Loire region of central France. The apocryphal 1898 origins of the dish stem from L'Hôtel Tatin, Lamotte-Beuvron, when the hotelier Stéphanie Tatin allegedly overcooked a traditional pie filling of apples, sugar, and butter. To disguise her mistakes, she covered the burnt results with a pastry topping and served it to the hotel guests, who were unexpectedly satisfied with the offering. Becoming a signature dish at the hotel, the desert was brought to national attention by Louis Vaudable, who reportedly stole the recipe with the use of a spy disguised as a gardener, and introduced the pie to his restaurant-cum-celebrity spotting ground, Maxim's of Paris.

· SAUCES ·

BÉCHAMEL

Béchamel, or white sauce, is the most basic of the French 'mother' sauces as set out by Antonin Carême. Made by whisking scalded milk into a *roux* paste of butter and flour, the sauce can have ingredients added to it to create myriad variations.

It is thought that seventeenth century chef François Pierre de la Varenne created the sauce for his seminal tome *Le cuisinier François*, naming the sauce in dedication to Marquis Louis de Béchamel, the chief steward of Louis XIV's household.

ESPAGNOLE

Espagnole's heritage derives from the French word for Spanish, and was allegedly so named to commemorate the chefs who added tomatoes to a brown stock at the wedding of Louis XIII, much to the delight of the assembled guests. The sauce is made by adding veal stock to a dark brown *roux*. Seasoning, bones, beef, vegetables, and tomatoes are also added, and the mixture is reduced and skimmed. *Espagnole* is the base to derivative sauces, such as *sauce bigarade*, *sauce bourguignonne*, *sauce aux champignons*, and *demi-glace*.

VELOUTÉ

Velouté, etymologically derived from the French word for "velvety", is a sauce made from a combination of light stock—predominantly with chicken, veal, or fish as a base—and a white *roux*. Also known as *sauce blanche grasse*, variations are often produced by adding ingredients such as cream, lemon, vinegar, parsley, or mushrooms.

ALLEMANDE

Based on the *velouté* sauce, *allemande* is produced with the addition of cream, egg yolks and lemon juice. Despite its derivative conception, it is still considered one of the four 'mother' sauces as laid out by Carême.

A traditional *béchamel* sauce.

·ENGLAND·

Previous pages: The Great Kitchen of Brighton's Royal Pavilion, circa 1897.

Opposite: Fifteenth century peasants work fields of wheat, whilst some take a break, eating bread and cheese.

Right: The physicality of preparing a Medieval feast is documented in this sequence from the *Luttrell Psalter*.

Social class, political situation and cultural changes have repeatedly been influential factors in the development of culinary traditions within English cookery. Food is in many ways a microcosm of the culture around which it is being prepared and enjoyed, and by examining the changes in cookery trends throughout England's history, we can better our understanding of the lives of the people eating it.

Unlike other European countries such as Spain, England's cuisine was not primordially shaped by ancient civilisations and Empirical occupation, but has rather been subtly adapted according to England's own conquests of other nations and their gastronomic traditions. England is, perhaps more than other nations, guilty of perpetuating a caste system, and the resulting differences between the cooking and eating practices of the upper and lower classes have been at odds with one another for centuries; even now the class divide is still evident, albeit not as strongly as it once was. English cuisine was once regarded as one of the finest in the world, but that image has slowly disintegrated with the passing of time, and the neglect of gastronomic pride from within England itself. However, thanks to the championing of English food by celebrity chefs, and new approaches to cooking from various multi-cultural influences, English cookery is looking to restore some of its lost value and importance.

In Medieval England, vast aristocratic estates provided the wealthy with an abundance of fresh meat, fish and crops. The Feudal System meant that agricultural workers would work the land for the land owners—the barons, earls and dukes—in return for tenancy of the land; although the farms could often produce an abundance of vegetables, it was the land owners who reaped the benefits. The upper and aristocratic classes of Medieval times would feast on this food over extravagant banquets serving spectacular dishes of jellies, pies, fritters, peacocks, seals, and even whales, although more 'down to earth' meats were also served, such as chicken, pheasant and beef, which was consumed in huge quantities. Aristocratic chefs flavoured foods with valuable spices such as caraway, nutmeg, cardamom, ginger and pepper; an ancient department at the Royal Court held its own 'spicery', built entirely with the purpose of holding huge

numbers of spice varieties. The puddings were dyed with sandalwood, saffron, or boiled black, to give them lurid colouring. Spectacle was everything at these lavish feasts, and they would be decorated with *sotiltees* (subtleties), large sugar sculptures adorning the tables in the shapes of mystical creatures, ships and castles. The food would all appear in one mass serving, rather than course by course, and diners could pick and choose from the huge variety of offerings depending on taste. The dining experience of the poor was, of course, vastly different. Although meat was occasionally available to them, it would mostly be pig—pickled and preserved to ensure its lasting benefits. Over 50 early Medieval cookery books are still in existence today, the most important of which is *The Forme of Cury*, an extensive collection of recipes put together by the master cook for King Richard II.

THE FORME OF CURY

The Forme of Cury is one of the English language's earliest known cookery books, dating from the latter part of the fourteenth century. Written by the master cooks to King Richard II, the manuscript details the great variety of culinary techniques and ingredients being put to work in the kitchens of the Medieval aristocracy and royalty. The book's content ranges from elaborate and unusual banqueting dishes containing rare and highly valued spices such as cardamom, nutmeg and black pepper, to "wholesome", "common" everyday dishes. The authors also note the traditional "physik", or medicinal properties of foods, whose uses date to ancient and prehistoric herbalist techniques. Elaborate, edible sculptures are also included in the book: made of sugar or jellies, these structures took the form of highly decorative architectural centrepieces and were seen on the tables of courts throughout Europe during the Medieval period.

Above: *The Forme of Cury*, a fourteenth century cookbook.

Opposite: A fifteenth century depiction of King Solomon and his wives, which reflects a contemporary fashion for dining alone.

Right: Early seventeenth century
herring fisherman pack their catches
in brine.

Opposite: A Tudor banquet held in the
honour of Sir Henry Unton; possibly
representing his wedding feast.

• THE TUDOR PERIOD •

The Tudor period, which lasted between 1485 and 1603, saw the population of England double from two million to four million; ten per cent of the population lived in cities and half of this total figure resided in London. For the poorer population, largely agricultural farmers, traders, and so on, four fifths of the average families income was spent on food, and their staple diet consisted of hunks of bread, cheese and the occasional offering of meat or fish. The menu for the average peasant was even worse. Poor relief from the church was a main means of income, and generally just a halfpenny loaf of bread was stretched between two people. The wealthy, however, continued with their banqueting traditions, but took the spectacle even

further, creating theatrical and excessive exhibitions for the art of dining. In 1508, the Duke of Buckingham held a feast for 460; the menu included swans, herons, peacocks, 12 pigs, ten sheep, 400 eggs and 260 flagons of ale, such was the levels of gluttony at these events. Modern celebrity chef Heston Blumenthal—who blends cookery with science, and is also the owner of The Fat Duck, lauded as one of the best restaurants in Britain—recreated a Tudor feast on *Heston's Feasts*. Using historical recipes, he served a sweet pudding of sausage, frog *blancmange*, and an exploding creature comprising a hog, turkey or sheep, filled with chicken, lamb and pork, creating a spectacle worthy of the Tudors applause.

A 1567 painting by the Master of the Countess of Warwick, showing Lord Cobham, his wife, sister-in-law and six children, who are eating a selection of fruit and nuts, indicating that fears surrounding fresh fruits and vegetables were beginning to disappear.

Frontispiece of *Paradisi in Sole Paradisus Terrestris*, 1629.

HERBALISM AND BOTANY

The frontispiece to John Parkinson's *Paradisi in Sole Paradisus Terrestris* of 1629, showing Adam and Eve in the Garden of Eden. Above the inscription can be seen an illustration of a pineapple, a rare commodity brought to Europe from the Americas by Christopher Columbus over a century earlier. An elaborate treatise on the cultivation of plants and their culinary and medicinal uses, or "the right ordering, planting and preserving of them and their uses and virtues", Parkinson employed his great experience of gardening to become not only a herbalist and botanist, but a founder member of the Worshipful Society of Apothecaries in 1617, a City of London Livery Company still in existence today. An expert in the traditional practise of herbalism, Parkinson was crucial in the development of botanical science in England, and was employed by King Charles I, to whose wife he dedicated *Paradisi in Sole*.

Candied fruits preserved in sugar.

SIR HUGH PLAT'S
DELIGHTES FOR LADIES

Sir Hugh Plat's activities during the late 1500s centred around the study of agriculture and animal husbandry, authoring numerous inventions and carrying out experimental projects in this field. It is with this background and experience that, in 1600, he wrote *Delightes for Ladies, to Adorne Their Persons, Tables, Closets, and Distillatories, With, Bewties, Banquets, Perfumes, and Waters.* A cookery manuscript focusing upon the preparation of sweets, Plat wrote to appeal to the aristocratic ladies that were his primary audience. Amongst 'ladies of leisure', the culinary art of fruit preservation was an established and respectable pastime, and Plat details the possibilities of sugaring, candying and modelling sweet products. His book makes reference to candied citrus rinds, or "sucket", and to "marchpanes", or marzipan.

English suspicions from this time resulted in a universal, although uninformed, fear of fresh fruit and vegetables. People regarded them with great suspicion and believed them to be the carriers of disease, thus all vegetables were thoroughly roasted before being consumed. Cooking techniques and attitudes towards food did, regardless, continue to develop, and the idea of cookery as an art expanded to new households and social circles. By the late 1500s, cookery books were being published with some regularity.

Sugar was an increasingly popular ingredient imported from the West/East Indies and Morocco. Tudor cooks would use it for everything, from preserving fruit, dressing vegetables, flavouring meat—it was even used in some remedies and medicines. Sugar was a luxury only afforded by the rich however, and the rottenness of your teeth was a good indicator of your wealth; Queen Elizabeth is said to have had nearly black teeth. Decaying teeth were not helped by poor irrigation, which also resulted in huge health problems. The water in Tudor times was so dirty, that ale was a common substitute, drunk throughout the day to avoid dehydration. The discovery of the "The New World" introduced new foods across Europe, and in 1580 Sir Francis Drake brought ingredients back from his travels to what is now Latin America, such as turkey, tomatoes, kidney beans and potatoes—food that is now taken for granted as part of English cookery.

Right: Robert May, from the frontispiece of his book *The Accomplisht Cook*, 1660.

Opposite: Preparations for a banquet in the Old Hall at Cothele, Cornwall. The Stuart style chairs, antlers and armour can clearly be seen.

• THE STUART PERIOD •

The 1600s and 1700s marked another great change in English history, beginning with the overthrowing of the monarchy in 1651. The English Civil War was a fight for power between the Parliamentarians and Royalists, which resulted in the trial and execution of King Charles I in 1649. The end of the monarchy saw many distinguished Royal chefs lose their jobs, so many turned to cookery book writing to make an income. The political changes also meant that there was suddenly a growing bourgeoisie, and these books by formally aristocratic cooks instructed the new middle class in the art of cookery and etiquette.

Due to the dissolution of the monasteries in the previous century, landowners began to force peasants off their land which in turn saw the evolution of commercial farming, as well as early population shifts from country to towns. During the 1600s English cuisine was influenced greatly by European menus, especially the French, and cooks acquired ingredient ideas such as anchovies, capers and wine from across the channel. Tea became a fashionable commodity in 1658, after the King, Charles II's, Portuguese wife, Catherine of Braganza, brought her love of the drink to England. Tea was however purely for the upper classes; at four pounds per pound, it cost as much as an artisan would make in three months, and a servant in a year.

ROBERT MAY

Robert May was one of the most important English cooks in the seventeenth century. May was one of many chefs sent to France by the Court to learn the art and trade of cooking as part of the popular trend of the time, where apprentice cooks would be sent to either France or Italy to study under the master chefs of aristocratic or courtly households. In 1660 he wrote his *The Accomplisht Cook, or the Art and Mystery of Cookery*, which he dedicated to those master cooks he had studied with abroad, and who allowed him to return to England with unusual new combinations of flavour, exotic Continental sauces, and culinary secrets. May had grown up in a courtly kitchen where his father had presided as a cook and organiser of magnificent banquets. It was here that May began to learn his trade, and where he developed a taste for spectacular menus, such as the pyrotechnic 'pie' he designed, from which would come "flying Birds and skipping Frogs". However, May also took care to detail simpler, accessible dishes more suited to readers with lower budgets, or those "whose Purses cannot reach to the cost of rich Dishes".

Opposite: William Hogarth's *Gin Lane*, produced as a political comment on the social implications of gin addiction.

Left: Detail of an illustration of *History of the Coronation of James II*, by Francis Sandford, 1687. The coronation feast was prepared by Patrick Lambe, and was an extravagant display of wealth and gastronomy.

Right: Hannah Glasse, whose book *The Art of Cookery Made Plain and Easy* helped to increase the number of proficient household cooks across the country.

PATRICK LAMBE

The illustration, above left, is taken from one of the most elaborate and ornate illustrated books of the seventeenth century, Francis Sandford's *History of the Coronation of James II*, a 'festival book' recording in detail the magnificent ceremonies of the occasion. The banquet shown here was served in the *à la française* style, with all "1,445 dishes of the delicious viands" served on the table at once, arranged in perfect symmetry. James II's Royal Cook for this banquet was Patrick Lambe, who was promoted in 1688 to "First Master Cook in the King's Kitchen", retaining this position through the reigns of William and Mary, and Queen Anne, in the early 1700s. In 1710 he published *Royal Cookery*, a seminal book in the field of aristocratic and courtly cookery, not only valuable for its practical applications but for the secrets, gossip, and intimate affairs that it revealed of England's royal tables. Lambe's influence was so great, and the extravagances and gluttonies of the Queen's table so attractive to its eighteenth century audience, that the wealthiest of England's population began to refer to elaborate banqueting dishes as "after Queen Anne's fashion".

HANNAH GLASSE

In 1747, Mrs Hannah Glasse published her volume of recipes, *The Art of Cookery Made Plain and Easy*, perhaps the most successful and enduring cookery book of its day. The head of a large household, Glasse applied this experience to her book, intending to prove that cookery need not be as extravagant or elaborate as the majority of books had previously suggested. It was advertised as "exceeding any thing of the kind ever yet published", with the intention of helping "ignorant and unlearned" cooks to realise the ease with which they might become proficient. The book's greatest audience would have been the aspirational middle classes, attracted by Glasse's time-saving and 'back to basics' approach, and her recipes included such lasting dishes as "Welsh rabbit", English muffins, and bread and butter pudding. Her advice on the aesthetics of food and its presentation would also have appealed, providing her readers an opportunity to display their new wealth through elegantly presented meals. Despite her book's success, Glasse, a serial entrepreneur—she also owned a dressmaking shop in Tavistock Street, London—would later be declared bankrupt and spend some months in prison.

By the early eighteenth century, there was a thriving pub scene in London, and although beer and ale was widely drunk, it was the introduction of gin that saw the popularity of pubs, and the number of alcoholics, soar. England began to develop a consumer culture, and various technological innovations altered cooking practices. Rolled sheet iron improved kitchen utensils, and superior fire grates also gave greater ease in the kitchen, therefore allowing further experimentation with previously complicated meals. Fresh meat became available all year round thanks to new winter feeding methods for cattle, and, now more than ever before, the classic roast beef was eaten widely across the country as a traditional family meal.

This new age of indulgence did, however, create health problems, such as gout, diabetes, heart and liver disease. Alcoholism was a much bigger issue than it had previously been, with poorer districts of towns encountering severe addiction problems amongst women and children as well as men. Many foods even contained poison; pepper was mixed with floor sweepings to increase its quantity and new copper and brass pans produced a poisonous layer of *vert-de-gris* when mixed with acidic foods. Cookery books were making a booming trade and were now a great commerce—books by prestigious chefs instructing housewives were more popular than ever. 'Celebrity chefs' who produced successful books included Patrick Lambe, Edward Kidder and Hannah Glasse.

EDW. KIDDER
Pastry-master.

EDWARD KIDDER

Edward Kidder, a self-proclaimed "pastry-master" was a renowned eighteenth century cook, best remembered for his book *Receipts of Pastry and Cookery*, published in London in 1720. The book included highly elaborate designs for the crusts of pies and pastries, made by placing templates onto the pastry and sculpting them with a confectioners tool. Such dishes were often very large, frequently containing a whole haunch of venison and made popular gifts which were often sent long distances—sometimes even abroad—so rye flour was used to make a hard durable crust which would not crack. Kidder, who died in 1739, taught the secrets of his trade at various cookery schools around London.

Above and right: Frontispiece and recipe from Edward Kidder's *Receipts of Pastry and Cookery*.

Opposite: A detail of a painting of oysters and fruit, by Jan Davidszoon de Heem, seventeenth century.

Overleaf: A banquet held to celebrate the coronation of King George IV in 1821.

Kidders Receipts. 11

Made Dishes.

Scotcht Collops.

Take the skin from a Fillet of Veal & cut it into thin Collops, hack and Scotch them with ye back of a knife, lard half of them with bacon & fry them with a little brown butter; then take them out & put them into another tossing pan, then set the pan they were fry'd in over the fire again, wash it out wth a little strong broth rubbing it with your ladle, then pour it to the Collops, do this to every panfull till all are fry'd; then stew & toss them up with a pint of Oysters, 2 Anchovies, 2 Shiver'd pallats, cocks combs, lambstones, & Sweetbreads blanch'd & Sliced, savory balls, onions, a faggot of Sweetherbs; thicken it with brown butter & garnish it with Slic'd Orange.

Olives of Veal

Take 8 or 10 Scotch Collops wash them over wth. the batter of eggs, then Season & lay over them a little forc'd meat, roul them up & roast them, then make for them a ragooe, & garnish it with Slic'd Orange.

Chickens forc'd wth Oysters.

Lard & Truss them, make a forcing of oysters, Sweetherbs, Parsley, Truffells, Mushrooms, & Onions; chop these together and Season it, mix it with a piece of butter the yolk of an egg then tye them at both ends and roast them; then make for them a Ragooe & garnish them with Slic'd Lemon.

F₃.

Afternoon tea at The Ritz.

• THE INDUSTRIAL REVOLUTION •

The early 1800s saw the further expansion of the city. The dawn of the Victorian era, with the Industrial Revolution in full swing, witnessed the need for new technologies in food production, preservation and transportation. These changes were partly profit driven, but also part of a genuine need to feed the ever growing population. From 1851 to the end of the Victorian era in 1901, the British population increased by 16.21 million. Canning technology and the new steam railways allowed for the easy transportation of foods around the country, and the country at large could now enjoy region specific specialities. However, some Victorian food contained several undesirable additives, including strychnine in rum and beer, lead in mustard, wine and cider and copper carbonate in sugar.

The Industrial Revolution saw the mass growth of the working class, and cheap, accessible, and nutritious meals were vital to keep the factory workers healthy. Fish and chips was seen as an ideal dish, and the lasting popularity of this great English meal is dated from the 1860s. Other popular take-away city foods included pie and jellied eels. Meanwhile, the upper classes were enjoying their afternoon tea at newly established top rate restaurants like The Ritz, where scones, jam and clotted cream were consumed with elegant dignity.

CESAR RITZ AND THE RITZ HOTEL, LONDON

In 1906, César Ritz opened The Ritz Hotel on Piccadilly in London. Already a world-famous hotelier, Ritz introduced a level of opulence and style to Victorian Londoners matched only by the Savoy, and his other famed enterprise, the Hôtel Ritz Paris. Its French neoclassical architecture provided the perfect setting for guests to eat at The Ritz Restaurant, where César Ritz hired French chef Auguste Escoffier as head of its kitchen. Escoffier's luxurious and creative cooking provided an extraordinary dining experience, suitable for the hotel's celebrity and royal clientele. Already a renowned *haute cuisine* chef, Escoffier built on and modernised Antonin Carême's technique, and went on to introduce the *à la carte* menu at the Carlton in London.

Ice cream sculpture moulds from Mrs Marshall's *The Book of Ices*.

The notion of new elegant dinner parties held in the home was invented by the Victorians. They were an excellent way for the urban middle classes to exert their new wealth with gluttony and social fineries, as well as an outlet for gentlemen to discuss business ventures and political opinions. The main course could comprise roast quail, whilst dessert might include ice cream, which was another fashionable delight of the Victorians, and Mrs Marshall's ice cream moulds allowed fabulous sculptures to be created and consumed.

MRS MARSHALL

During the Victorian period, the moulds that had been traditionally used to form savoury puddings and jellies took on an utterly novel purpose. New refrigeration techniques meant that ice—previously harvested from frozen lakes during the winter season—could finally be artificially formed in the domestic environment. Flavoured ice creams, although already in existence some decades earlier, could now be produced easily and economically at home, and moulded ices and fruit sorbets became quite common and *de rigeur* at dinner parties. In 1880, Agnes Bertha Marshall published *The Book of Ices*, an instructive manual that illustrated the colourful and extravagant edible ice structures one could create. It also provided her with an opportunity to advertise some of the domestic ice cream machines she herself invented. These were in fact similar to ice cream makers still in use today, operating by a hand crank to turn the cream mixture. Mrs Marshall, as she was known, is also reputedly responsible for creating the edible cone. Although the cone's invention is often attributed to American origin, in 1888 she presented a book of cookery that includes a recipe for cornets and cream, which is in principle the same idea as the cone we use today.

A VICTORIAN DINNER PARTY

The image here shows many of the nuances of the etiquette that was required for a Victorian dinner party. To begin, it was required that the room be lit with white candles, and it was considered to be most appropriate if lighting was also placed next to walls so that it could bounce off and create a warm atmosphere. The tablecloth was always to be of the highest quality that the host could afford, but there were to be no other ostentatious displays of wealth. Obstructions of view were to be taken into account and there was to be nothing to prevent guests from seeing one another across a table. Low flowers were only acceptable if they did not have a scent and each guest was provided with a place card so that he or she would know where to sit. Likewise the silverware was determined with care and included two large knives, a knife and fork for fish, three large forks, a spoon for soup and an oyster fork, along with a plate and a water glass.

An engraving of a high Victorian dinner party, circa 1870.

Opposite: A portrait of Alexis Soyer from the frontispiece of *Pantropheon*.

Below: The Reform Club, of which Alexis Soyer was head chef; he designed the layout of the kitchen himself.

Industrialisation sped up the homogenisation of the English diet, so the various social classes generally ate similar foods and drew their culinary inspiration from the same nationally distributed cookbooks, which were a must have in kitchens up and down the country. Popular chefs from the time producing influential books included Mrs Beeton and Alexis Soyer. Tastes from the Empire were also starting to exert an influence over British palates, as Indian flavours and cooking traditions began to find their way into English recipes. Anglo-Asian cookery originated during the British Raj in India, and included mulligatawny soup, still popular today. The cuisine often combines Indian spices with ingredients more reminiscent of English foods, for example roast meats combined with chili and mild coconut or yoghurt-based sauces. Restaurants such as Veeraswamy in London were among the first to introduce this modern cuisine to the public as a fine-dining cuisine, and in the present day Indian restaurants are among the most prevalent and popular locations for both restaurant and take-away dining.

ALEXIS SOYER

Alexis Soyer was the most famous and celebrated chef in Victorian London. Born in Meaux-en-Brie in France, he was expelled from school in 1821 and moved to Paris to work as an apprentice at the restaurant G Rignon. He fled to England during the Revolution, where he worked in several aristocratic kitchens, eventually becoming known as the best chef in England. In 1837 Soyer became head chef at the Reform Club, a private gentlemen's club in London, where he himself designed the kitchen in which he was to work. In 1847 during the Great Irish Famine, Soyer was sent by the government to Ireland where he was able to put into practice his idea for a soup kitchen. Known for implementing the most up-to-date and innovative gastronomic inventions, in the 1850s he created a portable stove for the armies involved in the Crimean War. He also initiated many other military reforms, including the introduction of a resident cook for each regiment. It was during this time that he made the acquaintance of Florence Nightingale, with whom he continued to work to improve catering and sanitation for army corps.

Still considered an important work for British military campaigns, *A Culinary Campaign* is Alexis Soyer's memoir of his work with the military during the Crimean War. Instructing on how to serve large groups with few resources, and how to cook in large portions, the book makes clear the revolutionary nature of Soyer's reforms to military cookery, including his field stove, which continued to be used by the British military well into the twentieth century.

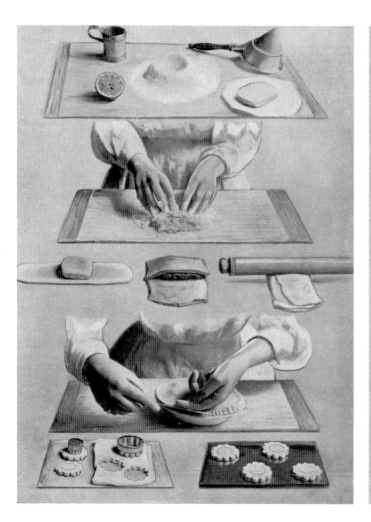

1

2

3

4

5

6

• SAVOURY PUDDINGS •

ELIZA ACTON, FROM *MODERN COOKERY FOR PRIVATE FAMILIES*

SAVOURY PUDDINGS.

The perfect manner in which the nutriment and flavour of an infinite variety of viands may be preserved by enclosing and boiling them in paste, is a great recommendation of this purely English class of dishes, the advantages of which foreign cooks are beginning to acknowledge. If really well made, these savoury puddings are worthy of a place on any table; though the decrees of fashion—which in many instances have so much more influence with us than they deserve—have hitherto confined them almost entirely to the simple family dinners of the middle classes; but we are bound to acknowledge that even where they are most commonly served they are seldom prepared with a creditable degree of skill; and they are equally uninviting and unwholesome when heavily and coarsely concocted. From the general suggestions which we make here, and the few detailed receipts which follow, a clever cook will easily compound them to suit the taste and means of her employers; for they may be either very rich and expensive, or quite the reverse. Venison (the neck is best for the purpose), intermingled or not with truffles; sweetbreads sliced, and oysters or nicely prepared button-mushrooms

in alternate layers, with good veal stock for gravy; pheasants, partridges, moorfowl, woodcocks, snipes, plovers, wheatears, may all be converted into the first class of these; and veal kidneys, seasoned with fine herbs, will supply another variety of them. Many persons like eels dressed in this way, but they are unsuited to delicate eaters; and sausages are liable to the same objection; and so is a *harslet* pudding, which is held in much esteem in certain counties, and which is made of the heart, liver, kidneys, &c., of a pig. We can recommend as both wholesome and economical the receipts which follow, for the more simple kind of savoury puddings, and which may serve as guides for such others as the intelligence of the cook may suggest.

BEEF-STEAK, OR JOHN BULL'S PUDDING.

All meat puddings are more conveniently made in deep pans, moulds, or basins having a thick rim, below which the cloths can be tied without the hazard of their slipping off; and as the puddings should by no means be *turned out* before they are sent to table, one to match the dinner-service, at least in *colour*, is desirable! Roll out a suet crust to

half an inch in thickness, line evenly with it a quart, or any other sized basin that may be preferred, and raise the crust from an inch and a half to two inches above the edge. Fill it with layers of well-kept rump-steak, neatly trimmed, and seasoned with salt and pepper, or cayenne; pour in some cold water to make the gravy; roll out the cover, moisten the edge, as well as that of the pudding; draw and press them together carefully, fold them over, shake out a cloth which has been dipped into hot water, wrung out, and well floured; tie it over the pudding, gather the corners together, tie them over the top of the pudding, put it into plenty of fast boiling water, and let it remain in from three to five hours, according to its size. The instant it is lifted out, stick a fork quite through the middle of the paste to prevent its bursting; remove the cloth quickly, and cut a small round or square in the top to allow the steam to escape, and serve the pudding *immediately*. Though not considered very admissible to an elegantly served table, this is a favourite dish with many persons, and is often in great esteem with sportsmen, for whom it is provided in preference to fare which requires greater exactness in the time of cooking; as an additional hour's boiling, or even more, will have little effect on a large pudding of this kind, beyond reducing the quantity of gravy, and rendering it very thick.

Some cooks flour the meat slightly before it is laid into the crust, but we do not think it an improvement: where fat is liked, a portion may be added with the lean, but all skin and sinew should be carefully rejected. Beat the steak with a paste roller, or cutlet-bat, should it not appear to be perfectly tender, and divide it into portions about the width of two fingers. Two or three dozens of oysters, bearded and washed free from grit in their own liquor (which should afterwards be strained and poured into the pudding), may be intermingled with the meat.

A true epicurean receipt for this dish directs the paste to be made with real-kidney suet, and filled with alternate layers *of the inside of the sirloin*, sliced and seasoned, and of fine plump native oysters, intermixed with an occasional small slice of the veal fat.

SMALL BEEF-STEAK PUDDING.

Make into a very firm smooth paste, one pound of flour, six ounces of beef-suet finely minced, half a teaspoonful of salt, and half a pint of cold water. Line with this a basin which holds a pint and a half. Season a pound of tender steak, free from bone and skin, with half an ounce of salt and half a teaspoonful of pepper well mixed together; lay it in the crust, pour in a quarter of a pint of water, roll out the cover, close the pudding carefully, tie a floured cloth over, and boil it for three hours and a half. We give this receipt in addition to the preceding one, as an exact guide for the proportions of meat-puddings in general.

Flour, 1 lb; suet, 6 oz; salt, ½ teaspoonful; water, ½ pint; rumpsteak, 1 lb; salt, ½ oz; pepper, ½ teaspoonful; water, ½, pint. 3 ½ hours.

RUTH PINCH'S BEEF-STEAK PUDDING.

To make *Ruth Pinch's* celebrated pudding (known also as beef steak pudding a la Dickens), substitute six ounces of butter for the suet in this receipt, and moisten the paste with the well-beaten yolks of four eggs, or with three whole ones, mixed with a little water; butter the basin very thickly before the paste is laid in, as the pudding is to be turned out of it for table. In all else proceed exactly as above.

MUTTON PUDDING.

Mutton freed perfectly from fat, and mixed with two or three sliced kidneys, makes an excellent pudding. The meat may be sprinkled with fine herbs as it is laid into the crust. This will require rather less boiling than the preceding puddings, but it is made in precisely the same way.

From *Modern Cookery for Private Families*, Eliza Acton, with an Introduction by Elizabeth Ray, published by Southover Press, 1993, pp. 336–337. Reprinted by permission of Equinox Publishing Ltd.

An early twentieth century
Oxo advertisement.

Customers at the Savoy Hotel enjoy the first class service and fine cuisine at the five star establishment, circa 1950.

• THE TWENTIETH CENTURY •

Although in the early stages of the Industrial Revolution eating and health standards were poor—especially amongst the working classes—but as the century progressed diet was improved amongst the masses. Vitamins and their various benefits were only discovered at the beginning of the twentieth century, and food standards gradually rose as a result. The early part of the 1900s saw the wealthy frequent restaurants and bars as part of evenings out, with the 1920s and 30s, in particular, representing a slight shift in the previously vast difference between the working, middle and upper classes. As the class system continued to dissolve, more people began to enjoy the modern life of capitalism and consumerism. Convenience foods were beginning to infiltrate English kitchens; Oxo cubes became popular as an easy alternative to home produced stock, and as an instant gravy to accompany roast dinner.

The Second World War impacted massively on English cookery, as rationing was introduced and those who could not fight were encouraged to keep up the home front by growing their own vegetables and eating as nutritiously as possible. Corned beef and Spam became popular during the war years, as they were cheap alternatives to large meat cuts, and although they were hardly as nutritious, they did still provide essential protein. During the war over 100 million pounds of Spam were shipped to help feed allied troops.

Precious CRUSTS

No scrap of bread is too small to save — it means saving valuable shipping space. Of course your best and most direct way of helping, is to take less bread into the house. Most households find they can do nicely with three-quarters of the bread they used to buy and yet can give every member of the family all the bread he or she individually needs.

The secret is in eating up every scrap of bread that comes in. Don't forget the end of the loaf. It's the bit that's apt to get left over. You always intended to do something with it. But how often was it thrown out, after all!

Half a slice of stale bread saved by everyone in this country every day, means a convoy of 30 ships a year freed to take munitions or men to our fighting fronts. If you explain this to your family you'll find them eager enough to help you save on bread!

Save Bread: Save Ships

4 things you can do

1 **Cut down your purchase (or making) of bread.** Most households find they can do nicely with three-quarters of the bread they used to buy.

2 Put the loaf on the dresser or side table. Cut only as required.

3 Use every crumb.

4 Don't eat bread whilst potatoes are on the table.

Some ways of using up STALE BREAD

CRISPY PIE-CRUST. Cut bread into dice ¼ in. thick. Cover a savoury pie with them, setting the dice closely together. Pour over them a little thin custard (salted) taking care that every piece of bread is moistened. Bake in a brisk oven.

SOAKED BREAD. This is the foundation of a countless number of puddings and cakes. No bread is too stale for it, and there is no need to remove any crust. Break into small pieces, put into bowl, cover completely with cold water and soak thoroughly. If the bread is to be used for a savoury, use vegetable boilings instead of water. Then squeeze the bread *hard*, put back in the bowl and beat with a fork until quite free from lumps and pieces of crust. The beating is most important and makes all the difference between a dull heavy pudding and a smooth, spongy texture.

MINCE SLICES. Mix 8 ozs. mince with 4 ozs. cooked mashed potatoes and 4 ozs. fine crumbs. Season to taste. Roll out on a floured board into an oblong ¼ in. thick. Cut into slices and fry in a very little hot fat or grill for 5 to 7 minutes. Serve with leek sauce.

MAKING RUSKS. Cut bread into neat figures, or fancy shapes, about ½ in. thick. Bake in a warm oven until crisp and golden brown. Pack in an air-tight tin. This is a valuable emergency store which will keep good for months.

TURN WASTE INTO DELICACIES!

A new taste-thrill!

Shredded raw cabbage in salads

Yes; here it is: clean-tasting, nutty, with a hint of " pep " to liven up war-jaded palates. Anyone who has not yet tasted a salad containing shredded raw cabbage is missing a real taste-treat.

Then, too, first class as are properly cooked greens and fresh fruits for giving you that feeling of well-being, for clearing the skin, for rosy cheeks, good teeth, and glossy hair, *uncooked* cabbage and other green-leaved vegetables are even better still. So why not brighten up your menus and do yourself and family good at the same time! Eat " something green and raw every day " as the Radio Doctor says. Just try these three ways of enjoying salads :—

Pilchard Salad

4 pilchards, ½ lb. cold cooked potatoes, cubed; 1 doz. radishes; 2 tablespoons chopped parsley; 1 finely chopped leek; 2 tablespoons salad dressing ; ½ lb. shredded cabbage or other greens; watercress.

Flake the fish and mix with the other ingredients except the cabbage and 1 tablespoon parsley. Add sufficient salad dressing to moisten well. Pile on the shredded greens and decorate with parsley, watercress and radishes. *To make the "flowers" if you wish, split long-shaped radishes nearly to base several times with sharp knife. Put into cold water and they will open out.*

(Instead of the pilchards, sometimes have cheese, hard-boiled dried egg, small pieces of meat, bacon, or other fish. With bread and butter or margarine and a milky drink any one of these salad combinations makes a complete meal.)

Palette Salad

For eye appeal and encouragement to appetite this salad takes some beating. Serve as a " side-dish " or as a separate course. *3 oz. shredded cabbage, 4 oz. grated beetroot, 2 oz. grated parsnip, 1 oz. chopped leek, 2 oz. carrot cut in strips. All the vegetables are used raw.* Lay shredded cabbage in oblong dish. Arrange a border of grated beetroot round edge of dish, and other vegetables as desired.

Salad Sandwiches

These are an excellent way to introduce salad-eating to young children, who sometimes " can't get through " a plateful of salad. Ring the changes by mixing with the shredded cabbage some watercress, mustard and cress, parsley or any other vegetables, chopped or shredded. Sprinkle with a little seasoning if liked. If you are making salad sandwiches for packed main meals, mix with the vegetables some body-builder such as hard boiled dried egg, grated cheese, chopped meat or bacon, or some fish. Mix with salad dressing.

TRY THIS SALAD DRESSING
(NO MILK REQUIRED)

2 oz. margarine ; 2 oz. flour, 1 pint well-flavoured vegetable water, salt and pepper, 3-4 tablespoons vinegar, 1-2 teaspoons made mustard, 1 teaspoon sugar. Melt the margarine and mix in the flour. When smooth add the vegetable water and stir till boiling. Boil 2-3 minutes and then add remaining ingredients to taste.

BETTER POT-LUCK

with Churchill today

THAN HUMBLE PIE

under Hitler tomorrow

DON'T WASTE FOOD!

WARTIME BRITAIN

During the Second World War, meat, eggs and dairy became luxuries that were saved for special occasions and the rich. This meant that the population was forced to create filling and nutritious meals based largely upon root vegetables and pulses. During this period, many cookery books were published and leaflets distributed, providing suggestions as to how to be thrifty with ingredients, and to tailor dishes to include rationed products such as dehydrated eggs. One example of a meal that became popular during the war is Woolton Pie: the recipe was created by the chef of the Savoy at the time and was named after Lord Woolton, the head of the Ministry of Food. The dish simply included potatoes, cauliflower, swede, carrots, onions, vegetable extract, and oatmeal. Intended to be cooked with just enough water to keep it from sticking to the pan, the mixture was spooned up with a potato crust. In the 1940s the government issued a campaign that suggested how women could help in the war effort by reducing how much food they used. As such, many women took part in "Dig for Victory" which encouraged them to sow gardens full of potatoes and other vegetables that would fill stomachs instead of using the other vegetables that were needed for the war effort.

Opposite: A Ministry of Food pamphlet on conserving food and eating healthily.

Left: A Second World War poster promoting the importance of eating economically.

Right: The front of a Sainsbury's store from 1905.

Opposite: A commentary by Banksy on the mainstream supermarkets.

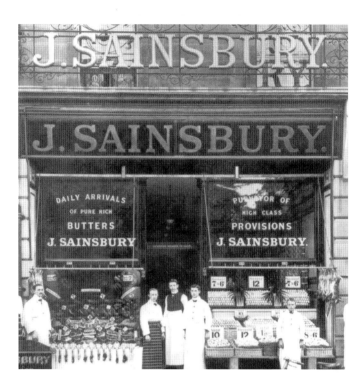

The Ministry of Food frequently produced pamphlets on how to use the food that was still available to cook healthy and hearty meals. After rationing was finally abolished in 1954, new trends in food started to emerge. Supermarkets sales were booming and the chain stores began to drive out local butchers and greengrocers, and further intensified the homogenisation of the English diet. Wimpy Bar, the UK's version of McDonalds, opened its first restaurants in 1954, and served American style hamburgers.

Whilst specific brands were becoming ever more popular, new waves of immigrants brought over their own culinary traditions, bringing new variety to English cookery. Indian curries continued to dominate the multi-cultural food market, but new menus such as Chinese, Thai and Caribbean also influenced the market. Today countless different cuisines sit next to each other in take-away shops and restaurants on the English high street. English cookery draws influences from many of them, so that the variety of visual images that can be conjured when considering contemporary English cuisine is vast.

SUPERMARKETS

Many people blame supermarkets as being partly responsible for the falling standards of the English diet. Although Sainsbury's had been open since the mid-1800s, it was the post-war years that really drove forward the notion of the modern supermarket, as self-service stores started to appear. The growing prosperity within England at the time, coupled with falling rationing restrictions, and changing trends in retail, all helped to encourage spending in the increasing numbers of Tesco, Marks and Spencer and Morrisons stores.

Today supermarkets have a massively unbalanced place within the market: Tesco for example owns 31 per cent of the market share, and takes 12.5 per cent of the total consumer spend within the UK. The influence supermarkets exert can potentially have a significant negative effect on farmers, the environment, as well as the quality of food that is available. Although supermarkets generally offer a variety of products, the majority of them also offer a 'value' range, the quality of which is highly questionable. Cheap battery reared chickens and eggs, additives and chemicals imitating flavour and fruit and vegetables flown half way across the world—raking up huge numbers of air miles—are just some of the problems that can be found on supermarket shelves. Celebrity chefs, including Jamie Oliver and Hugh Fearnley-Whittingstall, amongst others, are campaigning to raise awareness of the implications of buying these products, and are calling for a return to natural, locally produced products and the great need for sustainable rural agriculture. However, without the co-operation of the supermarkets these aims are unlikely to be achieved.

GROWING YOUR OWN

There has been an increasing trend towards home-grown produce as the widespread use of preservatives, colourings and pesticides in supermarket have become increasingly unappealing to consumers. The Royal Horticulture Society and the BBC have led the way in promoting home-grown vegetables as a resourceful way to save money and perhaps more importantly as a way to combat climate change during a period when these issues have begun to achieve widespread recognition. Riding a wave of enthusiasm for do-it-yourself home-growing, many websites and books have proliferated that are devoted to planning and laying out a garden with helpful hints on technique as well as other practical considerations such as soil preparation and general maintenance. The Soil Association is a Bristol-based charity that champions the importance of organic, locally produced, seasonal foods, and publishes standards that they believe should be met by farmers and retailers. Although supermarkets do sell organic produce, farmers markets are becoming ever more popular as consumers become more conscious of issues surrounding air miles and a greater desire for fresh, locally sourced food.

Runner beans, beetroot, carrots, tomatoes, rosemary and mint, all organically grown in an allotment.

A thai steak salad served in an English gastropub.

• MODERN CUISINE •

In an age of instant gratification, the quality of food has reduced as people's need for quick meal fixes increases, reflecting the busy, fast paced lifestyle of much of the country's population. There is a fear surrounding the decline of family/home cooking, as well as concerns over growing obesity—figures indicate that 22 per cent of English adults are obese. This has arisen as a result of the over saturated, emulsified and mass-produced fast food and cheap supermarket produce. It is fair to say that it is largely amongst the poorer families that weight and dietary problems predominate, so in some ways English cookery is still divided by class. On the other hand, England is home to some of the most prestigious restaurants in the world, such as The Fat Duck in Berkshire, L' Autre Pied in Mayfair and Claridges in Brook Street, London. New developments in gastronomy as well as a growing nostalgia and demand for traditional hearty English foods such as roast beef, steak and kidney pie, toad in the hole and of course fish and chips—such dishes are favourites at 'gastro pubs' across the country—are marking a new resurgence in English cookery. England is home to a number of prestigious celebrity chefs and their esteemed restaurants, and the cult of the celebrity chef is perhaps stronger in England than elsewhere in the world. as such English cuisine, in its varied historical and cultural influences, is still worthy of a place amongst the great cuisines of the world.

FANNY CRADOCK

During the 1950s Fanny Cradock was the face of home cookery on the BBC. Her rise to culinary celebrity was swift. Following the success of her book *The Practical Cook* in 1949, Cradock began penning a food column in *The Telegraph* entitled "Bon Viveur" with her partner Johnnie, which the Queen Mother was to claim was responsible for raising the standard of cooking in England. With *The Telegraph* the pair also travelled the country staging cookery shows of "Kitchen Magic" in theatres, during which they would cook elaborate French dishes and serve them to their audience. Cradock's cooking style aimed to bring the traditions of French *haute cuisine* to the English home; however by the 1960s her sometimes over-the-top cooking was already becoming dated. She was known for her eccentricity, presenting her cookery shows dressed in ball-gowns and heavily made-up, exclaiming that "cooking is a cleanly art, not a grubby chore".

A woman of extremes, Cradock was perhaps best known for her ambivalent relationship towards Christmas, declaring it at once "pagan, revolting and commercial", and yet insisting that preparations should begin a year in advance. Beneath her harsh exterior, she was driven by a desire to champion quality cooking on a budget and campaigned successfully against artificial flavourings and fertilisers.

• CELEBRITY CHEFS •

The modern trend of the celebrity chef applies variously to restaurateurs who have become well-known in the media, to food writers and cooks without backgrounds in professional chefing, such as Delia Smith. Predecessors of today's celebrity chefs include Martino da Como in the fifteenth century who was renowned for his cooking throughout Italy, and Marie-Antonin Carême, whose reputation followed him to the most celebrated courts and aristocratic houses of Europe and Russia. In 1805, cook Maria Rundel's book, *A New System of Domestic Cookery*, which was targeted at women and instructed them on the running of the household, as well as etiquette and reliable, nourishing recipes. Certain chefs and the phenomenon of celebrity chefs as a whole has had a considerable impact upon the English population's culinary habits and awareness, from the popularisation of French gastronomic traditions by figures such as Fanny Cradock, to the simplification and accessibility of cookery by Delia Smith and Jamie Oliver—although Smith has controversially published books advocating the use of battery farm eggs and using cheaper tinned produce over fresh, an attitude to cooking which is at odds with Oliver's.

DELIA SMITH

Delia Smith is one of England's most eminent and respected celebrity chefs. She began her gastronomic career at The Singing Chef in Paddington, London, shortly after leaving school at the age of 16. Beginning as a dish-washer, Smith's thirst for culinary knowledge, much of which was gained in the British Library's reading rooms, pushed her into practical cheffing. The late 1960s and early 1970s saw her writing for publications such as the *Daily Mirror*, *Evening Standard*, and the *Radio Times*.

She first appeared on television in her 1973 BBC series *Family Fare*. Since then she has subsequently appeared as the presenter of such successful series' as *Delia Smith's Cookery Course*, *Delia Smith's Winter Collection*, *Delia Smith's Summer Collection*, and *Delia's How To Cook*, most with corresponding—and equally successful—publications. Her 2008 title *How To Cheat At Cooking*, an update of her 1971 book of the same name, was received with some controversy due to its focus on "kitchen shortcuts", but became an immediate success. The popularity of her televised and written output has made her one of the BBC's most recognisable faces and placed her amongst the country's most trusted cooks.

GORDON RAMSAY

Gordon Ramsay is probably the most successful restaurateur, chef and television personality of the present-day in England. In Michelin starred awards, Ramsay is ranked third in the world, behind only the French chefs Joël Robuchon and Alain Ducasse. An injury curtailed a professional football career in his earlier years, allowing Ramsay's interest in cooking to flourish. Having trained with such gastronomic luminaries at Marco Pierre White, Guy Savoy, and Albert Roux, he founded his first restaurant, Gordon Ramsay at Hospital Road, in Chelsea, London, in 1998. He is famed for his straight-talking style, which can be seen in his television series *The F-Word*, *Ramsay's Kitchen Nightmares*, and the reality television competition, *Hell's Kitchen*.

NIGELLA LAWSON

Nigella Lawson has enjoyed enormous success in recent years as both a food writer and a television cook. Her book *How to be a Domestic Goddess*, 2000, was a bestseller and won numerous awards, and later that year she hosted her first programme, *Nigella Bites*. She became immediately famous for her openness about the sensual and emotional aspects of food, and for championing the pleasure and enjoyment of cooking. Lawson's most recent series *Nigella Express*, released in 2007, encouraged the quick cooking of tasty, nutritious food through simple means, and again emphasised her status as an accessible home cook that the public can relate to.

HUGH FEARNLEY-WHITTINGSTALL

After schooling at Eton, Hugh Fearnley-Whittingstall studied at Oxford University, following his graduation with a period of conservation work in Africa. He began his culinary career as a sous-chef at the River Café but was made redundant, an early blow that he has claimed helped define his current career. His early television programmes *Cook on the Wild Side* and *TV Dinners* earned him a reputation for eccentricity, as he was seen foraging for and cooking roadkill animals, and infamously cooking a human placenta.

Fearnley-Whittingstall's present success came about through his television series *River Cottage*, based on a project he started in Dorset in 1997 where he established a small-holding. The River Cottage project and many television series have seen Fearnley-Whittingstall growing and rearing his own food in an effort to get closer to the processes of food preparation. The project continues to operate by its principles of self-sufficiency, organics, food integrity and the use of locally produced, seasonal food. The River Cottage HQ also runs courses in everything from foraging to butchery, and is supported by a canteen and local produce store which provides food according to the River Cottage philosophy. River Cottage has cemented Fearnley-Whittingstall as a respectable chef, and has placed him alongside fellow television chefs Jamie Oliver and Gordon Ramsay in the campaign to encourage sensible eating using responsibly sourced ingredients. He has also publicly campaigned extensively against the rearing of chickens in battery cages, and the mass-distribution of these animals at low cost through supermarkets.

JAMIE OLIVER

After first appearing on British television as *The Naked Chef* in 1998, Jamie Oliver has become one of England's best loved chefs. His parents own a pub, The Cricketers, in Clavering, Essex, and Jamie grew up fascinated by the going ons of the kitchen, and helped out with food preparation from the age of eight. He left school at 16 to go to Westminster Catering College, and then spent time in France absorbing the gastronomic atmosphere. His television career came about after he made an impression on producers when he appeared on a documentary about the restaurant he was working in; *The Naked Chef* was quick to follow. Jamie Oliver has used his reputation as a celebrity chef to champion various causes through his television shows. *Jamie's Kitchen* saw him setting up 15 London restaurants and the 15 Foundation Charity, which exists to give young people who come from disadvantaged backgrounds the chance to work in Jamie's restaurants and give them training in chefery. *School Dinners* was an attempt to show the country the poor standards of the processed food that is served up in school canteens, and appealed to the government to provide children with nutritious lunches; as a result of the programme the government pledged to spend £280 million over three years to improve the standards of food in school canteens. Other programmes such as *Jamie at Home* and now *Jamie's American Road Trip* see Oliver championing the use of home grown, simple and nutritious ingredients to make hearty and delicious meals, that as Jamie would say, are "pukka".

English Asparagus, a seasonal speciality
officially 'in season' from 1 May–21 June.

· BREAKFAST ·

FULL ENGLISH BREAKFAST

A full English breakfast—also variously referred to as a "fry up", "full English" or an "Ulster fry"—is a traditional meal popular both in home-cooking and at cafes where is commonly served as a hearty "all-day breakfast". The dish typically consists of fried bacon and eggs accompanied by a combination of sausages, baked beans, grilled tomato, fried mushrooms, black pudding, and fried bread. It is usually served with a cup of tea or orange juice.

Another traditional English breakfast food is kippers, or smoked herring, although this is much less commonly served today. The traditional 'leftovers' dish "bubble and squeak"—a fried mixture of mashed potato and cabbage—is also a popular component of the breakfast meal. The Northern Ireland variation, the "Ulster fry", is distinguished by the addition of a flat triangular "farl" of soda bread, and the meal is typically fried in lard.

PORRIDGE

Porridge is another traditional, but still popular, breakfast meal. It is made by boiling oats in milk, water, or a mixture of both. It is generally served with salt or sugar, depending on taste. Although eaten all over the world, porridge has strong ties with Scotland, where it is conventionally prepared with a "spurtle"—a fifteenth century cooking utensil rather like a spatula.

Porridge making has even become a competitive game—the World Porridge Making Championships are held annually in Carridge, Inverness-shire. During Victorian times the poorest sector of the population ate a very watery version of porridge which was known as gruel. This formed a staple, although unpleasant, part of their diet.

KIPPERS

A kipper is a herring that is split open from head to tail. The English eat their kippers grilled or fried for breakfast.

In the early twentieth century the urban working classes consumed kippers as part of high tea or supper, and today they are a widely enjoyed nostalgic treat. They are particular favourites in the Scottish Highlands, East Anglia and Northumberland. Overfishing of herring has led to a decline in kipper consumption; however the town of Hastings on the southeast coast of England produces especially fine herrings that are then prepared as kippers. This has led The Marine Stewardship Council to recognise Hastings for their sustainable herring fishing methods.

"Kipper time" historically refers to the prohibited practice of salmon fishing in the River Thames between 3 May and 6 January, as enforced by an Act of Parliament.

• FISH •

JANE GRIGSON

I remember as a child listening to my father's tales of going out with the herring boats from South Shields or Tynemouth. He talked about the cold and the fierce sea, the sudden energy required and the cups of strong sweet tea that kept people going. When the nets were pulled in, the silver catch tumbled into the boat for what seemed like hours, the mesh stuck solid with the fish. He came to appreciate Scott's remark in *The Antiquary*, "It's nae fish ye're buying, it's men's lives."

Such things had gone on for ever, would go on for ever. The vast shoals would appear as usual at the expected times and places, even if they had not been predicted by the annual arrival of the Scottish fisherwomen. These women knew the seasons and would appear up and down the coasts ready to gut and barrel the herrings, a vast trade for export. They were a tough, loud, cheerful lot, who swore with the best of the men and worked in bitter conditions. Modern methods and refrigeration put an end to this picturesque trade, but the herring still appeared in the sea.

The name herring means army, and even a small shoal in an aquarium is an impressive, unnerving sight,

millions of 'soldiers' blindly moving on. Some shoals were the width and breadth and depth of towns, which meant weeks of enormous catches.

It never occurred to most of us that herrings might vanish from our shops. They were eternal, a natural plunder that would never fail. But they did fail. Nets and trawling techniques became so efficiently Hoover-like that even the vaster shoals were sucked up. So depleted were they that for several years herring fishery was forbidden. Only in 1984 was it allowed again.

Herrings are on the slab once more, it is true, but what has happened to them? The ones I see are poor limp things compared to the crisp bright herring of the old days. Is this because they are kept too long in ice between catch and sale? Is it because local fishmongers do not buy the top of the catch, but second and third rate fish? Is it because we fished the heart out of the herring tribes and the few years' peace we allowed them has not been long enough to restore their vigour? It seems to me that they very often have a grey pappiness, that unpleasant softness you sometimes encounter with farmed salmon. Once, a plain grilled herring, well salted and nicely

browned, was a treat. All it needed was bread, butter and a squeeze of lemon juice. Now such herrings as I can buy need zippy handling, a tonic of sharp and savoury ingredients to disguise the weariness of what should be one of our finest and most health-giving fish. But perhaps this is just a Wiltshire peculiarity—we are not spoiled in the matter of fish.

Perhaps because herrings were once a cheap and abundant fish, they did not appear much on polite English dinner tables. I wonder, too, if this was because their oily flesh does not stand up well to poaching and papillote treatments? To my mind, they need a high heat, whether in the oven or under the grill, so that the skin becomes brown and crisp in places, even a little burnt at the edges. This leads to strong smells which people worried about far more in the past than they do today—perhaps it is easier to air our houses. The smell of a herring on the grill over hot coals is one of the most captivating I know, it's the smell of holidays in the sun, relaxed parties out of doors.

Since herrings go from 150-350 g (5-11 oz), you will find it easy to adapt sardine or mackerel recipes to them.

They all have similarly oily flesh and need contrasts of sharpness (lemons, gooseberries, sharp apples, sorrel) and a hint of sweetness. They stand up well to spicy piquancy (mustard, anchovies, spices, bacon).

The scales of herring fall off easily enough—for this reason they are described as deciduous—under the tap with the minimum of help from a knife. Gutting can be done via the gills, or by slitting the belly with a pair of scissors. Any trace of blood remaining can be removed by dipping a finger in salt and rubbing the mark away.

The head is not usually cut off unless you want to bone the fish or remove the fillets.

Herring roe is much prized, especially the soft kind. It will be of better quality, coming from the fish, than the roe you buy from thawing blocks at the fishmongers. Dip the roes in flour seasoned with salt, pepper and cayenne, fry them in butter and serve on toast with parsley. Alternatively, crush both soft and hard roes together with a little butter, a few crumbs and parsley, and use them to stuff the fish for baking. Roes can also be kept as a filling for omelettes or they can be liquidised with egg and cream or milk as a filling for tarts.

DEVILLED HERRINGS
Serves 6

6 very fresh herrings with soft roes
3 level tablespoons Dijon mustard
2 teaspoons sunflower or groundnut oil
a level teaspoon cayenne pepper
salt
100 g (3 1/2 oz) fine dried white bread crumbs
100 g (3 1/2 oz) butter, melted
sprigs of parsley

Gut the herrings, extracting the roes carefully. Leave the heads in place. Rinse the fish and dry them, slashing them diagonally two or three times on each side. Rinse and dry the roes.

Mix together the mustard, oil and cayenne pepper with a little salt. Brush the roes with this mixture and put them back into the herring cavities. Brush the herrings with the same mixture. Tip the bread crumbs on to a baking tray and roll the herrings in them.

Preheat the grill. Line the grill pan with foil. Carefully lay the herrings on top of the rack, sprinkle with melted butter and slide under the grill. Baste the fish from time to time, and turn them once. Total cooking time, including time for basting, will be about 12 minutes.

Transfer to a dish and garnish with parsley. Serve with buttered, boiled new potatoes and a sprig or two of rosemary.

"Fish" from *A La Carte*, from *The Enjoyment of Food: The Best of Jane Grigson*. Copyright © Sophie Grigson, 1992. Published by Penguin. Courtesy of David Higham Associates.

· LUNCH ·

CORNISH PASTY

An original Cornish pasty is a d-shaped wrapped pastry, typically consisting of beef (no less than 12.5 per cent), sliced potato, turnip and onion, although many other fillings are popular today. The earliest documented recipe for the Cornish pasty is dated 1746, but they became universally popular in the late 1800s.

Tradition states that the pasty was originally designed for the tin mine workers in Cornwall; the sturdy crust acting as a kind of handle which prevented the miners from contaminating their food with arsenic (often found in the mines). This 'handle' could be eaten around, and also allowed miners to re-heat the pasty without burning their fingers. The pastry casing is designed to keep the innards warm for long periods of time down the mines, and gives the meal a safe sturdy shell; it is said that a good Cornish pasty should be able to survive a fall down a mine shaft.

The Cornish Pasty Association has applied for the Protected Geographical Indication of the pasty. This will ensure that all products labelled as Cornish Pasties must have been made in Cornwall, and produced to a traditional pasty recipe.

FISH AND CHIPS

Though fish and chips have given way to curry as the 'national' fare of London, there is no shortage of fish and chip houses, also known as "chippies." Originally, the dish was served in rolled-up newspaper. A handful of chips were topped off with a piece of fried cod, salt and malt vinegar. However, fish and chips has its roots in French and Jewish cookery; the former invented chips or chipped *pommes de terre à la mode*, the latter brought *pescado frito* (fried fish) to England in the eighteenth century. The first fish and chip shops opened in the mid-1800s–"Mr Lees" shop opened in Mossley near Oldham, Lancashire in 1863, and Joseph Malin opened his in Cleveland Street, London, in 1860. Fish and chips initially gained popularity with the working class as a cheap and relatively nutritious meal. Before the war, fish and chip shops gained a bad reputation as being unsanitary because of the smell of frying grease, but during the war they escaped rationing, encouraging people to eat from them and increasing their popularity. Today fish and chips are still a massively popular take-away dinner; there are approximately eight chippies for every single McDonalds outlet. Although cod is traditionally the key fish served in fish and chips, concerns over declining populations and over-fishing have resulted in more sustainable fish, such as pollock, being used as an alternative.

PIE AND MASH

A traditional English dish is pie and mash. It can come with a variety of fillings but will most often contain steak and kidney, steak and ale, or minced beef. In the nineteenth century it was also common with steak and oyster, as oyster was then a cheap ingredient. Originally, the dish was minced beef pie, mash and jellied eel, making an affordable serving for the working class of East and South London, to which the dish has been associated since the eighteenth century. During the heavy industrialisation of London the Thames was badly polluted, but eel could still survive there and were served as a cheap food for East Enders, typically sold from family-run outlets. The dish traditionally comes with a green parsley sauce called "liquor", despite it being non-alcoholic, but today it is common to use gravy instead. Pie and mash is still a popular dish with both tourists and local Londoners, now also made with vegetarian fillings. At some pie shops oysters have even been reintroduced.

ROAST BEEF

Traditionally, roast beef is a focal ingredient in an English Sunday lunch, served up with gravy, roast potatoes and Yorkshire pudding. Once a regal dish enjoyed only by the privileged few, roast beef has gradually integrated itself into the British home kitchen. Under Henry VII, The Yeoman of the Guard became known as "Beefeaters" due to the large quantities of meat that were granted to them through their rations. Historical references to the English penchant for roast beef and its reputation as a dish good for the body and mind are littered throughout English culture. Henry Fielding in his play *The Grub-Street Opera*, 1731, included a patriotic ballad "The Roast Beef of Old England" which included the lines "When mighty roast beef was an Englishman's food, it ennobled our brains and enriched our blood."

Later, caricaturist William Hogarth stole the name for one of his paintings depicting beef smuggling activities at the Gate of Calais. William Shakespeare also made a reference to the reputation of beef in his play Henry V, in which the Constable of France says: "Give them great meals of beef and iron and steel, they will... fight like devils." Notably, a French nickname for the English was *les rosbifs* ("the roast beefs"), as they considered roasting to be a plain, basic and boring form of cookery. The roast dinner is perhaps the most typically English dish, although the modern rise in single households has resulted in the decline of this traditional Sunday meal. Beef is considered the original roast dinner meat, but roast chicken, pork and lamb are also widely eaten, as are nutmeg roasts for vegetarians, or roast turkeys for Christmas dinner.

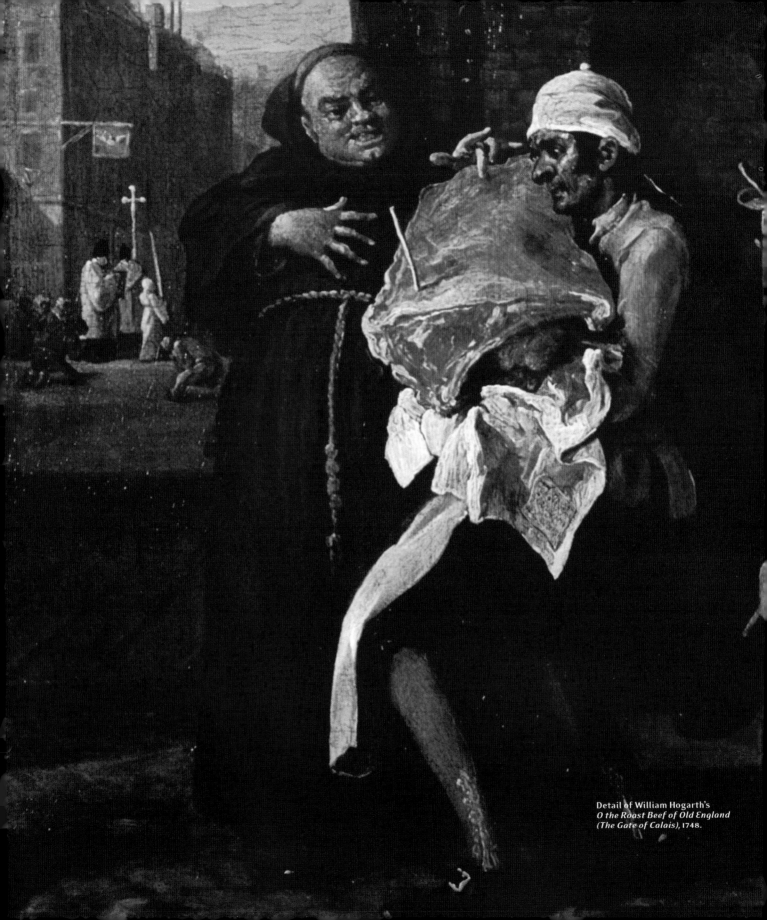

Detail of William Hogarth's
*O the Roast Beef of Old England
(The Gate of Calais)*, 1748.

· AFTERNOON TEA ·

AFTERNOON TEA

Afternoon tea is a light meal served between three and five o'clock in the afternoon, consisting of a spread of light food as well as loose tea served with milk and sugar. Although this practice would have once been common throughout the British Empire, today it is rarely taken except on formal occasions. The Ritz Hotel in London is one of the few remaining locations at which afternoon tea can still be had: the Palm Court with its baroque interior and furnishing provides an opulent setting in which to enjoy fine sandwiches such as cucumber, egg and cress, ham or smoked salmon. Scones are also a traditional choice and are served with clotted cream and jam. Finally, pastries are often included such as Victoria sponge or a Battenberg cake. The Palm Court counts Sir Winston Churchill, King Edward II, Noël Coward and Judy Garland amongst its guests.

The Ritz Restaurant in 1906. © The Ritz Hotel London.

SCONES AND WELSH CAKE

Generally acknowledged as part of a traditional Devonshire tea, scones actually originate from Scotland. The Scottish variation, a "bannock", is still eaten today. Resembling a kind of cakey bread, a scone is made with wheat, barley or oatmeal and baking powder, although there are many different family specific recipes and methods. Scones can be sweet or savoury, and blended with different ingredients varying from cheese, currants, raisins or dates. A traditional English afternoon tea would see scones served with jam and clotted cream. Welsh cakes are similar to scones, and are also known as "bakestones" or "girdle scones". Unlike scones, however, they are eaten on their own, rather than as an accompaniment to tea and cake. They are sometimes sold split open and filled with Welsh jam.

English tea pots, tea cups and tea sets from *Mrs Beeton's Book of Household Management*.

TEA

The English are famously great tea drinkers, and there is a long established tradition of tea drinking in England's history. The drink became popular around 1660, after Charles II's new wife, Catherine of Braganza, brought her love of tea to England. The English aristocracy was happy to indulge in the consumption of tea, but the drink remained an upper class luxury due to extortionate prices. It was not until a merchant, Thomas Twining, began selling tea in his coffee house in 1706 that it began to become a more accessible drink. Twining's was amongst the first coffeehouses to serve women, and this undoubtedly helped popularise tea. Twinings is still one of the biggest brand producers of tea, and sells many different varieties including Earl Grey, Darjeeling and assorted herbal flavours. Black tea is the tea most commonly drunk in England, with most tea nowadays being manufactured in the form of tea-bags for added convenience.

ENGLISH CRUMPETS

Crumpets were created by the Anglo-Saxons, who baked them as hard, thick pancakes on a griddle; it was not until the Victorian era that they were baked with yeast to produce a spongy texture, and the characteristic holes were developed later in London and the Midlands by adding extra baking soda. The Victorians ate them as part of afternoon tea, flavoured with jam, honey and lemon curd. Today they are consumed at breakfast.

VICTORIA SPONGE

Victoria sponge is named after Queen Victoria, whose favourite offering of cake enjoyed with afternoon tea was sponge. Two slim sponge cakes are melded together with jam and sometimes clotted cream, producing a kind of sweet sandwich; the top of the cake is left plain, or sometimes sprinkled with a small amount of icing sugar. Today the Victoria sponge is typically sold at country fetes, and although in some ways a nostalgic cake, it is still widely baked and eaten.

· DINNER ·

BANGERS AND MASH

Bangers and Mash is a simple dish, popular in England and Ireland as a staple working class meal. "Bangers" are sausages, which in England are made of fresh meat rather than smoked or dried meat as in other cuisines. There are many regional specialities. Cumberland and Lincolnshire are two of the most popular varieties of sausage; the former is long and curled, the latter mixed with herbs. Cheap sausages may include suspicious low-quality meats and large amounts of connecting tissue, rusk and fat, although there has been a backlash against this in recent years. As a result of this backlash, butchers now use higher quality meats to produce premium quality sausages. Other sausage varieties include pork and apple, beef and Stilton, and pork and leek. Smooth and fluffy mashed potato is best achieved by using thinly sliced potatoes that have been boiled for around 40 minutes at 70 degrees centigrade. Butter is added after mashing, with optional additions such as cheese, rosemary and bacon. Bangers and Mash is typically served with onion gravy.

SHEPHERD'S PIE

Once known as Cottage Pie, this meat and potato pie combination dates from around 1790, when potato was being introduced as an edible and cheap vegetable for the poor. Originally made using the leftovers of any roasted meat, lined and covered with a mashed potato topping, shepherd's pie has remained a popular and hearty meal in Britain. The use of 'shepherd' over 'cottage' did not appear until 1885. Many maintain that cottage pie should only refer to a beef filling, and shepherd's pie to a lamb or mutton filling, however shepherd's pie today is generally used to refer to both varieties of the dish.

• RECIPE •

1/2 lb of cold mutton
1 lb of mashed potato
1 oz of butter or dripping
1/2 pint of gravy or stock
1 teaspoonful of parboiled
and finely chopped onion
salt and pepper

—Cut the meat into small thin slices, or mince coarsely.
—Melt half the butter or fat in a stewpan, add to the potato and stir over fire until thoroughly mixed.
—Grease a pie-dish, line thinly with potato, put in the meat, sprinkle each layer with onion, salt and pepper, pour in the gravy, and cover with potato. The potato covering may be given a rough appearance by scoring it in every direction with a fork.
—Bake in a moderate oven until the surface is well browned.

TOAD IN THE HOLE

Toad in the Hole consists of sausages contained inside an extra large Yorkshire pudding, usually served with gravy and vegetables. Although the origins of the name are unclear, it is widely thought to refer to the 'poking out' of the sausages through the batter. This is meant to resemble a toad poking its head out of a hole. Another origin of the name could be from a pub game, originally called 'frog in the hole', where discs were thrown into holes on a table. The game dates as far back as the 1700s, and 'frog' has replaced 'toad' over time. Toad in the Hole is relatively cheap and easy to make, and it is a popular dish with the working classes, although nowadays the dish is also served in gastropubs with a much higher price tag.

CURRY

The influence of Indian food in England has been so significant that in 1997 curry officially supplanted fish and chips as the nation's favourite food. The most popular curry in England falls under the category of 'Indian', although many curry houses were originally established by Bengali immigrants, and Punjabi restaurants are increasing in the North of the country. Many Bengali citizens settled in London's East End during large waves of immigration, most notably in Brick Lane, also known as "Banglatown", and today home to copious curry houses. Although the dishes served in Indian restaurants are given traditional names, the actual tastes are often not quite so authentic. Most dishes are a fusion of Anglo-Asian cooking, tailored to suit the tastes of the British population that have developed in the 250 years since 'currey' was first introduced. Popular British curries include *jalfrezi*, *madras* and *rogan josh*. Chicken *tikka masala*, the most widely eaten curry in the country, was allegedly created in Glasgow by a Bengali chef after a customer complained that his dish was "too dry". The chef quickly put together a sauce made of Campbell's soup, yoghurt and spices. Today *tikka masala* is considered by many to be "Britain's true national dish", and Glaswegians have even attempted to obtain a Protected Designation of Origin, which would specify the dish as having originated in Glasgow.

BUBBLE AND SQUEAK

Bubble and squeak is a meal comprising the leftovers of a Sunday roast. It is generally comprised of potatoes and cabbage, fried together in a pan. In its traditional form cold meat was included, but this practice faded out during the Second World War, probably due to rationing restrictions on meat. Bubble and squeak can also include pickles, carrots, peas or Brussels sprouts. According to a 1785 text, *Dictionary of the Vulgar Tongue*, the dish's name comes from the sound of the vegetables bubbling and squeaking in the pan as they cook. In Scotland a similar dish is known as "Rumbledethumps"; the Irish equivalent is "Colcannon". Although Bubble and Squeak has always been a cost effective way of ensuring all food is eaten after a big meal, it is now also available in supermarkets as a microwave ready meal.

• RECIPE •

a few thin slices of cold boiled beef
potatoes
butter
cabbage
1 sliced onion
pepper and salt to taste

—Fry the slices of beef gently in a little butter, taking care not to let them dry.
—Lay them on a flat dish, and cover with fried greens. The greens may be prepared from cabbage sprouts or green savoys. They should be boiled till tender, well drained, minced, and placed, until quite hot, in a frying pan with butter, a sliced onion, and seasoning of pepper and salt.
—When the onion is done, the dish is ready to serve.

HAGGIS

Haggis is famously a Scottish dish, although some historical sources indicate that it was actually created in Lancashire in the north of England; the earliest reference to it is in a verse cookbook from 1430, *Liber Cure Cocorum.* It was, however, immortalised as a Scottish dish by Robert Burns in his poem *Address to a Haggis*, and haggis and Scotch whisky are consumed and celebrated every Burns night on 25 January. Haggis is sheep's heart, liver and lungs mixed with onions, suet and spices, boiled together in a sheep's stomach for approximately three hours—although artificial stomachs today exist which can be used as a substitute for the real thing. It is traditionally served with "neeps and natties"—swede, mashed turnip and creamed potatoes. Today is can be bought as a take-away food in Scotland, where it is deep-fried in batter and served with chips as "Haggis Supper".

KEBAB

The increased Turkish population in England has led to a plethora of shops selling kebabs. The doner kebab, a favourite late night snack among club and pub goers, is usually made using either lamb or chicken. Large chunks of meat slowly spin on a spit, and servings are shaved off thinly then presented in a pitta or with chips.

Equally popular is the shish kebab, which consists of cubes of skewered meat and vegetables cooked over a grill. Turkish tradition upholds that the roots of the shish can be traced back to Medieval soldiers roasting meat on the end of their swords, but this is essentially a romantic notion disputed by historical evidence.

GAMMON STEAK WITH A POACHED EGG

Gammon comes from the French term *jambe*, meaning the hind-leg of a pig, and a popular serving in England is gammon steak accompanied by a poached egg. Gammon steak can be served with pineapple and sometimes peppercorn sauce. The dish is a popular pub food, especially in chain establishments. Brewers Fayre, which owns over 150 different pubs across the country, identifies gammon steak as one of its best selling meals. Gammon steak is sometimes served as part of a 'mixed grill', comprising lamb chops, beef, tomatoes and mushrooms.

· PUDDING ·

BREAD AND BUTTER PUDDING

A hearty and warming dessert, bread and butter pudding is a popular English winter dish. It is made by layering buttered bread with currants, adding an egg and milk mixture flavoured with nutmeg or vanilla, then baking the combined ingredients in an oven and serving with cream or custard. It forms a simple but rich and filling dessert. In the 1600s, a similar dessert existed called "whitepot" or "marrow pudding", where bone marrow was used in place of butter.

SPOTTED DICK

Spotted dick is a traditional English pudding similar to roly-poly pudding and is often associated with school dinners. It is made from a flat sheet of suet pastry scattered with currants and raisins and rolled into a circular pudding. The earliest documented recipe for spotted dick is in Alexis Soyer's *The Modern Housewife* or *Menagère*, from 1850. There are a number of theories on the origin of the strange name. It could have evolved from the word "pudding", becoming first "puddink", then "puddick" then simply "dick". An alternative is that it could be a corruption of "dough". The "spotted" comes from the appearance the currants and raisins give the dish.

ROLY-POLY PUDDING

Roly-poly puddings have been enjoyed since the 1800s, and an early recipe for them can be found in *Mrs Beeton's Book of Household Management*. Suet (raw beef or mutton fat) is pressed out flat, slathered with jam, and rolled up to form a circular spiral. Roly-poly pudding was once also known as shirtsleeve pudding, as it was steamed and served from inside an old shirtsleeve to help preserve its shape.

APPLE CRUMBLE

Many different fruit crumbles are enjoyed in England, but apple crumble is the most popular. Made with stewed fruit and covered with a crumbly topping made of butter, flour and sugar, crumbles were popularised during the Second World War. This is largely due to the fact that they were seasonal, easy to make, and the ingredients required to make them were not heavily rationed.

CUSTARD

Custard is an accompaniment to many English desserts. Dessert custard is made from cream, egg yolks, vanilla and sugar, all slowly heated in a saucepan. Getting the mixture to set without over heating and curdling is a time-sensitive operation, as just a few degrees centigrade separate the two consistencies. Custard can be traced back to the early fourteenth century, and cookery texts such as *Crustardes of Flessh* and *The Forme of Cury* detail its use in custard tarts, where it was baked in pastry.

PLUM-PUDDING

Plum pudding, also known as Christmas pudding, has for centuries been a hallmark of 'Britishness' with a long and complex history. Originally a Harvest Festival dish, it is believed that the first recorded reference to the "Christmas" pudding is in *Modern Cookery for Private Families*, 1845, by Eliza Acton, one of the nineteenth century's most acclaimed cookery book authors. The origins of this well-known dessert can be traced back to the 1420s, when it was used as a means of preserving meat, whereby livestock slaughtered in the autumn would be mixed with dried fruit and stored, encased in a suet pastry. This savoury steamed pudding, or "pottage", was based on the Ancient Roman technique of slow-cooking meat, vegetables, dried fruits, and spices. In the late Middle Ages, prunes would be added to the traditional concoction of meat, bread and currants, giving it the name of "plum pottage". It was often eaten as an accompaniment to that most traditional of British meals, roast beef. However when methods for preserving food improved, the dish became something of want rather than necessity, and the sweet aspects of the pudding began to dominate the savoury ones. According to tradition, the pudding would be made the week before advent, each child in the household taking part in its preparation. The children would stir the pudding and make a wish. Likewise it was common to bake a sixpence into the dessert, and it was believed that the coin's finder would be granted wealth in the upcoming season. Today there are as many recipes for plum pudding as there are houses that prepare them, though the basic ingredients include dried fruit, nuts, suet, brandy and dark treacle.

Boiled Pudding, Pudding Mould, Pudding garnished with Preserves, and Baked Pudding Mould, from Eliza Acton's *Modern Cookery for Private Families*, 1845.

TRIFLE

Trifle is an English dessert made from sponge cake soaked with fruit and sherry, covered with thick egg custard and topped with a layer of whipped cream. The dish has been traced back to the late 1500s where the combination of cake or biscuits soaked in alcohol and served with cream boiled thick and flavoured with ingredients such as sugar, rosewater and ginger are found. According to contemporary cookery book recipes it was not until the 1700s that fruit was introduced to the dish, making it more or less comparable to the English trifle of modern days. In some homes it is used as an alternative to the heavier Christmas pudding.

Various cheeses illustrated in *Mrs Beeton's Book of Household Management*.

CHEESE AND BISCUITS

Cheese and biscuits are sometimes served after a large dinner as either an alternative to pudding, or as a fourth course served after a sweet. Diners are presented with a cheese board, from which they can select from around five different cheeses, eaten with plain biscuits or crackers. England is a great producer of cheese, and key regions are known for their specific varieties; Cheshire is the oldest known cheese—it can be traced back to Roman times, and is even mentioned in the *Domesday Book*. It is a moist and crumbly mild cheese, with a salty but acidic 'tang'. Lancashire cheese is sharp, hard and salty, and finer varieties, appropriate for cheese boards, are unpasteurised and matured for at least six months. Double Gloucester cheese is made in a wheel and protected by a rind; it is mild with a smooth texture. Red Leicester is waxy, mild, and has a lemony 'tang'. It is coloured using *annatto*, although carrot was historically used to give it its deep colour. Stilton is produced in Nottinghamshire, Leicestershire and Derbyshire, where it holds a Protected Designation of Origin. It is most widely known as a blue cheese, although there is also a white variety. During manufacture the cheese is pierced with steel needles which impregnate the 'rounds' with a bacteria that produces its characteristic blue veins. In the 1700s, it was served with a spoon, so that diners could scoop up the maggots that it was served complete with. Another popular blue cheese from England is Beenleigh Blue, produced in Devonshire with sheep's milk, and similar in taste to the French Roquefort. Somerset Brie, an English version of the French cheese, is the countries biggest selling soft cheese. Golden Cross is a well-known goat's cheese produced in East Sussex.

A whole 'round' of Mrs. Kirkham's Lancashire cheese.

· ITALY ·

Previous pages: Long strips of macaroni being hung out to dry.

Opposite: *Summer*, by Giuseppe Arcimboldo, 1573, is one of a series of portrait paintings by the artist, made from the seasonal fruits, grains, and vegetables.

Right: Jacobo Chimenti da Empoli's *Kitchen Still Life*, from the late sixteenth century, depicts a typical rural Italian store cupboard with hanging game birds, sausage, *Parmesan* cheese, truffles and garlic.

Italian cuisine is characteristically regional, with great emphasis given to fresh, seasonal produce. Items such as pasta and *polenta* have long been a staple in the typical Italian household's store cupboard, evolving over time as different cultures influenced the national cuisine. Initially a Greek and Roman influenced fare, Italian food gradually became subject to Arabic influences, with herbs and spices such as jasmine and saffron being introduced, alongside ingredients and flavours from the Americas and Europe. The discovery of the New World in the sixteenth century led to the introduction of items that are now essential to modern Italian cuisine—the potato, maize, and most notably, the tomato. Whilst developing on a global scale, Italian cuisine simultaneously developed on a localised level due to the regional separation of Medieval Italy. The legacy of this can be seen today, as the variation from region to region of ingredients and national dishes fast became synonymous with Italian cooking. Varieties of fare—from cheese to wine—play different roles in the dining experience of Italy's regional culinary landscape, particularly with the emphasis in recent decades on a return to traditional Italian cookery.

Right: Apicius' *De Re Culinaria* is believed to be one of the oldest surviving cookbooks in the world. The first edition was published between 1483 and 1486. Depicted here is the front cover of a privately printed 1705 edition.

Opposite: Detail from a Roman mosaic depicting different species of fish plentifull at the time.

• ANCIENT ROME •

The origins of Italy's culinary history lie in the Ancient Romans' passion for food and wine. Food, and in particular the art of dining, permeate throughout Roman literature and art and can be considered as central to Roman culture. A highly sophisticated civilisation, the Romans developed expansive areas of farmland to cultivate crops and breed animals and were responsible for introducing numerous plants and fruits to northern Europe. Whilst the geography of Greece naturally led its ancient inhabitants to base their cuisine on the sea, the Romans looked to the land for their sustenance. Their foodstuffs were divided basically between *fruges*—products of the soil—of which cabbage and broad beans were favourites, and *percudes*—those foods linked with the ritual sacrifice of animals—such as ham, mutton and hare. The consumption of sacrificial meat, which was generally reserved for the upper classes, identified the properly 'civilised' members of a community.

APICIUS

The earliest written cookery book to survive, Apicius' *De Re Culinaria* is a collection of banquet recipes dating from the late fourth or early fifth century Italy. Containing ingredients as exotic and unorthodox as flamingo, nightingale tongues and camel heels, and served with many costly spices, this was clearly intended for use in events at which no expense was to be spared. Of the approximately 420 surviving recipes, roughly 200 are for rich sauces, highlighting the Roman trend for heavy, pungent flavours that often rendered the main ingredients of dishes unrecognisable. With chapters that would not seem out of place in a contemporary recipe book, the text is written in the Vulgar Latin spoken by the lower classes, and was most probably used as an *aide-mémoire* for those working in the kitchens of the wealthiest households in Italy. Since many of the foods identified with the country today, such as pasta and tomatoes, were not available in ancient times, this text is useful for reconstructing the dietary habits of the Romans. Marcus Gavius Apicius, the culinary expert who lends the book his name, is reported to have poisoned himself when he realised that he no longer had enough money to maintain his standard of living.

FEAST OF BACCHUS

The Romans knew Bacchus, or Dionysus to the Greeks, as the god of wine. The son of Jupiter and Semele, he was known as the inspirer of ritual madness and ecstasy, and for inducing the frenzy *bakcheia*. As well as being the patron deity of agriculture and the theatre, Bacchus was considered the "Liberator", freeing people from their normal selves through madness, ecstasy, or wine. Originally the Roman god of fertility, Bacchus was often depicted in paintings eating, drinking and wearing a wreath of vines and grapes. Worship of Bacchus began to extend to festivals, *bacchanalia*, which originated in Rome and were held in secret, with only women initially being admitted. Over time, men were gradually allowed into the festivals, with celebrations being held five times a month. The festivals became infamous, with a variety of crimes and political conspiracies supposedly planned at the gatherings. This led to a decree of the Senate being declared in 186 BC, prohibiting *bacchanalia* from taking place anywhere in Italy. Despite the harsh consequences of violating the decree, the festivals were not stamped out in Italy for many years to come.

Taddeo Zuccari, *Bacchanal*, detail, 1551.

The Roman day was structured around two main meals: *prandium*, a midday snack usually consisting of little more than the previous day's leftovers, and the *cena*, or in its grander form the *convivium*—meaning "living together"—a lavish affair that involved eating with guests whilst reclining. Due to fears over the safety of such a richly extravagant gastronomic experience (Ancient Romans believed that only fresh ingredients were pure and uncorrupted, and that the very act of cooking led to corruption and rottenness) there was a constant stream of laws attempting to regulate the number of guests that one could invite and what one could serve them. It is generally agreed that the correct number of guests for a Roman dinner party was nine and that they would be arranged reclining in a U-shape around a table, propped up on their left arm, whilst they ate and drank with their right hand.

Meals were structured around three courses the *Gustatio*—an "appetizer" of which eggs, oysters and sausage were popular, often washed down with *mulsum*—a sweet, honeyed wine; *Primae Mensae* or "main course" of meat, fish, seafood, porridge or pulses; and, *Secundae Mensae*, comprising nuts, fruit or honey cake. The ambitious cooking skills of the Romans led to them enhancing their food with a variety of flavours—pepper, cumin, fennel, dill, coriander, oregano and thyme; alongside a pungent fish sauce or *garum*, similar to the Asian fish sauce of today. Grain was a staple of the Roman diet, with bread being eaten as an accompaniment throughout the *Gustatio* and *Primae Mensae*.

Opposite: A fourteenth century Italian
corn market.

Right: The pomegranate was first
introduced to Italy during the Middle
Ages by Arabic invaders.

• MEDIEVAL ITALY •

The culinary excesses of the Roman period were
dissolved with the onset of the Middle Ages. Medieval
Italy consequently became divided and fragmented,
existing as a collection of city states rather than a
unified whole and, as a result, cuisine developed on a
regional level. Impressive mountain ranges coupled
with poor transport facilities meant that a myriad
of different styles and techniques emerged all over
the country. Regional geography was a key factor in
the subsequent development of an Italian cuisine,
especially if the province was close to the sea or the
mountains. And if a region was land-locked by several
other countries, such as those in northern Italy, this
would also affect the cuisine in that particular area.
The elaborate concoction of flavourings synonymous
with Roman food gradually became less salient in the
preparation of meals with Italians learning to cook the
simplest of food such that it tasted good, whilst using
the freshest local ingredients. During this period,
lack of refrigeration meant that chemical or physical
methods of food preservation were used. This involved
foods such as meat and fish being smoked, dried and
kept on ice, whilst salt and brine were used to preserve
items such as pickles and herring. Brine, oil and vinegar
were also used to preserve root vegetables that had
been parboiled and items such as honey, liquor and
sugar were employed to preserve fruit.

Adjacent to the southern-most tip of Italy, the island
of Sicily played a crucial part in the development of
Italian cuisine during the ninth century. For 200 years
Arabic invaders maintained control over the island,
and whilst Sicilian food had originally been shaped by
the culinary traditions of Rome and Athens, Sicily's
new inhabitants began to significantly influence the
island's cuisine. Introducing North African and Middle-
Eastern ingredients and flavours—including spinach,
rice, couscous and, most notably, pasta—although

the latter was not fully democratised until the
seventeenth century; along with the 'sweet' flavours
of jasmine, almond and pomegranate, which sparked
a new trend of sweet and savoury food. Another
major Eastern influence on Italian cooking was the
introduction of sugar and with it the development
of traditional desserts, such as ice cream and sorbet.
Due to problems with the cultivation of sugar cane,
however, it was not until the latter half of the Middle
Ages, that refineries began to appear along the
island's coast.

CRISTOFORO DI MESSISBUGO

Born in Ferrara at the end of the fifth century, Cristoforo di Messisbugo was court administrator and steward to the dukes of Este, previously Ferrara: a role that demanded the organisation of many banquets in honour of his household. One of his most renowned achievements was the banquet of 24 January 1529, held in the honour of the Duke of Ferrara. In his book, *Banchetti: Compositioni di vivande et apparecchio generale*, 1549, translated as *Banquets: Compositions of Food and General Equipment*, he describes in unparalleled detail the logistics of managing and staging one of these lavish, formal, ceremonial feasts, from the conception of the idea to the departure of the very last guest. The book was published a year after Messisbugo's death in 1549, and is considered one of the most imaginative and comprehensive gastronomic manuals of the sixteenth century.

Messisbugo's cuisine was characterised by its richness and extreme attention to detail. Going further than many of his contemporaries, Messisbugo adapted foreign and exotic recipes to local produce, as well as creating recipes and refining popular dishes. Recipes for pies and tarts were included in the publication, with an extensive list of 124 fillings for the dishes. He also presented his more exotic and experimental dishes alongside already popular foods such as vegetable soups. Most notably, many of Messisbugo's recipes emphasised the use of Eastern sugar and spices, something that was otherwise diminishing in national cooking recipes. Messisbugo's influence can still be seen in modern day cuisine: for instance, combinations such as *tortellini* with spinach, and *porchetta* milk with mustard, were originally suggested by Messisbugo.

Left: A 1549 woodcut of a Renaissance kitchen by Cristoforo di Messisbugo.

Opposite: A banquet in the Palazzo Nanni on the Giudecca, eighteenth century.

• RENAISSANCE ITALY •

The increasing urbanisation of the country and consequent new concentrations of wealth towards the end of the Middle Ages saw the Italians re-discover lavish Roman dining practices at the dawn of the Renaissance period, alongside a re-appreciation of the food writers of previous centuries—in particular Apicius. Italian Renaissance cookery was far more extravagant than that of previous years, as its various cultural influences became more apparent. Sugar was soon discovered to be a useful flavouring for many foodstuffs, both sweet and savoury, and was referred to as "Indian Salt".

The banquet flourished in Renaissance Italy from the mid-fourteenth century to the early seventeenth century. Originating as a specifically secular celebration, the very word "banquet" derived from the Italian for "a long bench or table". Often in honour of an individual or occasion, the banquet was a lavish, ceremonial meal that gave households the opportunity to impress their neighbours. Reports of mid-fourteenth century banquets tell of fountain centrepieces spurting five different types of wine and decorative salt and sugar sculptures adorning the tables. Food and taste often lost out to spectacle, abundance and luxury with the banquet becoming the new indicator of political power and status in the courts. Numerous courses of hearty food were offered, serving extravagant dishes of peacock, veal and trout. The inclusion of musical performances and visual spectacles lent an air of theatricality to these affairs with the guests fulfilling the role of spectators in a show, which ultimately glorified its host.

Illustrations from Mattia Giegher's *Trattato*, 1639, showing some of the seemingly infinite possibilities of napkin folding.

NAPKIN FOLDING

In the banquet halls of Renaissance Italy, the arrangement of tablecloths and the folding of napkins played an important role in the ritual of feasting. Starching techniques allowed napkins to be prepared as folded cloth sculptures. Mattia Giegher's manuscript dedicated to this art was published following the end of the Renaissance, at a time at which napkins had ceased to perform a practical purpose and instead became purely ornamental table decorations.

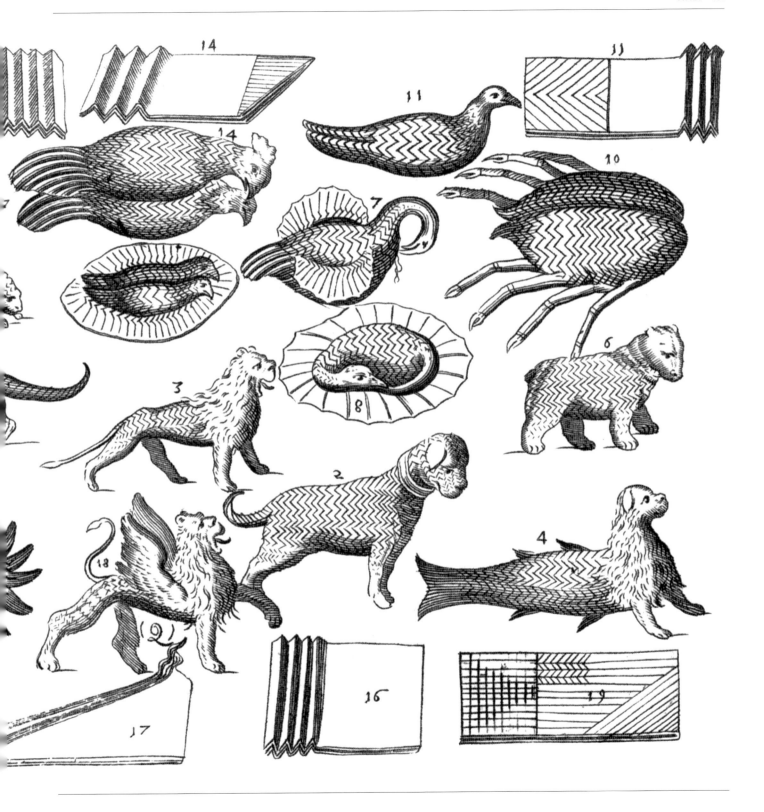

BARTOLOMEO SCAPPI

In 1570, Bartolomeo Scappi published his six-volume opus, *Opera di Bartolomeo Scappi*. A spectacular compendium of over 1,000 recipes and beautifully illustrated, *Opera* is surely the most important work of its kind, and Scappi the ultimate Renaissance cook. From 1536, Scappi found employment with several Roman cardinals, before, in 1564, becoming the private cook to Pope Pius IV. Scappi's illustrations demonstrate the revolving spits, open roasting fire, and suspended cauldrons of the Renaissance kitchen, and individually describe the vast range of knives, colanders and pots employed there. It is testament to both Scappi's culinary passion and imagination, and Renaissance Rome's status as a gastronomic capital, that the recipes of the *Opera* document the extensive regions from which Scappi sourced his produce. Scappi describes olives imported from Spain, Bolognese cabbage, Genoese sardines, and speciality cheeses from Florence, and details *ravioli*, *tortellini* and dried pastas, early versions of Spanish-inspired stewing dishes, and regional Italian specialities, many of which are still found today. It was Scappi that first provided what might be called a "national" Italian cuisine, drawing upon different regions, combinations of flavour, and technical innovation to create a way of eating still influential today.

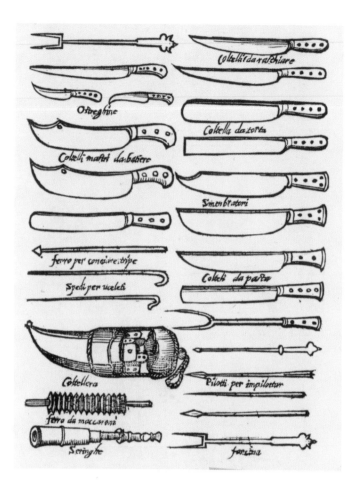

Left: Image from *Opera di Bartolomeo Scappi*, 1570.

Opposite: A woodcut from Cervio's book showing a turkey (*gallo d'India*) and peacock (*pavone*). From Ancient Rome to the high Renaissance table, the peacock was a most revered and precious bird, and took pride of place amongst the most lavish banquets.

Vincenzo Cervio draws a comparison between peacock and turkey, their apparent physical similarity an exciting prospect for sixteenth century cooks. The peacock was thought to be a rare bird, while the newly discovered New World turkey was an exotic and plentiful import: the two are labelled to instruct carving and boning techniques.

As the grand eating practices of the Renaissance banquet gained recognition, so did the importance of table manners. The table was seen as a site of social discipline, and part of the spectacle of the banquet, with importance placed upon seating, place settings and cutlery. Significantly, the first recorded instance of a fork dates back to fourteenth century Italy. The rise of humanist thought—a balance of dietics and eating well also began to influence the direction of Italian cookery during the Renaissance, with meat and fish generally being regarded as healthier than fruit and vegetables.

VINCENZO CERVIO

Vincenzo Cervio was in the service of Guidobaldo II, Duke of Urbino and then, after 1540, in that of Cardinal Farnese in Rome. He travelled widely throughout Northern Europe and was decidedly unimpressed by the abilities of the carvers he encountered there. According to Cervio, the carver should be a gentleman of handsome presence, well dressed in white, ready to please his master and careful to deport himself in such a manner as to set himself apart from the surrounding menials. His catalogue of carving, *Il Trinciante* or *The Carver* published in 1581, is unrivalled, treating everything from game to melons, providing a detailed account of the carving process. Cervio states that no worthy carver would ever cut up a roast on a dish: instead they would carve it in the air. The *Trinciante* was no longer a servant who merely served and distributed food; he was a senior court official expected to turn a commonplace operation into a visual feast and choreographed display of talent.

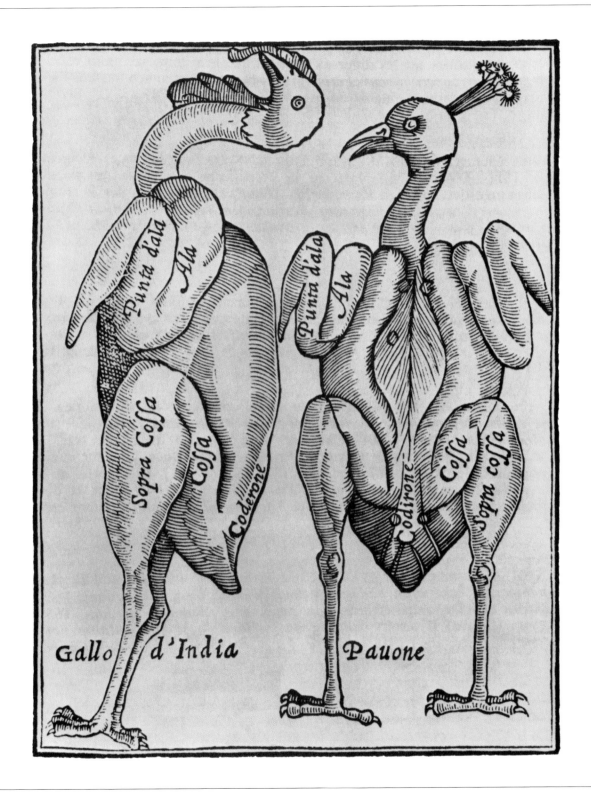

Right and opposite: Illustrations of herbs and plants from *Tacuinum Sanitatis*, circa 1390–1400. Myrtle: fennel; lemon tree; nutmeg; basil.

Overleaf: Botticelli, *The Banquet in the Pinewoods: Scene Three of the Story of Nastagio degli Onesti*, 1483.

TACUINUM SANITATIS

The *Tacuinum Sanitatis*, translated as the "Maintenance of Health", refers to a medical manuscript that initially surfaced in the eleventh century and formed a basic reference point for physicians studying food and wellbeing. The text itself describes in detail the beneficial and harmful properties of plants and food, with each entry beautifully illustrated. Aimed at a cultured lay audience, the *Tacuinum Sanitatis* takes a predominantly herbalist approach to the subject. The publication suggests six key elements to wellbeing: sufficient food and drink in moderation, fresh air, alternation between activity and rest, alternation between sleep and wakefulness, secretions and excretions of the bodily humours, and the effects of states of mind. The book goes on to state that illness was a result of an imbalance between these factors, and concludes that a healthy life is one lived in harmony. Many passages from the text were translated into Latin in mid-thirteenth century Palermo and Naples, both prime locations for inter-cultural communication between the Islamic and European worlds. In the Late Middle Ages, the *Tacuinum* became popular in Western Europe, where it served as a quick reference guide for those studying food and wellbeing, as well as those studying medicine. As well as its significance to the study of Medieval medicine, the *Tacuinum* was also of interest to those studying agriculture and cooking. For example, the earliest recognisable image of the carrot is found within the text.

Fenicultui.

Natur. c. et f. in. t. melior et eo. comestie. Juuamentu
in eftillibus. nocumenti. ficui mesnion. remotto
nci. eg notcis et karie.

Limoni.

Natur. f. q. h. i. f. melior er eis. maturi et nttes. Juuamé
ti. collerias agautr uisu. nocuméciz stomacis frigrois.
remono noci. cu comedur cu carnib calidis q asana

Basilici gariofolan.

Al. natur. c. i. et. f. i. t. meli ereo. ocouiferum. Juuamenti.
subitantia stringit. fuceas laxar. nocumétus. obtenebrar in
remouo nocumenti. cu foleis pozulace.

Mirtus.

io. natur. f. i. et. t. melius ereo. grosi et rccentes.
Juuamenti. et in pistatra. nocumentu. inglas.
remono noci. cu uiolis recntti s.

• PASTA ASCUITTA •

The European voyages to the New World during the late sixteenth century saw items such as potatoes, maize and the tomato being brought back to Italy but not necessarily consumed. The onset of the seventeenth century, however, saw many of these foodstuffs along with other previously dismissed ingredients rapidly gain popularity. Pasta, easily the best-known Italian dish, brought to Italy as early as the twelfth century from the East, did not go into commercial production until the 1700s in Naples. At one point it seemed the entire population of the city was consuming the savoury dish on a daily basis, offered to them from open-air stalls throughout the city. This was particularly the case with the *lazzari*—the paupers of Naples—who were infamous for their incorrigible laziness. Once they had earned enough money to buy their desired amount of *maccheroni* for the day, they would "cease worrying about tomorrow" and stop working. Before long, Neapolitans became known as *mangiamaccheroni*, meaning *maccheroni*-eaters, a title that had previously been claimed by Sicilians. Gradually, pasta became a staple of the Italian kitchen and remains so to the present day. There are now thought to be over 300 acknowledged varieties and shapes of pasta, many of which are regional varieties.

Opposite: Anonymous, *The Pasta Eater*.

Above: *Mangiamaccheroni*, Apulia, Italy, 1909.

• PASTA ASCIUTTA •

ELIZABETH DAVID, 1954

On the fifteenth of November 1930, at a banquet at the restaurant Penna d'Oca in Milan, the famous Italian futurist poet Marinetti launched his much publicised campaign against all established forms of cooking and, in particular, against *pastasciutta*. "Futurist cooking", said Marinetti, "will be liberated from the ancient obsession of weight and volume, and one of its principal aims will be the abolition of *pastasciutta*. *Pastasciutta*, however grateful to the palate, is an obsolete food; it is heavy, brutalising, and gross; its nutritive qualities are deceptive; it induces scepticism, sloth, and pessimism."

The day after this diatribe was delivered the Italian press broke into an uproar; all classes participated in the dispute which ensued. Every time *pastasciutta* was served either in a restaurant or a private house interminable arguments arose. One of Marinetti's supporters declared that "our *pastasciutta*, like our rhetoric, suffices merely to fill the mouth". Doctors, asked their opinions, were characteristically cautious: "Habitual and exaggerated consumption of *pastasciutta* is definitely fattening." "Heavy consumers of *pastasciutta* have slow and placid characters; meat eaters are quick and aggressive." "A question of taste and of the cost of living. In any case, diet should be varied, and should never consist exclusively of one single element." The Duke of Bovino, Mayor of Naples, plunged into the fight with happy abandon. "'The angels in Paradise', he affirmed to a reporter, 'eat nothing but *vermicelli al pomidoro.*'" To which Marinetti replied that this confirmed his suspicions with regard to the monotony of Paradise and of the life led by the angels.

Marinetti and his friends proceeded to divert themselves and outrage the public with the invention and publication of preposterous new dishes. Most of these were founded on the shock principle of combining unsuitable and exotic ingredients (*mortadella* with nougat, pineapple with sardines, cooked *salame* immersed in a bath of hot black coffee flavoured with eau-de-Cologne, an aphrodisiac drink composed of pineapple juice, eggs, cocoa, caviar, almond paste, red pepper, nutmeg, cloves, and *Strega*). Meals were to be eaten to the accompaniment of perfumes (warmed, so that the bald-headed should not suffer from the cold), to be sprayed over the diners, who, fork in the right hand, would stroke meanwhile with the left some suitable substance—velvet, silk, or emery paper.

Marinetti's bombshell contained a good deal of common sense; diet and methods of cookery must necessarily evolve at the same time as other habits and customs. But behind this amiable fooling lurked a sinister note: the fascist obsession with nationalism and patriotism, the war to come. "Spaghetti is no food for fighters." In the "conflict to come the victory will be to the swift", "*Pastasciutta* is anti-virile…. A weighty and encumbered stomach cannot be favourable to physical enthusiasm towards women." The costly import of foreign flour for *pastasciutta* should be stopped, to boost the national cultivation of rice. The snobbery of the Italian aristocracy and *haute bourgeoisie*, who had lost their heads over American customs, cocktails parties, foreign films, German music, and French food, was damned by Marinetti as *esterofil* (pro-foreign) and anti-Italian. In future a bar should be known as a *quisibeve* (here one-drinks), a sandwich as a *traidue* (between-two), a cocktail as a *polibibita* (multi-drink), the *maître-d'hôtel* would be addressed as *guidopalato* (palate-guide), an aphrodisiac drink was to be called a *guerra in letto* (war-in-the-bed), a sleeping draught a *pace in letto* (peace-in-the-bed). Marinetti's tongue was by no means wholly in his cheek. A message from Mussolini, to be published in *La Cucina Futurista* (F Marinetti, 1932), was dedicated "to my dear old friend of the first fascist battles, to the intrepid soldier whose indomitable passion for his country has been consecrated in blood."

Marinetti's effort was not the first that had been made to reform the Italian diet. In the sixteenth century a Genoese doctor had denounced the abuse of pasta. Towards the end of the eighteenth century a campaign was instituted against the consumption of excessive quantities of *macaroni*. Innumerable volumes from the hands of eminent scientists and men of letters proved unavailing. Not only was the passion for *pastasciutta* too deeply rooted in the tastes of the people, but there was also a widely diffused superstition that *macaroni* was the antidote to all ills, the universal panacea.

Another effort was made in the first half of the nineteenth century by the scientist Michele Scropetta; he,

again, achieved nothing concrete. Had it not been for the war Marinetti's campaign might have achieved a certain success; but however aware enlightened Italians may be of the unsuitability of pasta as a daily food, the fact remains that the majority of southern Italians (in the north it is replaced by rice or *polenta*) continue to eat *pastasciutta* at midday and probably some kind of pasta in *brodo* at night. Considering the cost of living, this is not surprising; freshly made pasta such as *tagliatelle* and *fettuccine* is cheap and versatile. According to circumstances it may be eaten economically with tomato sauce and cheese, with fresh tomatoes when they are cheap, with butter and cheese, with oil and garlic without cheese. The whole dish will cost rather less than two eggs, is immediately satisfying, and possesses the further advantage that every Italian could prepare a dish of spaghetti blindfold, standing on his head in his sleep.

Figure-conscious Italians claim that no fattening effect is produced by pasta provided no meat course is served afterwards; vegetables or a salad, cheese and fruit, are quite sufficient. People mindful of their digestions will also tell you that the

wise drink water with their spaghetti and wait until it is finished before starting on the wine.

SOPHIA LOREN

In 1971, Academy Award-winning actress and international sex-symbol Sophia Loren published her cookbook *In cucina con amore*, published in England as *Eat With Me*. Merging Hollywood glamour and womanly sex appeal with the notion of the classic Italian mamma, the cookbook united powerful and contradictory notions of womanhood in the singular Loren persona. The dishes in her book are hearty, traditional, and display the regionality crucial to Italian cuisine: Neapolitan *pollo alla cacciatora*, Bolognese *tagliatelle al ragu*, Sicilian *caponata*. Loren's culinary prowess was never in doubt: "I can perform miracles with a bony or third-rate, stringy piece of meat." The image of mamma perpetuated by her book found its way, in the following years, into the advertising world. In reality, the heritage of the classic Italian mother figure was dwindling due to the pressures of women trying to reconcile work, motherhood and housewifery, while advertisements marketed products based on the notion of the sacrosanct mamma's 'approval'.

REGIONALISM

The character of Italy's cuisine is shaped significantly by its regional flavours. Stark contrasts in cooking habits between the north and south are particularly noticeable—where the north's staple food is rice, with most dishes cooked using butter, the south's is pasta and olive oil. The geographical culinary differences pervade much further than this, however, with each region being host to their own specialities and cooking practices.

The food of Italy's northern regions of Trentino Alto Adige, Friuli Venezia Giulia and Veneto all show influences of the cuisines of the countries with which northern Italy shares its borders. Veneto, in particular, has a highly distinguished culinary past, with its

food paying homage to the regions history as one of the most famous maritime trading cities in the world. These northern regions are also home to the rich and fertile Po valley, famous for its rice. As the Po Valley extends through the region of Emilia Romagna, the cooking remains rich and robust in flavour; the region's *prosciutto*, *parmigiano* and balsamic vinegar being renowned as the best in the country.

Travelling south, the regions of Toscana and Umbria combine the robust cooking styles synonymous with the north with the lighter Mediterranean cooking of the south to create a characteristically rural cuisine. Both regions have a rich agricultural history, with hearty

vegetable soups or *minestre* replacing pasta on the menu. Toscana is famed for its beef and poultry in particular, alongside its olive oil. Umbria is also well known for its meat, especially its pork, and game. The cooking of Lazio is best known for its dishes *alla Romana* alongside its vegetables—in particular the Roman artichoke.

Dried chilli is abundant throughout the cookery of southern Italy, as is the tomato. Pasta and pizza, originating from Naples—Campania's capital— are both incomplete without the famous Neapolitan *passata*; Buffalo *mozzarella* is another Campanian speciality. The region of Puglia is responsible for much of Italy's grain, vegetable and fruit production, whilst the wheat and olive trees of Basilicata

are grown to make the bread, pasta and oil vital in southern Italian cookery. Calabria's vegetables, wild fungi and chestnuts give the region's seasonal cuisine a distinctly earthy flavour, whilst the area's vibrant citrus groves give evidence to the Middle-Eastern influence upon Italian cuisine during the Middle Ages.

And finally, the island of Sicily and its influence upon Italian cookery must be mentioned. The Greek and Middle-Eastern invasions of the island significantly shaped the national cuisine, bringing with them an abundance of flavours and ingredients prominent in Italian cookery today. A diet of pasta and fish is favoured by the Sicilians, alongside sweets of sorbets and *gelati*.

Opposite: Italian actress Sophia Loren prepares an Italian dish, circa 1965.

Above: Dried chillies popular in the cooking of southern Italy.

The Pizza Seller, from a nineteenth century illustration.

• IL POMODORO •

It took nearly two centuries from its introduction into Italian fare before the tomato began to be used regularly in cooking, with many initially considering the *pomo d'oro* or "golden apple" inedible. This soon changed, however, with Italy's warm climate proving ideal for the tomato's growth.

When peasants of the Naples area began adding tomatoes to baked flatbreads during the eighteenth century, the dish—now commonly known as pizza—quickly gained popularity and became a firm regional favourite. Rapidly becoming an extremely popular street food—particularly with the original *marinara* topping of tomato, olive oil, garlic, basil and oregano—pizzas were sold from stalls, by street peddlers and out of shop-fronts. Coinciding with the establishment of two of modern Italian cooking's most famous foodstuffs—pasta and pizza—the work of a chef also emerged as a recognised profession during the eighteenth century, shortly followed by the common restaurant of the nineteenth century.

Opposite: A Cirio advertisement, circa 1921.

Right: De Cecco *fettucine*.

• THE INDUSTRIAL AGE •

Italy's unification in 1861 and the rapid industrialisation that followed gladly welcomed the commercialisation of Italian cookery as reflected in the burgeoning success of companies such as the food preservation giant Cirio. Canned food rapidly gained popularity, allowing for seasonal produce to be available year round, with dried pasta and tinned tomatoes becoming a staple in the Italian store cupboard. However, along with the commodification of Italian cooking, a greater appreciation for regional dishes also arose, which coincided with the publishing of the first regional Italian cookbook. It was also around this time that "Russian" dining became popular, whereby dishes were served in succession of each other—*primo*, *secondo* and *dolce*.

However, the Italian Fascist regime, from 1922 to 1943, saw an authoritarian emphasis placed upon Italian cookery. Italians were urged to dismiss traditional recipes and methods of producing food, with the objective of creating a 'modern' national food culture, in which regional traditions were dismissed—ultimately being seen as backwards—in favour of faster, more commercially viable foods. During the Second World War nationally produced food was promoted through a system known as *Autarchia* which encouraged economic self-sufficiency. This food austerity, enforced throughout the Fascist regime, permeated throughout the period and into that of its aftermath, with the Italians avoiding food experimentation until the late twentieth century.

• SLOW FOOD •

The 1980s was a turning point in the history of Italian cookery. Alongside the rise of *nouvelle cuisine*, the country also became accustomed to fast food, with the opening of the first McDonalds restaurant in Rome. In an effort to counteract the fast food movement, a Slow Food movement arose whose interests lay in regional food and traditions. Releasing their *Slow Food Manifesto* in 1989, the movement works to increase the enjoyment of good food, combined with an effort to sustain regional and traditional Italian food products that have been increasingly replaced by a prevalence for convenience eating and fast food. Today, Italian food has come full circle, and with the help of movements such as Slow Food, a regional culinary tradition has been rediscovered, reviving Italy's eclectic culinary past.

CARLO PETRINI
Carlo Petrini came to prominence in 1986, when he and the Arcigola movement protested against the intended opening of a branch of McDonald's near the Spanish Steps in Rome. In 1989, this would become the Slow Food organisation, founded in Bra, Italy by Petrini as a reaction to the growing trends of fast food, and a faster life. The movement actively works to preserve local food traditions worldwide, and to increase awareness of the consequences our eating habits have on our health and the environment. Today the Slow Food movement counts 85,000 members in 132 countries.

Top: Hanging *Mortadella* ham from Emilia Romagna.
Bottom: Carlo Petrini.

San Marzano tomatoes, balsamic
vinegar and garlic.

• THE SLOW FOOD •
INTERNATIONAL MANIFESTO

Our century, which began and has developed under the insignia of industrial civilisation, first invented the machine and then took it as its life model.

We are enslaved by speed and have all succumbed to the same insidious virus: Fast Life, which disrupts our habits, pervades the privacy of our homes and forces us to eat Fast Foods. To be worthy of the name, *Homo Sapiens* should rid himself of speed before it reduces him to a species in danger of extinction.

A firm defense of quiet material pleasure is the only way to oppose the universal folly of Fast Life.

May suitable doses of guaranteed sensual pleasure and slow, long-lasting enjoyment preserve us from the contagion of the multitude who mistake frenzy for efficiency.

Our defense should begin at the table with Slow Food. Let us rediscover the flavours and savours of regional cooking and banish the degrading effects of Fast Food.

In the name of productivity, Fast Life has changed our way of being and threatens our environment and our landscapes. So Slow Food is now the only truly progressive answer.

That is what real culture is all about: developing taste rather than demeaning it. And what better way to set about this than an international exchange of experiences, knowledge and projects.

Slow Food guarantees a better future.

Slow Food is an idea that needs plenty of qualified supporters who can help turn this (slow) motion into an international movement, with the little snail as its symbol.

Courtesy of the Slow Food Archive.

A selection of regional Italian meats.

Lasagne Bottura.

MASSIMO BOTTURA

Massimo Bottura is perhaps the most avant-garde chef working in Italy today, mastering the traditional Italian cuisine as well as the most innovative techniques available to the contemporary kitchen, creating new dishes with the creativity of an artist. His culinary background began with the influences of his mother and grandmother who taught him the techniques of the traditional Italian kitchen. Later, as he had opened his first restaurant, he was invited by Alain Ducasse to spend time in his kitchen, which inspired Bottura to leave behind the excessive styles of the 1980s plate. In 1995 he opened his restaurant Osteria Francescana in Modena, where his beautiful and unorthodox creations are made from the meeting of tradition and innovation, with an emphasis on the quality and taste of the raw ingredients. His work earned him two Michelin stars in 2005. Recently he spent time working in the kitchen of Spanish chef Ferran Adrià, with whom he not only shares the fascination of the new techniques adapted to the kitchen but also the passionate approach to food as an art. To Massimo Bottura the personal history and cultural traditions of the chef cannot be separated from the mastering of new technology and techniques, just as the quality of the raw ingredient must never be compromised.

CARLO CRACCO

Carlo Cracco is considered to be one of the leading figures of the contemporary new Italian cuisine. Cracco originally trained at the Scuola Alberghiera in Recoaro Terme and later with some of the world's most renowned chefs, such as Alain Ducasse, Alain Sanderens and Gualtiero Marchesi. He soon became head chef at L'Enoteca Pinchiorri in Florence, which was appointed three Michelin stars in 1993–1994. He was then invited by Marchesi to help establish the kitchen of L'Albereta, which he left after three successful years to open his own restaurant Le Clivie, quickly earning his first Michelin star. He later entered into a seven year collaboration with the Milanese Peck delicatessen, opening the Cracco-Peck Restaurant and gaining two Michelin stars in the process. In 2007 Carlo Cracco took over the restaurant in his own name, as Ristorante Cracco: here he continues to intrigue and excite his guests with dishes such as buffalo *mozzarella*-crusted oyster with pepper cream, and salad of *puntarelle* rice, *Mortadella* and black truffles.

Left: Oyster salad.
Right: Carlo Cracco in his kitchen.

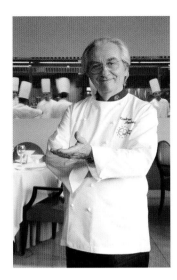

GUALTIERO MARCHESI

Gualtiero Marchesi is one of the most influential figures in the development of new Italian cuisine. Fusing traditional Italian culinary traditions with a love for Japanese food, Marchesi works from a culinary philosophy he calls "total cuisine" that demands precise attention to every detail. Opening his first restaurant in 1977, he was awarded his first Michelin star after just six months; and in 1985 became the first Italian chef to receive three Michelin stars. He finds inspiration in Goethe's words on art, applying them to his cooking—proclaiming that artists "are not those that say something new but those who know how to say a well-known thing as if it had never been said before". Indeed, twentieth century visual artists such as Wassily Kandinsky, Joan Miró, Jackson Pollock and Jean Arp inspire many of his dishes. However, Marchesi's early culinary inspiration came from working in the kitchen at his father's restaurant, L'Albergo del Mercato, Milan, where he learned to prepare traditional dishes from simple and flavourful ingredients. He undertook his studies in Switzerland and later went on to work at several restaurants in France, amongst which was the Maison Troisgros, then run by the forerunners of French *nouvelle cuisine*—Jean and Pierre Troisgros. Today Marchesi is involved in a number of restaurants and gastronomic projects, but is primarily based in Erbusco working at his Ristorante Gualtiero Marchesi, where he serves his guests elegant dishes based upon regional ingredients, created using the complex techniques of *haute cuisine*. One of his signature dishes is a version of the traditional dish *Risotto alla Milanese*, seasoned with saffron and decorated with a gold leave—which not only adds to the visual style, but also enhances the true taste of the saffron.

Clockwise from top left: Gualtiero Marchesi; *Raviolo Aperto*; Marchesi's signature *Risotto alla Milanese*.

Fresh spinach and *ricotta tortellini*.

· ANTIPASTI ·

Most Italian mealtimes begin with a dish of *antipasti*—meaning "before the meal". Varying from region to region, popular *antipasti* include *salame* sausage, *prosciutto* with figs, artichokes, *funghi* in vinegar, *pimentos*, olives, fennel and broad beans. *Antipasti* of fish are also popular and are generally fried in oil or marinated in vinegar sauces. These include anchovies, prawns, mussels and oysters; of which the latter can be traced back to Ancient Rome. Hot *antipasti* also make an appearance on the menu, of which *crostini* are popular. The use of olive oil is crucial within *antipasti*, used as a marinade or seasoning.

Asparagus and finely grated *Parmesan crostini*.

CROSTINI

Garlic infused *ciabatta*, toasted, and then drizzled with olive oil and seasoned with salt and pepper is the traditional basis for *crostini*, from which popular toppings of cheese, tomatoes, olives, beans, anchovies and *prosciutto* can be added.

INSALATA CAPRESE

Originating from the island of Capri, situated off the coast of Campania, the *Insalata Caprese* is a simple salad of tomato, *mozzarella* and basil. Served as both an *antipasti* dish and also as an accompaniment to *primo* and *secondo* dishes, the *Insalata Caprese* is evidence of Italians dedication to using fresh, local ingredients. Traditionally made using the celebrated *San Marzano* tomato and buffalo *mozzarella* originating from southern Italy, the salad is typically dressed with olive oil, salt and pepper, with the occasional addition of balsamic vinegar.

Insalata Caprese drizzled with olive oil, salt, pepper and basil leaves.

The Elegant Snack by Christian Berents, eighteenth century

PROSCIUTTO

When discussing *antipasti*, Italian cured ham or *prosciutto* must be mentioned, traditionally distinguished between *Prosciutto Crudo*—"raw" or dry-cured ham—of which *Prosciutto di Parma* and *Prosciutto di San Daniele* are two notable versions; and *Prosciutto Cotto*—cooked ham. Traditionally, after cleaning and salting, *Prosciutto Crudo* can be air-cured for up to three years, after which it is popularly enjoyed as antipasti with fresh melon or figs, or a simple piece of bread such as *grissini*. It is also often used as part of the *primo* or *secondo*, within pastas or to accompany other meats. *Prosciutto* is listed by the European Union Protected Designation of Origin, under which *Prosciutto di Parma* is distinguished by its flavour and method in which it is made, where by the pigs are fed with the regions Parmigiano-Reggiano. Similarly, local sea salt used in the production of *Prosciutto di San Daniele* alters the flavour of the ham and gives it a darker colour than some Italian hams, while *Prosciutto di Norcia*, from Umbria, is made from local white pigs and cured with black pepper.

· PRIMO ·

Considered to be the main source of carbohydrate in the Italian meal, the *Primo* is typically a dish of pasta, *polenta*, *risotto*, *gnocchi* or soup.

GNOCCHI

Gnocchi is the traditional Italian version of a boiled dumpling or soft noodle, made with a base of potato or durum semolina, and in certain regions plain wheat flour—a method more akin to the German *spätzle*. *Gnocchi* can be combined with varying sauces and flavourings, often according to region, such as saffron in Sicily, *ricotta* in Trentino-Alto Adige, or *Parmesan* cheese *alla Romana* in Lazio. *Gnocchi* is particularly popular in the North of Italy, in provinces such as Emilia-Romagna.

Taking place on 17 and 18 May each year, the Gnoccata Festival of Guastalla in the Emilia-Romagna province showcases the many different regional varieties of *gnocchi* on offer. On the evening of the first day, there are gastronomic tastings followed by a torch lit procession through the town celebrating the coronation of King Serpo XI; the evening concludes with the Grand Court Ball and fireworks. The following day begins with a Proclamation reading and Coronation speech, preceded by a historical parade. Aside from the gastronomic tastings, there are local craft stalls and court entertainment, with two *gnocchi*-based dinners taking place in between. The day culminates in a parade, with carts hauled through the streets by horses or oxen, displaying a selection of local produce and *gnocchi* and a final proclamation of "King Gnocco".

· RECIPE ·
GNOCCHI ALLA ROMANA

1 pint of milk
200 g semolina
3 eggs
110 g Parmiggiano-Reggiano cheese
60 g butter
pinch of salt
pinch of nutmeg
pepper

—Bring the milk, nutmeg, salt and pepper to the boil. Gradually add the semolina, whilst continually stirring the mixture to a thick consistency.
—Remove from the heat.
—Beat the eggs and *Parmesan* and add to the mixture.
—Transfer mixture to a greased baking tray and spread until even.
—Refrigerate for at least an hour, after which cut into small circles, baste with melted butter and cover with finely grated parmesan cheese.
—Place in a preheated oven (Gas mark 6) for around 15 minutes.

The core ingredients used to make pasta.

PASTA BOLOGNESE

Bolognese pasta originates from the Bologna region—often considered to be the gastronomic centre of northern Italy. Typically served with a *ragu*—consisting of onions, carrots, tomatoes and beef—*Bolognese* pasta is best known for its *tagliatelle*. Made with the local wheat in a laborious process involving sieving, kneading and rolling, *tagliatelle* is renowned for its fine, light appearance. From the same dough both *tortellini* and *lasagne* have evolved, giving the people of Bologna claim to three of Italy's best-loved pastas.

Ragu, or *Bolognese* sauce is typically served with *Lasagne Verdi* in the Bologna region but can be served with a variety of pastas, topped off with finely grated *Parmesan* cheese.

• RECIPE •

800 g lean minced beef
2 onions
2 cloves garlic
1 dried chilli (optional)
1 carrot, thinly sliced
1 green pepper, thinly sliced
2 tins chopped tomatoes
1 tin tomato puree
bunch flat-leaf parsley chopped
mixed herbs
salt and pepper
glug of olive oil
tagliatelle
Parmesan cheese

—In a large saucepan fry the garlic, onion, chilli, carrot and pepper in the olive oil until soft.
—Mix the mince, parsley, herbs, chopped tomatoes and tomato puree in a bowl. Add to the pan.
—Simmer on a low heat for 50 minutes to one hour.
—Leave to cool whilst cooking the tagliatelle.
—Serve with finely grated *Parmesan* cheese.

POLENTA

Polenta—a golden-yellow cornmeal, made from ground maize—is a traditional Italian dish, particularly in the northern regions, and can be served both hot and cold. When served hot, typically accompanying meat dishes, it is called "wet *polenta*" and is often served with butter and cheese. It can also be left to cool and cut into pieces, which can then be grilled or fried and served layered with different sauces. One such version is the *polentone alla carbonara* in which cooled polenta is layered with meat sauce and cheese. Originally a peasant's dish, *polenta* can now be found on the menus of even the most high-end restaurants. The regional diversity of the Italian kitchen is reflected in the many varieties of polenta: a Venetian version—*Polenta e Osei*—is made with the meat of small birds; whilst a Lombardian version—*Missultin e Polenta*—is cooked with fish from Lake Como; and a Milanese version—*Polenta Pasticciata*—is served as a sort of *polenta* and mushroom pie. Every year *polenta* festivals are held all over Italy to celebrate the many different local ways of preparing this very traditional staple; such as *Festa della Polentone alla Carbonara* in Piobbico.

Polenta, by Pietro Longhi, eighteenth century.

Making *polenta* at the *polenta* festival, Bormio, Italy.

Minestre of cabbage, tomatoes, pepper and pasta.

RISOTTO ALLA MILANESE

Rice was introduced to Italy during the twelfth century but was not cultivated until the sixteenth century. As Europe's largest rice producer, Italian cooking often features rice within its recipes. Of all Italy's rice dishes the *risotto* is best known, of which *Risotto alla Milanese* is a favourite. Originating from the fertile Po Valley—famed for its butter and slow-cooking rice—*Risotto alla Milanese* is made with a mixture of chicken stock, onions, butter, wine and Parmesan, and is often distinguished by its use of saffron. Although generally served as a primo dish, when accompanied by the Milanese dish of *Ossobucco*—a hearty dish of braised veal knuckles—*Risotto alla Milanese* can be served as a *secondo* dish.

A bowl of *risotto* rice, grown in the Po Valley.

ZUPPA

Originally considered as a peasant's food, soup now plays an important part in the Italian meal, evoking a sense of culinary tradition. Divided into two variations: *minestre* or *minestroni*—in which vegetables, herbs and pulses are combined with pasta to produce a hearty soup; and, *zuppa*—soup without pasta. Common ingredients used in the *minestre* include cabbage, carrots and artichokes. Another addition to Italian soups are the regional fish soup variations found along Italy's coast, traditionally made with leftover fish that the fishermen could not sell.

· SECONDO ·

The *Secondo* is typically a robust dish of meat or fish, often accompanied by a side dish *Contorni* of vegetables or salad.

PESCE

Italian national and regional cuisines are directly influenced by the country's geography and location on the Mediterranean Sea, with fish featuring prominently on the menu. Fairly uncomplicated in style, *Secondo* fish dishes are reflective of the simplicity of Italian cooking as a whole. Popular dishes include fried sardines, baked sea bream and salt roasted cod; alongside an abundance of shellfish, with recipes dating back to Ancient Rome. Effort is focused upon the cooking process itself, rather than on complicated sauces and marinades, with methods of frying, grilling and roasting being preferred.

Detail from a Roman mosaic.

BACCALÀ ALLA VICENTINA

La Vigilia or "Feast of the seven fishes" is a time-honoured Christmas Eve celebration in Italy. Traditionally a Roman Catholic meal consisting of seven different seafood dishes, it is now popular throughout the country. A popular La Vigilia dish is baccalà alla vicentina—a salt cod dish traditionally associated with the impoverished areas of Southern Italy. Made using dried cod, onions, anchovies, olive oil, Parmesan and parsley and then baked in the oven and served with polenta, Baccalà alla vicentina has become synonymous with Christmas in Italy.

SARDE IN SOAR

A traditional Venetian fish dish, Sarde in Saor is prepared using fried sardines and onions cooked in vinegar, and dressed with pine nuts and raisins. Traditionally eaten by Venetian fishermen—sweet and sour ingredients were used to preserve the fish on long voyages—Sarde in Saor highlights the Arabic influence on Italian cuisine during the Middle Ages. The dish can be traced back to Bartolomeo Scappi's Opera.

• RECIPE •

for the Scappi marinade
1 tbsp olive oil
300 g/10 oz onions, finely sliced
4 tbsp white wine
4 tbsp wine vinegar
6 tbsp vino cotto (strongly reduced red wine);
if unavailable, eliminate the wine, wine vinegar and
vino cotto from the ingredients and use 10 tbsp
balsamic vinegar instead
100 g/3 oz sugar
pinch saffron powder

for the sardines
1 kg/2 lb 3 oz very fresh sardines, cleaned, gutted and
scaled
salt, to taste
plain flour, for dusting
olive oil, for shallow frying

—For the marinade, heat the oil in a pan and fry the onions until softened. Transfer the onions to a large bowl and mix with all the remaining marinade ingredients. Set aside.
—For the sardines, lay the sardines on a board and sprinkle with salt. Dust with flour.
—Heat a generous amount of oil in a pan and fry the sardines until golden-brown on both sides.
—Place the sardines into the bowl with the marinade and stir to coat.
—You can eat the sardines immediately, with lemon juice or finely chopped parsley sprinkled on top. Otherwise, for proper Sarde in Soar, leave the sardines in the marinade for a day to absorb all the flavours. They'll keep in the fridge for a few days.

CARNE

Much like fish, Italian meat dishes are characteristically simple. Traditionally veal, beef, pork and lamb are the preferred meats to cook with in Italy—roasted, grilled or made into a hearty stew. The regions of Tuscany and Florence are particularly well known for their meat, offering robust dishes made using the freshest ingredients. Famed for its beef, the Tuscan Chianina cows are thought to be the oldest breed of cattle in Europe, dating back to Ancient Rome. Although veal is the Italians favoured meat, Chianina beef is known as *vitellone* or "grown-up veal" due to the cattle's fast growth. The Chianina steak—*bistecca alla fiorentina*—is one of the best-known Florentine dishes.

Chianina cattle roaming the Tuscan countryside.

OSSOBUCCO

Ossobucco—literally translating as "bone with a hole"—is a traditional Milanese dish made using braised veal shanks, onions, garlic, white wine and tomatoes. Originally known as *Ossobucco in Bianco*, the dish was made without tomatoes before they were introduced to Italian cookery in the eighteenth century. Braised in a sauce of cinnamon, allspice, bay leaves and wine, and garnished with *gremolata*—lemon zest, parsley and garlic—*Ossobucco* is an incredibly tender dish. Traditionally the dish is to be served with *Risotto alla Milanese*.

ABBACCHIO AL FORNO

Abbacchio al forno is a classic Italian Easter dish of fragrant lamb or *agnello* roasted with garlic, olive oil, rosemary and white wine. The dish is typically served with potatoes cooked in the wine and the lamb's juices.

POULTRY AND GAME

Poultry and game have been popular within Italian cookery for centuries, with recipes dating back to Ancient Rome. Goose, chicken and turkey are all favourites on the menu, alongside small birds prized for their delicacy and tenderness. Game–predominantly hare, deer, and wild boar–also features prominently within Italian cooking.

Wild rabbit, prepared for roasting with rosemary and bay leaves.

ROAST WILD BOAR

The following method for preparing and cooking Boar *Cinghiale* is taken from Apicius' *De Re Coquinaria.*

APER ITA CONDITUR: WILD BOAR IS PREPARED THUS:

It is cleaned; sprinkled with salt and crushed cumin and thus left. The next day it is put into the oven; when done season with crushed pepper. A sauce for boar: honey broth, reduced wine, raisin wine.

ALITER IUS IN APPROPRIATE: ANOTHER SAUCE FOR BOAR:

Crush pepper, lovage, origany, celery seed, laser root, cumin, fennel seed, rue, broth, wine, raisin wine; heat, when done tie with roux; cover the meat with this sauce so as to penetrate the meat and serve.

Cinghiale ragu on a bed of *polenta*.

Authentic Neapolitan pizza.

· PIZZA ·

PIZZA MARGHERITA

The pizza's long and mercurial history has developed in many stages from the ancient Roman, Greek and Middle Eastern variations on bread and flatbread. It is known, for example, that the ancient Greeks ate a flatbread flavoured with herbs and garlic called *Plakous*; while Apicius describes the addition of ingredients such as meat, pepper, cheese and oil to a hollowed-out loaf or trencher. The addition of tomatoes did not arrive until the eighteenth century when Rafaele Esposito of the Pizzeria di Pietro e Basta Cosi—now Pizzeria Brandi—allegedly topped a pizza with the patriotic colours of buffalo *mozzarella*, tomatoes and basil to celebrate Queen Margherita of Savoy's visit to Naples in 1889. Pizzeria Brandi still proudly displays a royal thank-you note dated June 1889.

NEAPOLITAN PIZZA

Made with tomatoes and fresh buffalo *mozzarella*, the Neapolitan pizza is synonymous with Italian food. This Italian food staple even has its own organisation—The Associazione Verace Pizza Napoletana (the Association of True Neapolitan Pizza)—that encourages strict ingredient and cooking guidelines.

· DOLCE ·

GELATI

Introduced to Italy by the Arabic settlers, who brought with them sugar cane and flavourings such as almond and lemon, the first *gelati* is thought to have been similar to sorbet. Milk was not introduced to *gelati* until the late seventeenth century, after the discovery of artificial freezing. *Gelati* rapidly gained popularity amongst the Neapolitans, with everyone from nobility to the poor consuming the delicacy, with the early *gelati* frozen within blocks to create the signature Neapolitan ices still popular today. *Gelato* differs from ice-cream in that it has a lower fat content, as it is made with milk as opposed to cream.

TORRONE

Another popular traditional Christmas-time sweet is the *torrone*, made of almonds encased in a nougat block. Its origins have been thought to date to ancient Greece and Rome, where the soft nougat mixture of cooled egg whites and honey could be carried over long distances by travellers, as the food preserved well. Traditionally, *torrone* should consist of approximately 60 per cent almonds, although pistachio nuts are also used in Sicilian *torrone*. Indeed, almonds were introduced to Sicily and southern Italy by the Arabs as early as the ninth century, who also brought cane sugar to the country. This would have contributed to the production of the hard, brittle version of torrone made using cane sugar. The *torrone* is also a very traditional Spanish sweet, where it is called *turrón*.

PANETTONE

The distinctive Milanese *panettone* is a round cake-like bread often prepared and eaten at Christmas time. It is thought that the bread has its roots in an ancient Roman recipe that sweetened bread with honey; today the cake typically contains candied citrus rind, and raisins. *Panettone* is prepared by leavening the dough over several days, giving it its tall shape and light texture, and was first mass-produced by Gioacchino Alemagna in the early twentieth century. It is often served with sweet wines and liqueurs such as *Amaretto* or *Moscato*, and sweet creams of *mascarpone* cheese or *zabaione*.

TIRAMISU

Contrary to what a lot of people think, *tiramisu* was only invented around 30 years ago. Supposedly originating from a restaurant in Treviso, Venice, the dessert gained far ranging popularity almost immediately, famed for its restorative properties. Originally being made from eggs, sugar and mascarpone, layered over coffee soaked biscuits, the dessert was initially served to children and the elderly; the celebrated addition of alcohol came later.

• RECIPE •

250 g mascarpone
30 g caster sugar
2 eggs, separated
150 ml coffee
250 ml whipped cream
1 packet of sponge ladyfinger biscuits
3 tbsp marsala (optional)
cocoa to dust

—Whisk the egg yolks, *mascarpone*, *marsala* and half the coffee.
—Fold in the cream.
—Beat the egg whites until they form soft peaks and fold into the mixture.
—Dip the ladyfinger biscuits into the remaining coffee and use them to line separate serving dishes.
—Spoon the *mascarpone* mix onto the biscuits and refrigerate.
—Dust with cocoa before serving.

· CAFFÈ ·

Originating in Ethiopia circa 1000 AD, coffee was not brought to Italy until the late 1500s, and has since become a mainstay of Italian culture. The most popular variation of coffee in Italy has to be the *espresso* or *un caffè*. A single shot of concentrated coffee, brewed through a process whereby hot water is forced through finely ground coffee granules and drunk in an instant, *espresso* is drunk throughout the day—particularly after meals. Italians drink *caffè latte* for their breakfast coffee. Again, coffee reflects the regionality of food and drink in Italy; whilst northern Italians prefer smooth, silky coffee; southern Italians prefer a comparatively robust cup, rich in flavour.

IL CAFFÈ FLORIAN

Italy's oldest café—Il Caffè Florian—opened in 1720 in
Piazza San Marco in Venice, serving coffee, alongside
soft drinks, pastries and the first Italian newspaper.
Famed as a cultural meeting place for artists, musicians,
poets and playwrights, Caffè Florian became a favourite
for everyone from Charles Dickens to Casanova. It was
also within the senate room at Florian that the idea for
a biennial art exhibition was first voiced in honour of
King Umberto and Queen Margherita of Italy. The first
Venice Biennale subsequently took place in 1895.

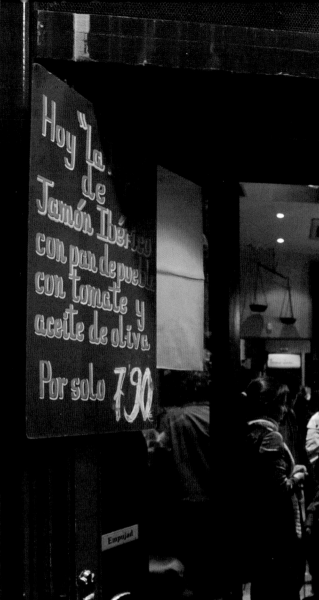

· SPAIN ·

The different regions of Spain, and the geographical characteristics of these areas, give Spain a rich and varied menu of diverse tastes, and culinary traditions. Typically Spanish fare consists of an abundance of fish and seafood from Spain's vast coasts, fine wines from the many distinguished vineyards, mountain reared pig meat, and classic Mediterranean dishes from along the Eastern coast.

The traditions and tastes that make up Spanish cuisine provide evidence for the country's history of occupation by various ancient civilisations, as well as Spain's own Empirical rule of other lands. Spanish culture, whether architecture, language or food, can often be traced back to the 800 year Muslim rule of the country; with many of what are now considered signature Spanish ingredients being introduced and cultivated in Spain by the Moors. The earlier occupations by the Phoenicians, Greeks and Romans also helped to shape Spanish culture, but their influence pales in comparison to that of the Moors. Later, Spain's own vast empire, stretching across the globe under the new Catholic rule, brought further developments to Spanish cookery, as well as an abundance of new foods from the Americas. The historical influences that have shaped Spanish culinary practice are so distinct, that a dish of Spanish food is itself rich in the history of the country that developed around it.

Previous pages: A *tapas* bar in Madrid.

Opposite: A seventeenth century confectioners' sign. Foods for banquets could be bought ready-prepared from confectioners in large towns.

Above: A Moorish tile of a pig from the Eastern Mediterranean coast of Andalusia.

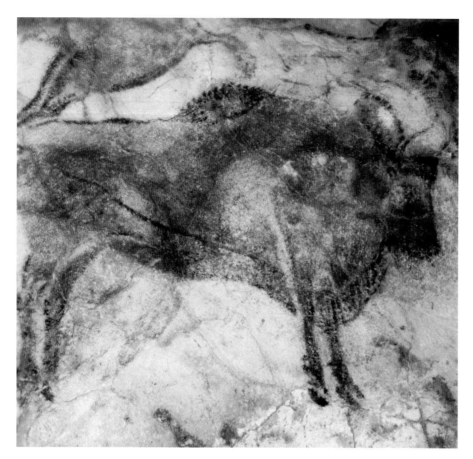

An early Iberian cave painting.

• ANCIENT IBERIA •

Approximately 1000 years BC, Indo-European tribes crossed the Pyrenees and settled on the Iberian Peninsula—now Spain, Portugal, Andorra and Gibraltar. This was the beginning of what would develop into the Iberian Age. The inhabitants of the land were tribal people: the Iberians on the Mediterranean side of the country, the Celts on the Atlantic, and the Celtiberians in central regions. Foods introduced onto the Peninsula in these early years included millet, lentils and cabbage; and developments in agriculture saw new food storing methods, the domestication of animals, and the use of iron and bronze tools.

The Iberian Bronze Age, from between the sixth and seventh centuries BC, brought the arrival of the Phoenicians, Carthaginians, and Greeks, who all founded colonies along the Mediterranean coast. These new neighbours massively affected the local Iberian tribes— the Phoenicians and their trading practises helped to establish the Iberian civilisation of Tartessos—modern day Andalusia. The Phoenician harbour of Gadir, now Cádiz, was nearby, and strong trading links existed between the two people, further developing the Iberian culture. The Phoenicians also introduced the olive tree onto the Peninsula, and founded the city of Barcelona.

The Núñez de Prado brand of olive oil is an unfiltered, certified organic and extra virgin olive oil. It comes from the town of Baena in Cordoba, Andalusia. The olives are crushed, not pressed, to release the oil. The Núñez de Prado family are considered to be amongst the finest producers of olive oil in the world.

OLIVE OIL

Spain is today one of the biggest exporters of olive oil in the world. There are two distinct historical reference points for Spanish olive oil, and these relate to the two different Spanish terms for olive—*oliva* and *aceituna*—the first deriving from the Latin *oleum* and the second from the Arabic *al-zait*. The Romans cultivated the Phoenician planted olive trees to produce oil, and while the fall of the Roman Empire saw the decline of the use of olive oil in other countries throughout Europe, the arrival of the Moors resulted in the continued use and development of Spanish *aceite de oliva*. After the successful conversion to Christianity in Spain, lard replaced olive oil as a key cooking ingredient. Although the health benefits of olive oil have always been extolled in Spain, it was not until the 1970s that it began to re-merge as a profitable and exportable product; although Italy cheaply imported large quantities of Spanish oil, re-labelled it as Italian, and sold it to foreign markets for double the price. Today, Spain is home to the largest number of olive trees in the world (over 300 million), and of the 2.1 million hectares of olive groves, 92 per cent of the trees are dedicated to the production of olive oil.

Opposite: Dried salt cod, or *bacalao*, is a popular *tapas* dish in Spain. The process of salt drying fish has been popular in the country for centuries and was introduced by the Romans.

Below: An Ancient Greek fisherman; the Greeks helped to popularise fishing in Ancient Iberia.

• GREEK ARRIVAL •

The Greek arrival around the fourth century BC brought stronger production and storage methods, resulting in a greater increase in grain production. The Greeks exported the grain to their other colonies and back to Athens, along with honey and other goods produced on the Peninsula. The Greeks were influential to the Iberians, and introduced wine, almond trees and grapes. The Iberians also began utilising their surrounding waters by fishing and collecting molluscs during their inhabitation of the Peninsula.

By the end of the second century BC, the Romans had settled on the Iberian Peninsula. Romanisation occurred quickly and easily, and Roman Hispania was established across the country, except for in the Basque and Cantabria areas. As with other Roman occupied lands across the Western hemisphere, agriculture, production, and transportation methods massively improved during their rule. At the end of the first century BC rural houses (*villae*) appeared as agricultural centres, and crop production intensified and extended—especially grain, but also vine and olive trees. The Peninsula became one of the greatest suppliers of olive oil to the Roman Empire, which was sent back to Rome in *amphorae*. Food preservation methods developed—fish was salted and air-dried, extending its shelf life and benefitting the fishing trade. *Garum*, a fish based seasoning produced in Cartago Nora (now Cartagena, Murcia) and invented by the Greeks was very popular in Roman Hispanic cookery.

Left: The Romans brought new fruits such as lemons to the Peninsula.

Below: A seventeenth century still life of Spanish grapes. Spain has long been known as a producer of fine wines; the Greeks introduced the drink to the Peninsula, with the Romans expanding grape crop growth.

• THE ROMAN INFLUENCE •

Roman stews filled with lamb, kid, pulse, vegetables, fish and poultry—including cranes and peacocks—were widely eaten, and recipes can be found in *De re Coquinaria* by Marcus Gavius Apicius, a key source of classical Roman recipes. The foods eaten by the Romans and the Hispanic people were, however, at odds with one another, with the Hispanic people enjoying far simpler foods. Wine consumption did increase, however, with spanish wines gaining popularity, resulting in the large expansion of grape crops.

Pulses were a key component of the Roman diet; lentils were staple foods of the Roman Army, and sustained them through long periods of service. The Romans considered fava beans sacred, and used them to decide the 'King' of the Saturnalia festival, held every December in honour of Saturn. *Pomeipolis* (*Pamplona*) hams also held great prestige in the empire, and the exportation of these was an integral part of Roman Hispanic economy. The Romans also introduced apricots, peaches, melons, and lemons to the Peninsula—all fruits that are still grown and enjoyed in modern Spain.

Below: Arabic spices sold at a modern market, *pimenton ahumado* (smoked paprika), *pimenton dulce* (sweet paprika) and *azafran molido* (ground saffron).

Overleaf: An eighteenth century painting showing new foods brought to Spain by the Moors.

• THE ANDALUSIAN AGE •

After the decline of Roman Empire in Hispania, the Visigothic Empire came into existence, led by the Germanic people. Food changed little during their reign, although there was a lesser variety of dishes available. The Visigothic occupation lasted little over 200 years, and as their empire declined the Muslim Berbers of North Africa took advantage of their weakness and entered Hispania in 711 AD. Christians from Northern Europe immediately began to try and conquer lands from the Moors, but this was simply the start of a very slow process. The Muslims inhabited the Iberian Peninsula for over seven centuries of the Andalusian Age, and left a deep cultural legacy still evident across contemporary Spain, especially in the South.

In the ninth century BC, Abou I Hassan arrived at the court of Cordoba and transformed cultural practices with tastes and fashions from the court of Damascus. Hassan introduced asparagus and brought new practices and manners that revolutionised Spanish dining. Music, attire and food underwent massive changes, as did table etiquette and Eastern cooking equipment. Originally in Andalusia, food at banquets was all served at once and eaten according to taste. Ziryab introduced the practice of eating by order of course—cold starters, then meat and poultry, pasta, couscous, and soups, then pies, cakes, and other desserts. The rest of Europe continued to eat in the old way until well into the Middle Ages.

The Moorish rule saw the introduction of many key Spanish cooking ingredients, as well as recipes and culinary techniques. They brought the widespread use of key pulses to the Peninsula by cultivating broad beans, chickpeas and lupines, and key vegetables including lettuce chard, artichokes, spinach, cucumbers, onions,

MOORISH CUISINE

The Moorish cuisine that developed over the Moor's 700 year residency on the Iberian Peninsula was shaped by Andalusian, Persian and Maghribian ingredients, and comprised a selection of basic foodstuffs, condiments, and cooking processes. The impact of the Moorish presence on the Iberian Peninsula shaped much of the culinary traditions of modern Spain, as well as impacting on a wider European scale through the proximity of Muslims and Christians during peaceful periods of the crusades. Spanish traditions of sharing food from the same dish, such as *paella* and *migas*, are examples of the Moorish influence over culinary traditions, still prevalent in modern Spain. The Moors introduced now staple ingredients of Spanish cooking, such as saffron, cumin, chickpeas, aubergine and asparagus, and popularised the use of honey and almonds in desserts. Traditional Moorish cuisine and its relationship with Spanish cookery is today celebrated worldwide; the Moro restaurant in London serves a fine selection of Andalusian recipes, and *The Moro Cookbook*, written by the owners of the restaurant, instructs on how to reproduce dishes at home.

garlic, eggplants, turnips, leeks, celery and squash. Many contemporary Spanish words also originate from Arabic, such as *alcahofas* (artichokes). Grains, especially wheat, millet, barley, oats, rye and sorghum, were at the heart of Andalusian cooking, alongside vast varieties of fruit introduced to the Peninsula. Amongst these were watermelons, figs, pomegranates, *membrillos* (quinces), grapes, apples, raisins, almonds, acorn palm hearts and dates. Elche in modern Spain is home to the largest date grove in Europe, which is mainly thanks to the Moors and their cultivation of the fruit. Key herbs introduced through Andalusian cooking included fennel, basil, coriander, caraway, mint, rosemary, saffron, pepper and cinnamon, and these were sold at market places, key to the trading of food.

Although rice was previously grown on the Peninsula, the Moors massively improved farming methods, bringing with them advanced irrigation and water technology, so that farming could be extended. Milk, cheese and other dairy products were key to Andalusian cooking and were basic ingredients in many popular dishes like cheese fritters. Meat was not widely eaten, being considered a luxury; and when it was necessary to slaughter an animal for meat it was carried out according to the Koran. A purified individual specifically selected for the task would face Mecca whist carrying out the slaughter, and kill the animal by slitting the throat with one deep slash across the neck.

SAFFRON

Saffron comes from the purple saffron *crocus sativus*, which was introduced to Spanish soil by the Moors more than a thousand years ago. Saffron is a delicate and sought after spice that comes from the bright red/orange *stigma* of the *crocus*. Retrieving these entails a slow handpicking process making it an extremely costly spice. Furthermore, each *crocus* only produces three threads each, needing an estimated 150,000 *crocus* flowers to produce just one kilo of saffron. Spain used to be the world's leading saffron producer, but now faces hard competition from the Middle East. The beautiful *crocus* fields are mainly grown in the province of Castilla La Mancha and bloom in autumn. In the Spanish kitchen you find saffron used in everything from *paella* to stew, roast suckling pig, soups, sauces and even ice cream. Saffron enthusiasts claim that Spain's Manchegan saffron is the best in the world.

Opposite left: Conservas Ortiz have been catching, canning and selling their fish products since 1891, and today it is one of the largest producers of canned goods in Spain. Conservas Ortiz anchovies are caught using purse seine nets, so named as the net resembles a purse's strings which engulfs the fish and then draws the net in till it closes itself.

Opposite right: Saffron threads, each individually hand picked from their flowers. Saffron sits amongst the most expensive spices in the world, and is a key ingredient in *paella Valenciana*, and is what gives the dish its distinct yellow colouring.

RICE

Rice plays a primary role in the Spanish kitchen and here rice is not just rice. There are many different distinctions and qualities to pay attention to depending on what dish you are looking to cook. Although rice is grown in many places in Spain today, it is not an indigenous crop. It is believed to have been introduced to the Iberian Peninsula during the Moorish rule, which is also indicated by the resemblance between the Spanish word for rice, *arroz*, and the Arab word *al-ruzz*. Most of the rice is cultivated in the Valencia region and not put on the export market, but the most sought after is grown in the village of Calasparra in Murcia. Here the perfectly plump grains, which remain firm during the taste absorbing cooking, are grown in still water using an irrigation system inherited by the Moors. During periods of the sixteenth to nineteenth centuries there were protests against rice crops as malaria was a common problem in the areas around the rice fields. Today that problem has been solved and now certain areas are protected by Denominacion de Origen.

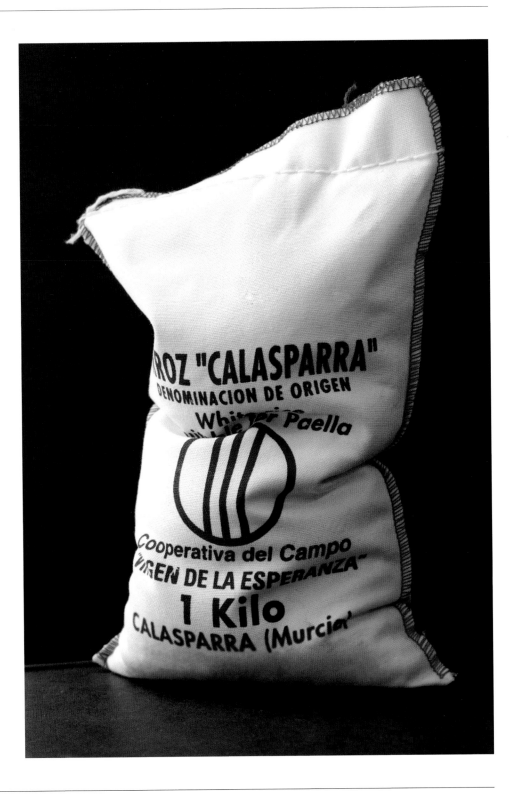

Left: *Bunyols*; a recipe for which can be found in the *Libre Sent Sovi.*

Right: A Moorish painting depicting Andalusian life taken from the *Tale of Bayad and Riyad*, a thirteenth century Arabic love story.

Opposite: Francisco De Zurbarán's religious painting of *St Hugo of Grenoble in the Carthusian Refectory*, 1633.

LIBRE SENT SOVI

The *Libre Sent Sovi* appeared in 1324, making it the oldest existing Spanish 'cookbook', and indeed one of the oldest surviving texts in Europe. It is a Catalonian collection of contemporary recipes and ingredients with no one identified author, which now exists as two separate manuscripts, one from Valencia, the other Barcelona. The *Libre Sent Sovi* shines a light on many of the cooking practices of the time, and includes recipes for soup, sauces, roasts and desserts, although fish and seafood dishes are noticeably absent. Popular ingredients that repeatedly appear throughout the text include chicken, game, almonds, and onions. The Moorish influence is clear; *esabèche* (fish poaching) techniques are described, and Arabic ingredients include rose water, bitter oranges and aubergine served with almond milk. The *Libre Sent Sovi* includes a recipe for *bunyols*, a dessert still eaten today that is similar to Arab fritters: small balls made from dough, eggs and grated cheese fried in pork fat and served with sugar.

The Spanish Middle Ages saw the formations of different kingdoms spreading across the Peninsula and becoming stronger. The late Middle Ages saw a mass population growth and move to the South, where agricultural exploitations increased. Food supplies were however sometimes scarce, and this issue was aggravated by the feudal structure of the country, which was based on an ever-growing gap between rich and poor. City dwellers relied on the market, whilst rural inhabitants were able to be self-sufficient. Vegetables, grains, and breads were the foods of the lower classes; whilst meat was a sign of distinction and power. Sardines and tuna were cheap, yet other fish expensive and rarely eaten—even in sea towns there was a poor variety. Wine was by now widely drunk. Attributed nutritious and therapeutic qualities; it was given to hospital patients, and used for medicines.

• CATHOLICISM •

The Moorish dominance in Spain declined throughout the later centuries of its 800 year occupation of the Peninsula, and by the 1400s Christian forces were taking control of more and more regions; and, in 1492 the Moors were driven out entirely. This was the beginning of the Spanish Renaissance. Under Moorish rule, the Islamic forces had tolerated Christians and Sephardi Jews, but the newly powerful Catholic Church demanded worshippers of other religions to either convert, or be expelled.

1492 was also the year that Columbus sailed to the Americas, and the arrival of food from the new found lands marked a turning point in European food, with Spain becoming the centre of the culinary changes introduced

CONVERSION TO CATHOLICISM

Almost as soon as the Moors arrived on the Iberian Peninsula, Christian troops began appearing in an attempt to conquer the land from the Muslim rulers. The years of this struggle are known as the *Reconquista*, and were century long attempts at increasing the Christian population and expanding Spain's Christian kingdoms. Over hundreds of years the Christians gradually claimed more and more territories, and by 1492 they had established rule over all the previously Muslim areas. The newly established Catholic Church exuded their influence over all facets of life—and food was key in this. Over 200 religious dates required fasting as penance for sins, where *bacalao* (salt cod) replaced meat, and many other foods were prohibited. There was a huge rise in the consumption of pig meat, and eating pork became a symbol of loyalty to the Catholic Church, and of disdain for previous Islamic traditions. The consumption of pork was also used as a means of proof of conversion for Muslims and Jews who had switched to Catholicism.

Diego Velázquez' 1618 painting, *An Old Woman Frying Eggs*. The realism gives a clear impression of a seventeenth century Spanish lower class kitchen, detailing tools, cutlery, plates and the earthenware stove.

from the New World. Vegetables such as peppers were quickly integrated into Spanish cuisine, however tomatoes took years to become popular. The Spanish Empire spread across South and Central America, Mexico, southern and western points of what is now the USA, cities in North Africa, parts of France, modern Germany, Belgium, Luxemburg, the Netherlands, most of Italy, Sicily, the Philippines, Guam and Mariana Islands. The empire established new trading routes, and the exchange of nation specific foods, traditions and gastronomic practices could influence one another more than ever before. Barcelona was the heart of the empire, and its cuisine benefitted from the Catalan maritime expansion and large-scale importation of spices from the east. Cookery books from this period indicate Renaissance cookery practices. The varied influences from Spain's new outposts were documented in texts such as *Arte de Cocina*, whilst our understanding of the more traditional eating habits of rural Central Spain can be grasped from other literary sources, such as *The Ingenious Hidalgo Don Quixote of La Mancha*, which gives an insight into the diets of rural peasants in Castilla la Mancha .

SEPHARDI JEWS

The Sephardi Jews lived in the Iberian Peninsula for centuries before being forced to leave in 1492. Their close connection to the territory is reflected in the word *Sephardim*, which by ancient Jewish scholars has been depicted as meaning (Jewish) inhabitants of Spain or the Iberian Peninsula. When expelled from Spain the Sephardic Jews moved to many different places around the Mediterranean. As a result contemporary Sephardic cuisine draws not only upon Spanish, Moorish and Portuguese cuisine but also the kitchens of Turkey, the Balkans and the Middle East, making it an incredibly rich amalgam of different flavours and tastes with essentially light dishes, with an emphasis on olive oil, salads, stuffed vegetables, vine leaves, lentils, chick peas and dried and fresh fruit. Due to their religious customs prohibiting any cooking on the day of the *Shabbat*, the Sephardi developed a slow-cooking technique where food would simmer on a low flame overnight, ready to be eaten on the following day.

A very famous illuminated manuscript on Sephardic Jewish traditions is *The Barcelona Haggadah*. The regions of Aragon and Barcelona had a large and thriving Jewish population in the fourteenth century, and the manuscript illustrates the origins of the holy festival Passover, or *Pesach*. Passover is an annual tradition celebrating God "passing over" and sparing the Jewish firstborn sons due to be killed in the Ten Plagues of Egypt. The Passover meal of the Sephardi Jews differs from other Jewish groupings, as it was normal for Jewish communities to adapt to their surroundings by cooking with the inexpensive ingredients available. During Passover, Sephardic cuisine includes *kitniyot*—rice, beans and pulses—which are forbidden for other Jewish groups but are rendered permissible by Sephardic rabbis as they are staples of Sephardic diet. The Sephardic *charoset* is commonly cooked and based on dates, raisins and figs, all fruits influenced by Spain's Arab history, while Eastern European or Ashkenazi Jews might add apples and honey to their uncooked version. Today the Sephardic diet has grown increasingly popular amongst some groupings of American Jews who have come to acknowledge the health benefits of the fish, grain, fruit and vegetable based kitchen.

The frontispiece of Ruperto da Nola's fifteenth century cookbook, *Libre del Coch*.

RUPERTO DA NOLA

Ruperto da Nola's fifteenth century *Libre del Coch* or *Libro de Guisados, manjares y potajes* is a landmark of Medieval and Renaissance Mediterranean cookery. Not much is known about the author other than that he was the head chef of King Hernando of Naples, the son of Alfonso V of Aragon. It is known that King Hernando held quite a cosmopolitan court, which explains the variety of cuisines the book draws upon, including Moorish, French, Italian and Catalan. Recipes include chicken or *capon* with egg and parsley sauce, and sautéed spinach. Of the various editions printed throughout the sixteenth century, only three survived: a Catalan edition from 1520, a Castilian edition printed in Toledo in 1525 and a later 1528 Castilian edition printed in Logroño.

FRANCISCO MARTÍNEZ MONTIÑO

Francisco Martínez Montiño had a long and successful career as the head cook of King Phillip II, III and IV of Spain. First published in 1611, *Arte de Cozina* was a seminal Spanish cookbook offering a variety of popular dishes from France, Portugal and Spain, documenting the influence of Islamic culture. The book describes recipes, tips on how to use ingredients and guidelines concerning the presentation and dispositions of meals. The book is extensive, including, for example, a range of recipes for the traditional Spanish *tortilla*: *Tortilla Blanca*, *Tortillas en agua*, *Una tortilla con agua y sal*, *Tortillas cartujas* and not least *Tortillas con queso fresco* and *Tortillas dobladas*. Francisco Martinez Montiño also wrote other books, giving account of such events as a dinner held for the Japanese ambassador, leaving behind great historical sources for insights into the etiquette and diet of seventeenth century Spain.

New and old editions of Martinez Montiño's *Arte de Cocina*, which has been re-edited and released copious times since it was first published in 1611.

JUAN ALTAMIRAS

Juan Altamiras, author of *Nuevo Arte de Cocina* (*The New Art of Cooking*), 1745, was in fact the pseudonym of monk Fray Raimundo of a Franciscan order. Emerging at a time when cooking as a refined art was spreading beyond the royal courts, Altamiras was one of the first to produce a culinary text that was widely accessible and available, enabling it to become Spain's most published cookery book until the nineteenth century. The study of food cultivation and the creation of culinary manuscripts had in fact been a practice in monasteries across Europe since the fifteenth century, but *Nuevo Arte de Cocina* marked a turning-point in its study, and the book's popularity reflected this.

SOUTH AND CENTRAL AMERICA

Christopher Columbus "sailed the ocean blue" on a voyage of discovery across the Atlantic in 1492, unexpectedly reaching the Caribbean, Cuba and Hispaniola. This was the beginning of the Spanish Empire's expansion to the Americas, where indigenous Aztec, Inca and other tribes were driven out and usurped by Spanish powers. The discovery of The New World brought a wealth of new foods to Europe, including potato, chocolate, corn, coffee, avocados, vanilla, squash and many pulses. The Native people of America taught the Spaniards how to use these new ingredients, and they have of course now been absorbed into European cultures. Spain's colonisation of the Americas shaped how the new lands evolved, especially in South and Central America, and the influence of Spanish cookery is evident across Latin America, although countries and regions have also developed their own traditions. Cuba for example is a fusion of Spanish, African and Caribbean foods, where the basic spice palette and food prepping techniques are very similar to that of Spain and Africa. Colombians eat similar dishes to Spaniards such as beans, rice and *chorizo*, but also *arepa* bread and *chicharrón*—fried pork rinds that are a popular dish across South America. Honduran cuisine is a combination of the indigenous foods of the Maya and Lenca people with Spanish and Mexican influences. Coconut is used in abundance in Honduran cookery, and regional specialities include fried fish, *carne asada* (roasted meat) and *baleadas* (wheat floured tortilla with mashed fried beans). Maize-based dishes with *tortillas*, *tamales*, or *pupusas* categorise many dishes across Latin America, as do *salsas* and other condiments such as *guacamole*, *pico de galo* and *chimichurri*. The potato—one of the most influential vegetables to have appeared in Europe in the advent of the discovery of the Americas, was once a staple ingredient of Incan cuisine.

Opposite: Fresh *churros* and dipping chocolate.

Right: A contemporary olive oil advertisement.

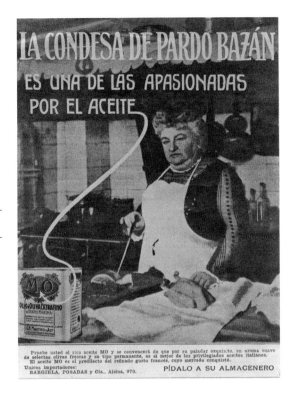

• DECLINE OF THE SPANISH EMPIRE •

With the decline of Spanish empire in the early nineteenth century, its influence lessened both politically and culturally. Cooking within Spain itself changed little and still held strong roots with ancient influences, as well as new influences from the Americas. The art of cooking began to spread throughout Spain, rather than being a pleasure purely afforded in aristocratic and upper class kitchens. Drinking chocolate became popular in the nineteenth century, and *chocolaterias* opened with the purpose of selling the new beverage. It was these *chocolaterias* that first introduced *churros*, the Spanish doughnut. Key chefs from the latter end of the nineteenth century include Ángel Muro and Emilia Pardo Bazán.

The Spanish Civil War (1936 to 1939) created massive food shortages for the people of Spain. Political rivalries resulted in the breakdown of food distribution, even when there was food available. Republicans faced the enormous task of feeding the most densely populated cities—Madrid, Barcelona, Valencia—exacerbated by an influx of refugees. The ration allowance was not enough, and the Spanish people would eat pulses for weeks on end. Broad beans, lentils, and chickpeas were popular. The Nationalists and their allies blockaded Republicans ports, and no imports could enter the towns, increasing the food shortages. The end of the Civil War saw the Nationalists emerge as victorious, and the resulting 35 year Franco led fascist regime kept Spain isolated from the rest of Europe.

EMILIA PARDO BAZÁN

Emilia Pardo Bazán was one of the most established scholars and authors of the Galician region in Spain and a central figure in the naturalistic movement of the country. Among a diverse and eclectic body of work, *Los Pazos de Ulloa* (*The Manors of Ulloa*), 1886, is perhaps the most popular and critically acclaimed. Towards the end of a successful literary life and career, Bazán published the seminal cookery book *La Cocina Espanola Antigua y Moderna* (*Traditional and Modern Spanish Cookery*) a unique contribution to Spanish gastronomic discourse. Given Bazán's predisposition towards a custom of writing and a stance traditionally defined as "masculine", it was not without a certain irony that she embarked on such a project.

Left: *Jamon Iberico Bellota.*
Right: Tinned baby squids in their own ink.
Opposite: A *tapas* bar and restaurant
in Plaza Mayor, Madrid.

• MODERN SPAIN •

Throughout time the different areas of Spain have developed their own regional dishes and traditions, and whilst they remain important to those areas, they have since spread across the country as a whole. The Catalan and Basque regions suffered greatly during Franco's regime, but after his death in 1975, these areas have had more freedom to express their cultural heritage, and celebrity chefs and world famous restaurants have emerged from these areas. The post-Franco years have seen a flurry of creative experimentation, and gastronomy is key in this. Spain's influence on other cuisines and the exports of its established produce make it one of the most universally enjoyed cuisines throughout Europe. Despite this, Spain has managed to maintain its ancient traditions and influences from its centuries of Greek, Roman and Moorish occupations, without too much interference from other cultures and colonies—with the exception of Latin America—which has greatly enriched and complimented the kitchens of Spain.

TXOKOS
Dispersed throughout the Basque country, the *Txokos* are closed, gastronomical societies. *Txokos* would traditionally admit members of the male sex only and as well as platforms for bonding and socialising, would provide an essential space to experiment with and learn new ways of cooking. Their popularity is still widespread in the Basque Country, with the small town of Guernica counting nine such societies. Women are nowadays allowed to enter, drink, eat and socialise but cooking is still a forbidden activity.

MEAL STRUCTURE
The meal structure in Spain is at odds with much of the rest of Europe, as lunch is the main meal of the day. *Desayuno* (breakfast) is a light affair, usually simply coffee, perhaps with a croissant or other pastry, so Spaniards are famished by the time they reach *comida* (lunch). Eaten between around two and four in the afternoon, *comida* is a several course meal—light soup or salad to start, followed by a main meat or fish dish, with fruit or Spanish flan or cake to finish. The famous *siesta* comes after this, which historically was intended for farm workers who would rest out of the hot afternoon sun and allow their food to digest before returning to work. *Cera* (dinner)

is eaten late, around nine to 11 at night, and could consist of a selection of *tapas*, or a salad or sandwich. Dinner is often concluded with *sobremesa*, literally translating as "over table", where the Spaniards stay at the table after eating, and enjoy the art of conversation and drinking.

TAPAS
Tapas is the name referring to a diverse variety of appetisers in Spanish cuisine. Dishes vary according to the gastronomic tradition of each Spanish region and range from mixed olives and cheese, to *bocadillos* (a sort of open sandwich, usually moistened with grated tomato) and minute shrimps or fried baby calamari. *Tapas* are often eaten as a full meal in themselves and are testament to a food culture based around sharing and communal eating. According to a tradition, the custom began when sherry drinkers in Andalusian taverns would cover their drinks with slices of bread, ham or cheese, a measure taken to protect the drink from the flies hovering around it—the word *tapa* means cover. Andalusia is famous for its *tapas*, including *cazón* (a type of small shark), and *frita malagueña* (mixed battered seafood); *charcuteries*, where hams are hanging over the bar, are an essential part of the tradition.

Left: Pumpkin oil caramel, from the El Bulli restaurant.

Right: Ferren Adrià, head chef at the famous El Bulli restaurant.

Opposite: Spherical *raviolo* and a minty pea salad, from the El Bulli restaurant.

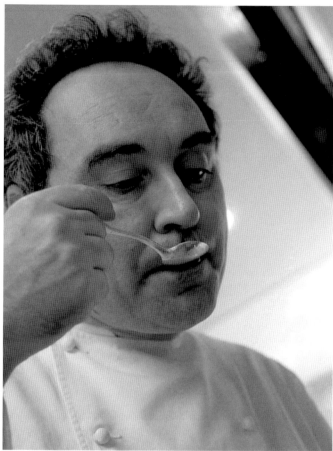

KARLOS ARGUIÑANO

Karlos Arguiñano Urkiola was one of the first TV chefs in Spain with his show *La Cucina de Karlos Arguiñano*, on which he is known for spicing up his cooking sessions with amateur singing and comedy. The show continues to run today but is now produced by Arguiñano's own production company. Arguiñano began his culinary career when at the age of 17 he enrolled at a cooking and hotel management school in the Basque country, where he trained under Luis Irizar. In addition to his TV show, Arguiñano also runs a hotel and restaurant in the Basque coastal village Zarautz, as well as a successful and prestigious cooking academy, Academia de Cocina Aiala. Arguiñano was, alongside other culinary personalities such as Juan Mari Arzak and Ramón Roteta, one of the leading figures in the development of the "new Basque" cuisine in the 1970s and 1980s. Influenced by French *nouvelle cuisine* they reworked traditional Basque dishes, giving the Basque kitchen some lightness, and have been hugely successful in making Basque cuisine more widely known throughout the world. Today the development and experimentation with Basque cuisine is famously represented by chefs like Ferran Adrià and Martin Berasategui.

FERRAN ADRIÀ

Ferran Adrià is considered one the most creative chefs of Spain. Head chef of the infamous restaurant El Bulli (located on an isolated Costa Brava beach), his cooking techniques have been admired and celebrated internationally. Although often associated with so-called "molecular gastronomy"—the application of science to culinary practices and cooking phenomena—Adrià has repeatedly referred to his cooking as "deconstructivist". Adrià has stated that his goal is to "provide unexpected contrasts of flavour, temperature and texture. Nothing is what it seems. The idea is to provoke, surprise and delight the diner." Culinary 'foam' counts amongst his most famous creations and is now used by avant-garde chefs around the world. It consists of natural flavours (sweet or savoury) mixed with a natural gelling agent; this mixture is placed in a whipped cream canister where the foam is then forced out with the help of nitrous oxide. One of his last, and rather controversial ventures, has been the opening of Fast Good—the first restaurant in a fast food chain, inside the premises of Madrid's NH Hotels group.

• SYNTHESIS OF EL BULLI CUISINE •

EL BULLI AND FERRAN ADRIÀ

In the mid-1990s a new style of cuisine began to be forged. Today, this style has been wholly consolidated and may be defined in the following terms:

1. Cooking is a language through which all the following properties may be expressed: harmony, creativity, happiness, beauty, poetry, complexity, magic, humour, provocation and culture.

2. The use of top quality products and technical knowledge to prepare them properly are taken for granted.

3. All products have the same gastronomic value, regardless of their price.

4. Preference is given to vegetables and seafood, with a key role also being played by dairy products, nuts and other products that make up a light form of cooking. In recent years red meat and large cuts of poultry have been very sparingly used.

5. Although the characteristics of the products may be modified (temperature, texture, shape, etc.), the aim is always to preserve the purity of their original flavour, except for processes that call for long cooking or seek the nuances of particular reactions such as the Maillard reaction.

6. Cooking techniques, both classic and modern, are a heritage that the cook has to know how to exploit to the maximum.

7. As has occurred in most fields of human evolution down the ages, new technologies are a resource for the progress of cooking.

8. The family of stocks is being extended. Together with the classic ones, lighter stocks performing an identical function are now being used (waters, broths, *consommés*, clarified vegetable juices, nut milk, etc.).

9. The information given off by a dish is enjoyed through the senses; it is also enjoyed and interpreted by reflection.

10. Taste is not the only sense that can be stimulated: touch can also be played with (contrasts of temperatures and textures), as well as smell, sight (colours, shapes, *trompe l'oeil*, etc.), whereby the five senses become one of the main points of reference in the creative cooking process.

11. The technique-concept search is the apex of the creative pyramid.

12. Creation involves teamwork. In addition, research has become consolidated as a new feature of the culinary creative process.

13. The barriers between the sweet and savoury world are being broken down. Importance is being given to a new cold cuisine, particularly in the creation of the frozen savoury world.

14. The classical structure of dishes is being broken down: a veritable revolution is underway in first courses and desserts, closely bound up with the concept of symbiosis between the sweet and savoury world; in main dishes the "product-garnish-sauce" hierarchy is being broken down.

15. A new way of serving food is being promoted. The dishes are finished in the dining room by the serving staff. In other cases the diners themselves participate in this process.

16. Regional cuisine as a style is an expression of its own geographical and cultural context as well as its culinary traditions. Its bond with nature complements and enriches this relationship with its environment.

17. Products and preparations from other countries are subjected to one's particular style of cooking.

The El Bulli kitchen in action.

18. There are two main paths towards attaining harmony of products and flavours: through memory (connection with regional cooking traditions, adaptation, deconstruction, former modern recipes), or through new combinations.

19. A culinary language is being created which is becoming more and more ordered, that on some occasions establishes a relationship with the world and language of art.

20. Recipes are designed to ensure that harmony is to be found in small servings.

21. Decontextualisation, irony, spectacle, performance are completely legitimate, as long as they are not superficial but respond to, or are closely bound up with, a process of gastronomic reflection.

22. The menu de *dégustation* is the finest expression of avant-garde cooking. The structure is alive and subject to changes. Concepts such as snacks, tapas, pre-desserts, morphs, etc., are coming into their own.

23. Knowledge and/or collaboration with experts from different fields (gastronomic culture, history, industrial design, etc.,) is essential for progress in cooking. In particular collaboration with the food industry and the scientific world has brought about fundamental advances. Sharing this knowledge among cooking professionals has contributed to this evolution.

Synthesis of El Bulli Cuisine.
Reproduced by permission of Restaurante El Bulli.

· SPANISH CUISINE ·

Many of Spain's key dishes differ in varying degrees according to area. Although two small villages miles apart may possess different recipes for the same dish, by simply examining Spain's cuisine by each autonomous region, it is possible to gain an understanding of the cooking practices and eating habits of the country. There are, of course, dishes and foods that are widely eaten across Spain, notably *tortilla de patatas* (potato omelette), *paella*, *Calamares a la Romana* (fried squid); and various uses of pig meat, including *chorizo* (a cured sausage usually seasoned with smoked *pimentón*), or *embutido* (hashed meat with herbs and spices, wrapped in the skin of a pigs intestines), or *morcilla* (blood sausage). *Jamón ibérico* and *jamón serrano* are also extensively eaten cuts of pig meat. Dessert across Spain is less region specific than other meals, and *arroz con leche* (rice pudding) and *churros* (Spanish doughnut) are enjoyed up and down the country.

GALICIA

Cold and wet coastlines define Galicia in the north of Spain, and fish and seafood caught off its shores are widely eaten. Galician people are generally descended from Celtiberians, whose ideas surrounding myth, legend and a belief in the mystique are still prevalent today. Known for its sauces, fish dishes and flavourful stews, Galician octopus is especially popular in the region. The catch is pounded well until tender, then cooked whole and seasoned with olive oil, paprika and salt, and served up on wooden plates. Cape Finisterre located on the far west coast provides more than half of the worlds mussels. *Lacón con Grelos* is the most famous dish from the area; *lacón* meaning boiled pig shoulder and *grelos* turnip leaves, are boiled together and served with *chorizo* and potato. Galicia is also known for its regional cheeses, such as *Tetilla* cheese, named after its shape which resembles a woman's breast. There is a long established tradition of distilling liqueurs in Galicia, such as the locally produced and strongly alcoholic brandy *orujo* (between 37 and 45 per cent) that is used to make the drink *queimada*, the "fire drink" of Galicia.

ASTURIAS

Miles of coastline give Asturias a high quality and varied selection of fish and seafood. It is also the largest salmon producing region in Spain. Over two-dozen different cheese varieties from cows, sheep and goats provide the milk for half of Spain's cheeses, with Asturias being known as "the land of cheeses". It is the home of *Fabada Asturiana*, a fava bean casserole made with pig blood and oak smoked sausages to give it a strong flavour—one of Spain's most famous exports, tinned and enjoyed all over the world. *Sidra* or cider has been a popular substitute to wine since ancient times, and is produced from a variety of Asturian apples. Locals gather together for *Espichas* or "first tasting", where the still fermenting cider is drank from the barrel.

A Moorish tile depicting *lenguado* or sole.

Calamari.

CANTABRIA

The Cantabrian Sea provides excellent fish and seafood to the region including exquisite squid and sardines, often served roasted. Hake is especially popular, cooked in *sidra* (cider). *Cachón en su tinta* is a particularly popular Cantabrian fish dish, and translates as literally "cuttlefish cooked in its own ink". Cantabria is also home to the Tudanca cow, considered one of the finest meats in Spain, and is distinguished by a Protected Denomination of Origin label, along with other 'Meats of Cantabria'. Cantabria is the host of the *Feria Nacional de Ganado* —the largest livestock fair in Spain—which is held in Torrelavega every year.

THE BASQUE COUNTRY

The Basque Country is famous for its strong gastronomic traditions, and arguably produces the best cuisine in Spain. Basque's spend on average twice as much of their disposable income on food as Americans and eat four times as much fish as the average Frenchman—favourites include *merluza* (Spanish hake), sole cod and the occasional baby eel. The Basques also have the largest fishing fleet in Spain. The geographical benefits of the Bay of Biscay and the Pyrenees help to define the Basque Country from other Spanish cuisines, as do the clear influences from France—as seen in the *nueva cocina vasca*, inspired by the *nouvelle cuisine* of France. The Juan Mari Arzak restaurant pioneered the new Basque cuisine, becoming one of Spain's first Michelin starred restaurants in the process, and helping to spread the *nueva cocina vasca* as a movement throughout Spain.

Key dishes from the Basque regions include *Marmitako*, meaning "from the pot"; a fish stew made from tuna, potatoes, onions, pimientos, and tomatoes. It originated as a dish eaten on tuna fishing boats in the Cantabrian sea, and its popularity is now spreading throughout Spain. *Talo* is made from cornflower and water, and is similar to tortillas. The Basques often eat it with *txistorra* (very thinly sliced *chorizo*) and *talo* an essential part of the Saint Thomas Fiesta. The colours of the Basque flag—red, green and white—are represented in the *Piperrada* dish, made with onion, green peppers, garlic, and tomatoes, sautéd in olive oil and flavoured with red *Espelette* pepper, perhaps with the addition of meat.

The Basque *nueva cocina vasca* has seen the number of Michelin starred restaurants in the area soar, with rare and unusual ingredients such as calves brain, snouts and sea urchins being experimented with in the kitchens of Basque chefs. There is a strong tradition of *pintxos*—dishes similar to *tapas,* but ordered and eaten individually rather than shared—a key component of Basque culture. In neighbourhoods such as Donostia-San Sebastian, bars line the streets and serve a delicious array of dishes, to be enjoyed with wines from nearby La Rioja or *Txakoli*, a light, acid and aromatic Basque wine.

Pinxtos are enjoyed in a bar in San Sebastián.

A *txoko* group get cooking in the Basque Country.

NAVARRE

Navarre is best known for *encierro*—the running of the bulls—in Pamplona (its capital city) during the San Fermín festival. The beef of the region is generally very healthy and naturally reared; the different cattle vary from Pyrenees, Alpine Brown and Charolais. Northern mountain dishes use local ingredients such as mushrooms with herbs, and roast quail in fig leaves. Vegetable stews, *Tudela* lettuce hearts and *Roncal* and *Idiazabal* cheeses are also popular. A fish dish from the coast is *truchas a la Navarra*—cod stuffed with bacon and cheese. The region is divided into Basque and Spanish speaking areas, and the cuisine of the north of the country is largely influenced by Basque traditions.

Idiazabal cheese.

ARAGON

Meat forms the basis for much of Aragon's dishes in what is one of the more straightforward cuisines of Spain. The mountain people of the northern regions possess a more rustic approach to cooking; lamb and goat are roasted on a spit and eaten with *espárragos montañeses* (mountain asparagus), which is in fact calves tails. Truffles and wild mushrooms grow in the upper river valleys of Jacetania, Gallego, Sobrarbe and Ribagorza. The birds that populate the area are regularly caught and eaten; pigeon is served in *salmorejo*, a garlic, tomato and vinegar cream, and partridges with chocolate. High up in the Pyrenees, a unique local dish known as *chireta*, or haggis, is eaten. Another locally eaten dish to Aragon is *Magras en Tomate*—slightly fried *Serrano* ham dipped in tomato sauce.

WHERE THE BOYS ARE
WHERE THE GIRLS ARE

ANTHONY BOURDAIN, *A COOK'S TOUR*

THERE WAS RARELY a sound to be heard in the empty streets of San Sebastian's *parte vieja*, just the clip-clopping of my boots on wet cobblestones echoing against four hundred year old buildings. It was late at night, and Luis Irizar and I carried food through the dark.

Luis was the main man at the Escuela de Cocina Luis Irizar, the cooking school that bears his name, a *capo*, maybe even a *consigliere*, in the city's vast culinary subculture. Had it not been so late, and the streets so empty, there would have been passersby waving at him, shopkeepers calling out his name, former students coming out to give him a hug, a handshake, and a hearty hello. Everybody who has anything to do with food in San Sebastian knows Luis. Where we were headed at this late hour was an institution particular to this food-crazy city, the Gaztelubide, an exclusive all-male clubhouse for one of San Sebastian's many gastronomic societies. If you love food, San Sebastian's got it all: an unwavering faith in its own traditions and regional products, a near-religious certainty that it's got the best cuisine in Spain, a language and culture that go back—literally—to the Stone Age. And more Michelin stars per capita than anywhere else in the world.

If you listen to the locals, San Sebastian isn't even really Spain. It's Basque Country, that vaguely defined, famously independent area of southwest France and northern Spain where the street signs are in Basque (lots of names with *t's and x's* and few vowels) and woe to anyone who too obnoxiously asserts obeisance to another culture. There's a bunch of good ol' boys here who call themselves ETA—and they make the IRA look like Mouseketeers. Screw with them at your peril. While the great majority of Basques look disapprovingly on car bombs and assassinations, their interest in independence and self-determination is right under the surface. Scratch lightly and it's in your face.

I wasn't worried about bombs or kidnappings. I've long ago found that nationalism bordering on militancy is often accompanied by large numbers of proud cooks and lots of good stuff to eat. San Sebastian is just about the best example of this state of mind. Good food, good restaurants, lots to drink—and 'Leave me alone!' Not a bad place for a hungry, globe-trotting chef, early in his quest for the perfect meal. Luis and I entered Gaztelubide with our supplies. We passed a wide, oblong-shaped dining area lined with wooden

tables and benches, then walked into a nice-sized, professionally equipped kitchen, crowded with men in aprons. The men were working earnestly on various individual cooking projects, the stovetops fully occupied with simmering pots and sizzling pans, while a few onlookers drank red wine and hard cider in the dining area and rear cloakroom. I was out of my element. First, I was at least 15 years younger than anyone there. This society hadn't opened the books to new membership in many years. Second, all these cooks were amateur—as opposed to professional—cooks (save Luis), guys who cooked for love, for the pure pleasure and appreciation of food. Third was the 'all-male' thing, an expression which, in my experience, is most often accompanied by signs reading PEEP-O-RAMA and BUDDY BOOTHS—or, worse, FOOTBALL ON THE BIG SCREEN! For me, a night out 'with the guys'—unless we're talking chefs, of course—usually veers into the territory of bar fights, Jager shots, public urination, and vomiting into inappropriate vessels. Without the civilising perspectives of women, too many guys in one room will almost always, it seems, lead the conversation, as if by some ugly, gravitational pull, to sports stats, cars, pussy, and whose dick is bigger—subjects I've already heard way too much about in 28 years in kitchens.

Virginia, Luis's daughter and the director of the cooking school, had put my mind somewhat at ease earlier, assuring me that I'd have a good time—"Go", she said—"You'll have fun… Tomorrow night", she added ominously, "you come out with the girls."

Now I was in the inner sanctum putting on an apron and preparing to assist Luis in the preparation of a traditional Basque meal—a tall glass of hard cider in one hand, a bucket of soaking *bacalao* (salt cod) in the other. "You dry the *bacalao* on the towel, like this", said Luis, demonstrating for me exactly how he wanted it done. He blotted a thick filet of cod on both sides, ready to make his move to an open burner on the crowded stovetop.

"Next you go like this—"

There was no argument about who was boss here. I happily complied as Luis slapped down a heavy skillet, added some olive oil, and began to bring it up to heat. When the oil was hot enough, I seared the pieces of fish lightly on both sides.

We were making *bacalao al pil-pil*, about as old-school Basque a dish as you are likely to find. After setting the seared fish aside, I covered the half-cooked filets in more hot olive oil. Then, moving over to a countertop and using a thick earthenware casserole, I followed Luis' example and carefully swirled in a gentle clockwise motion until the natural albumen in the fish bound with the oil, creating a thick, cloudy emulsion. At the very end, Luis spooned in some *piperade* an all-purpose mixture of tomato, peppers, and onions, which gave the sauce a dark pink- and-red-flecked finish and an inviting spicy aroma.

"Keep it warm here", said Luis, balancing the casserole dish between two simmering stockpots.

Next: *cocoches*, the salt-cured cheeks of hake, soaked in milk, then seasoned, floured, dipped in egg, and fried until crispy and golden brown. Luis walked me through the process while frying serrano ham-wrapped langoustines on skewers on the flattop next to me, charring them lightly on both sides. People kept refilling my cider glass and handing me glasses or *txakaoli*, a sort of greenish white wine similar to *vino verde*. I was beginning to feel that warm buzz, an artificial sense of well-being

and inflated self-image so conducive to enjoying a fine meal. We were joined by a brawny and gregarious former student of Luis', who explained the society's drinking policy: drink as much as you like—on the honor system. At the end of the night, count up your bottles, fill out a ticket totaling the damage, and leave the money in a hanging covered pot by the untended bar.

The food almost ready, Luis showed me to a table, set down some glasses and high-poured me a big drink of *patxaran*, the deadly local brandy made from berries and anise. With the bottle held about two feet over the glass, he did the same for himself, winked, and gave me the Basque toast of "*Osassuna!*" before draining his glass in one go. I was beginning to understand what went on here. Soon, we were well into the *patxaran* and happily tearing at our food. The cheeks were terrific, the pil-pil, served at blood-warm temperature, surprisingly sweet and subtly flavored, the *piperade/*oil emulsion a nice counterpoint to the salt cod and much more delicate than I'd expected. The langoustines were great, and a surprise addition of wild mushroom *salpicon* in a sort of rice-paper *vol-au-vent*—another cook's contribution, I think—was wonderful.

All the other cooks' food seemed to be coming up at the same time, and the tables were soon crowded with burly, barrel-chested men animatedly devouring their creations in food-spattered aprons, the clatter and roar of conversation punctuated by exclamations of "*Osassuna*".

We were having a jolly time at my table, and visitors from other tables frequently swung by to say hello to me, Luis, and his former student. Conversation ranged from the exact frontiers of Basque territory (Luis's friend claimed everything from Bordeaux to Madrid—wherever there was good stuff to eat) to the incomprehensible aversion to mushrooms shared by most non-Basque Spaniards. Luis was quick to point out that the Basques, not Columbus, had discovered America. When I mentioned that some Portuguese friends had just made the same claim, Luis waved a hand and explained everything. "The Basque are fishermen. We were always fishermen. But we were also always a small country. When we found cod, we didn't tell people about it. And we found a lot of cod off America. Who should we have told? The Portuguese? They'd have stolen it all. Then we'd have had nothing." Things seemed normal in the large room, a big crowd of happy eaters, speaking in a mixture of Spanish and Basque, glasses clinking, more toasts.

Then things got weird.

An old, old man, referred to as "*el niño*" ("the Baby"), on account of his advanced age, sat down at an old upright piano and began pounding out what was clearly the introduction to the evening's entertainment. I broke out in a cold sweat. My most terrifying nightmare scenario is that I might someday be trapped on a desert island with only a Troupe of cabaret performers for diversion—and menthol cigarettes to smoke—doomed to an eternity of Andrew Lloyd Webber and medleys from *South Pacific*. A guy in a dirty apron stood up and launched into song, his tenor voice impressive. Okay, I thought, opera, I can handle this. I had to hear this at home when I was a kid. I should be able to handle it now.

What I was not prepared for was the chorus. Suddenly, everyone in the room began pounding their fists on their tables, rising, then sitting down in unison to provide alternating verses of chorus. This was the wackiest thing I'd seen in quite a while. It was a little frightening. Then, one after the other, every man in the room—tenors, baritones—got up to sing, belting out arias and other solos in heartfelt, heart-wringing renditions. Then came a really creepy—but funny—duet between two lumberjack-sized fellows, one doing what was clearly the male part, the other doing the female in a scary but good falsetto, accompanied by appropriate gestures and expressions. You have never seen such sincere, evocative grimacing, agonising, chest pounding and garment rending, such earnest cries of feigned torment, pain, and bold challenge. These men could cook. They could drink like heroes. And every damn one of them could sing like a professional. I gathered they practised—a lot.

Just when I was beginning to fear that soon we'd all be stripping down to our Skivvies for a little towel snapping in the steam room, the mood became decidedly nationalistic. No more opera. Instead, lusty anthems of Basque independence, marching songs, songs about battles won and lost, loud homages to dead patriots, nonspecific vows to take to the streets in the future. The men were all lined up together now, two rows of raised fists, swinging in time, feet stomping, shouting triumphantly. A few more glasses of *patxaran* and I'd be storming the barricades myself. It got only louder and more festive (and my table wetter, from all the high pouring) as the evening progressed. The ranks of empty bottles near me grew from platoon to company strength, threatening to become a division. "We don't do this in New York", I told Luis. I don't remember much after that.

I woke up in the Hotel Londres y Angleterre, one of the many Victorian piles built on San Sebastian's English seaside-style strand, which curves around a beautiful scallop-shaped bay. Should I tell you about castles and forts and Crusade-era churches, the unique and lovely facades on the buildings, the intricate wrought iron, the old carousel, the museums? Nah, I'll leave that to *Lonely Planet* or *Fodor*'s. Just believe me when I tell you that the city is beautiful—and not in the oppressive way of, say, Florence, where you're almost afraid to leave your room because you might break something. It may be beautiful, but it's a modern city, sophisticated, urbane, with all the modern conveniences artfully sandwiched into old buildings. The French vacation there in large numbers; so there are all the fashionable shops, brasserie-type lunch joints, *pâtisseries*, nightclubs, bars, internet cafes, and cash machines you'd expect of a major hub—along with the homegrown cider joints, *tapas* bars, small shops selling indigenous products, and open-air markets you hope for. As San Sebastián is is still spain, there is the added benefit of being part of a society that has only recently emerged from a repressive dictatorship. If you're looking for hard-living, fun-loving folks, Spain is the place. During the days of Franco's dictatorship, the Basque language was illegal—writing or speaking it could lead to imprisonment—but now it's everywhere, taught in schools, spoken in the streets. The supporters of ETA, as in any good independence movement, are profligate with the use of graffiti, so there's an element of Belfast to the walls and parks and playgrounds—except they're serving two-star food across the street.

With a crippling hangover, I limped out of the hotel and back to the *parte vieja* in search of a cure, noticing a few surfers getting some nice rides off the long, steady curls in the bay.

Chocolate and *churros*. A thick, dark, creamy cup—almost a bowl, really—of hot chocolate, served with a plate of deep-fried strips of batter. *Churros* are kind of like flippers: sweet dough forced through a large star-tipped pastry bag into hot oil and cooked until golden brown, then piled onto a plate, powdered with sugar, and dipped into chocolate. The combination of sugar, chocolate, hot dough, and grease is the perfect breakfast for a borderline alcoholic. By the time I was halfway through my cup, my headache had disappeared and my worldview had improved dramatically. And I needed to get well fast. I had, I suspected, a big night ahead of me. I'd seen that look on Virginia's face before, when she'd told me that I'd be going "out with the girls". It was a look that made my blood run cold as the memories came rushing back. Vassar, 1973. I was part of a tiny minority of men, living in a little green world run by and for women. I'd fallen in—as I always do—with a bad crowd, a loosely knit bunch of carnivorous, brainy, gun-toting, coke-sniffing, pill-popping manic-depressives, most of them slightly older and much more experienced than I was at 17. Sitting each morning in the college dining facility and later the neighborhood bar with eight or ten of these women at a time, I'd learned, painfully at times, that women have nothing to learn from men in the bad behavior department, particularly when they travel in packs. They drank more than I did. They talked about stuff that made even me blush. They rated the sexual performance of the previous night's conquests on a scale of one to ten, and carved up the class of incoming freshmen ahead of time–drawing circles around their faces in the *Welcome to Vassar* pamphlet introducing the new fish–like gangsters dividing up building contracts.

I was afraid. Very afraid.

When I showed up at the cooking school, a whole posse of women was waiting for me: Luis' daughters Virginia and Visi (also a chef), and three friends, their faces brimming with mischief, I'd compounded the danger factor by bringing along my wife. Nancy, a woman with her own limitless potential for causing mayhem, and I knew, just knew, that the all-male adventure the night before was a trip to Disneyland compared to what was in store for me now. There's an expression in Spain that translates as "a little bit–often", a phrase usually invoked before setting out on a *poteo*–what we might call a "bar crawl". Essentially, the way a *poteo* works is this: you bounce around from one *tapas* joint to another, eating what they

call *pintxos* (the local term for *tapas*) and drinking *txacoli*, red wine, in measured amounts. Drop in, eat what's great–and only what's great–at each particular bar, then move on.

We had the TV crew lurking ahead and behind us as we set out through the streets of the *parte vieja*, and I was keeping a sharp, worried eye on Nancy, who hated the idea of making a television show, hated being near a camera, and had already taken a serious dislike to the producer for keeping me busy most of the day shooting "B-roll", meaning scenery, shots of me walking around and pretending I was thinking deep thoughts, while she stewed, neglected, in a hotel room. If the producer elbowed her out of a wide shot one more time, I knew, she was going to sock him in the neck. I'd seen her use that punch before–on a too-friendly woman at a sailors' bar in the Caribbean. She'd leaned behind me, drawn back, and walloped a much larger woman two stools down, straight in the carotid. The woman went down like a sack of lentils. I didn't want to see that again. I made out–Matthew, the producer, walking backward in the darkness and decided there would be no contest. Nancy could take him with one arm behind her back. Besides, she already had allies. She

was now commiserating with Virginia and Vist and their friends behind me. I could hear them all laughing; the other women immediately sympathising. If things degenerated into senseless violence, I'd just walk away and leave Matthew to his fate. Besides, I was still pissed about the Jerry Lewis incident.

The girls–that's how they referred to themselves–were all sharp, attractive, fiercely independent women in their mid to late thirties, happily single and totally unneurotic about sex. When a camera guy, making casual conversation, asked one of the friends if she liked to dance, she shrugged and said, "I like to fuck"–not an invitation, by the way, just a casual statement of fact. I felt, in spite of the lingering potential for violence, reasonably comfortable and among friends. These women acted like... well, cooks.

It takes experience to navigate the *tapas* bars of San Sebastian the way we did that night. Temptation is everywhere. It's hard not to gorge too early, fill up too soon, miss the really good stuff later in a haze of alcohol. The first place was a good example: Ganbara, a small semicircular bar with no seats and room for about 20 people standing shoulder-to-shoulder. Laid out in a breathtaking display on clean white marble was the most maddeningly enticing spread of bounty: snow-white anchovies glistening in olive oil, grilled baby octopus salad, roasted red and yellow peppers, codfish fritters, marinated olives, langoustines, pink-red fat-rippled serrano, *pata negra* and Bayonne ham, stuffed chillies, squid, tarts, *empanadas*, *brochettes*, salads—and the most awesome, intimidatingly beautiful mountain range of fresh wild mushrooms: gorgeous custard-yellow *chanterelles* and hedge-hogs, earth-toned *cèpes*, morels, black trumpets. Cooks seared them to order in black pressed-steel pans and the room was filled with the smell of them. Visi cut me off before I started blindly eating everything in sight; she conferred with the cooks for a moment while a bartender poured us small glasses of red wine. A few moments later, I had a pungent mound of searingly hot sauteed wild mushrooms in front of me, crispy, golden brown, black and yellow, with a single raw egg yolk slowly losing its shape in the center. After a toast of red wine, I ran my fork around the plate, mingling yolk and fungi, then put a big forkful in my mouth. I can only describe the experience as "ready to die"—one of those times when if suddenly and unexpectedly shot, at that

precise moment you would, in your last moments of consciousness, know that you had had a full and satisfying life, that in your final moments, at least you had eaten well, truly well, that you could hardly have eaten better. You'd be ready to die. This state of gustatory rapture was interrupted by more wine, a tiny plate of tantalising baby octopus, and a few sexy-looking anchovies. I was at first confused by an offer of what looked to be a plate of fried *zucchini* sticks, but when I bit inside and found tender white asparagus, I nearly swooned.

"Let's go", said one of the girls, tearing me away from a long, lingering look at all that ham. "Next place is famous for fish cakes." We walked six abreast down the cobblestone streets, the girls laughing and joking—already best pals with my wife—who speaks no Spanish and certainly no Basque. I felt like part of the James/Younger gang. At the next joint, Luis' former student recognised me from the street, entered, took one look at the female desperadoes I was keeping company with, and bolted immediately from the premises, badly outnumbered.

"This place is famous for hot food—especially the fish cakes. You see? Nothing on the bar. Everything here

is made to order in the kitchen", said Visi. We drank more red wine while we waited for the food. I was soon digging into a hot, fluffy fish cake of *bacalao*, onions, and peppers, smeared onto a crust of bread, followed by the even better *morro*, a braised beef cheek in a dark, expertly reduced *demi-glace*. Yes, yes, I was thinking. This is the way to live, perfect for my short attention span. I could easily imagine doing this with chef friends in New York, ricocheting from *tapas* bar to *tapas* bar, drinking and eating and eating and drinking, terrorising one place after another. If only New York had an entire neighborhood of *tapas* bars. The whole idea of the *poteo* wouldn't work if you had to take a cab from place to place. And the idea of sitting down at a table for *pintxos*, having to endure a waiter, napkins, a prolonged experience, seems all wrong. Another joint, then another, the red wine flowing, the girls getting looser and louder. I don't know how one would translate "Uh-oh, here comes trouble", but I'm sure we heard it in our rounds as our crew swept into one tiny bar after another. I remember anchovies marinated in olive oil, tomato, onion, and parsley, cured anchovies, grilled anchovies, fried sardines, a festival of small tasty fish. More wine, more toasts—I recall stumbling through an old square that had once been a city bullring, apartments now overlooking the empty space. Past old churches, up cobblestone steps, down others, lost in a whirlwind of food.

At San Telino, a modern, more upscale place (inside an old, old building), I found a more *nouvelle* take on *pintxos*. Wine was poured as soon as we entered. I had, I recall, a spectacular slab of pan-seared *foie gras* with mushrooms—and, glory of glories, a single squid stuffed with *boudin noir*. I hunched protectively over my little plate, not wanting to share.

More wine. Then more.

The women still looked fresh. I felt like I'd awakened under a collapsed building, the room beginning to tilt slightly. I was speaking Mexican-inflected kitchen Spanish, which is always a bad sign when wondering if I'm drunk or not—and the girls had only begun.

After a few more places, I finally called it a night. Somehow, we'd gotten into the tequila by now. I'd seen a chunk of hash cross the bar, there was a fresh row of shot glasses being lined up, and Nancy was looking at one of the crew's idle cameras like she was going to use it as a blunt object. It was time to go. One seldom leaves a good impression on one's hosts by suddenly sagging to the floor unconscious.

It's great, sometimes, to be a chef. It's even great, sometimes, to be a well-known chef—even if one is well known for things completely unrelated to one's skill in the kitchen. There are perks. It's even better when you're with a better-known chef, a longtime resident of the community in which you're eating, and you're looking to get treated well in a really fine restaurant. No one gets fed better in good restaurants than other chefs. And when you're really, really lucky, you get to sit at the chefs table, right in the kitchen, attacking a three-star Michelin tasting menu in the best restaurant in Spain.

Which is where I was, sipping from a magnum of Krug in the kitchen of Arzak, a family-run temple of Nouvelle Basque on the outskirts of San Sebastian, the best restaurant in town, I was assured by just about everyone I'd met—which, of course, means it was also the best restaurant in Spain, and therefore the world. I'm not going to weigh in on the 'who's best' issue, but I will tell you that it was a flawless, remarkable, and uniquely Basque experience. Yes, yes, there is that other place, where they serve the seawater foam and the desserts look like Fabergé eggs, but I wasn't going there, so I can't offer an informed opinion, though I'm happy to sneer at it in principle. Chef/owner Juan Mari Arzak was one of the fabled "Group of Ten", back in the heady, early days of French *nouvelle cuisine*. Inspired by the pioneering efforts of French chefs like Troisgros, Bocuse, Verge, Guerard, et al, Arzak and a few others had determined to move the traditional elements and preparations of Basque cuisine up and forward, refining it, eliminating any heaviness, redundancy, silliness, and excess. He took a much-loved, straightforward family restaurant and turned it into a cutting-edge three-star destination for serious gourmets from all over Europe, a must-see whistle-stop on every self-respecting chefs world tour. And he did it without compromising, without ever turning his back on his roots or on Basque culinary traditions.

Luis and Juan Mari greeted one another like two old lions. The chef showed us around his immaculate white-tiled kitchen as if we were guests in his home, sitting down at the table with us while the chef de cuisine, his daughter, Elena, took charge of the cooking.

Apologies to Elena—and Juan Mari—but I have to tell you, just to set the scene properly, that later, back in New York, when I raved about the meal I had at Arzak to a tableful of multistarred New York chefs (all of whom had already eaten there), they wanted to know only one thing: "Was Elena there? Ohhhh God." There is nothing sexier to many male chefs than a good-looking, brilliantly talented young woman in chef whites, with grill marks and grease burns on her hands and wrists. So Elena, if you ever read this, know that thousands of miles away, a tableful of *New York Times* stars were moved to spontaneous expressions of puppy love by the mere mention of your name.

Elena walked us through each item of food in near-perfect English, apologising (needlessly) for her accent. The kickoff was pumpkin ravioli with a squid-ink sauce infused with red pepper. Next, little toast points with a puree of Basque sausage and honey, a tiny cup of sheep's-milk yogurt with foie gras—almost obscenely good. Like all my favorite *haute* chefs, the Arzaks don't mess about with the extraneous or nonsensical. Presentations represented the food to best effect and never distracted from the ingredients. The Basque elements were always front and center; you knew, at all times, where you were. There was crayfish with eggplant caviar, olive oil, and parsley, and then an alarmingly shrewd yet deceptively simple creation I'd never seen nor even heard of before: a fresh duck egg, whole, yolk and white undisturbed, which had been removed carefully from the shell, wrapped in plastic with truffle oil and duck fat, then lightly, delicately poached before being unwrapped and presented, topped with wild-mushroom *duxelles* and a dusting of dried sausage. It was one of those dishes that, while absolutely eye-opening and delicious, inevitably makes me feel small, wondering why I could never have come up with such a concept. Eating it was bittersweet, the experience tinged as it was with the certain knowledge of my own bad choices and shortcomings. How did they come up with this? Did the idea appear like the theory of relativity appeared to Einstein—in dreams? What came first? The egg? The duck fat? It was so good. It hurt to eat it.

The menu kept coming. A vegetable tart with chestnuts, white asparagus, baby *bok choy*, and wild mushrooms; sea bass with a sauce of leek ash, a green sauce of fresh herbs, and garnish of one flawless diver's scallop; wild duck, roasted in its own juices, the defiantly fat-flecked *jus* allowed to run unmolested around the plate; a duck *consommé* with roasted tomato. It was one of the best meals I'd ever had. In one of those "It can't get any better than this" moments, an ashtray appeared, allowing me to enjoy a postmeal cigarette inside a three-star kitchen. Life was good.

Listening to Luis Irizar and Juan Mari Arzak discuss cuisine, the things they'd accomplished, was like listening to two old Bolsheviks reminisce about storming the Winter Palace. I envied them that they were so good at what they did, that they were so firmly grounded in a culture, a place, an ethnoculinary tradition, that they were surrounded by such limitless supplies of good stuff—and the clientele to appreciate it fully. Would such advantages have, in my time, changed my own trajectory? Made me a better chef? A better cook?

As another American writing about Spain famously said, "Isn't it pretty to think so?"

'Where the Boys Are/Where the Girls Are' from *A Cooks Tour*, ©2001 Anthony Bourdain, published by Bloomsbury Press.

CATALONIA

Considered by many to be the finest cuisine in Spain, alongside the Basque Country, Catalonia's menus are a fusion of Mediterranean and French cooking, with less Moorish influences than other areas of Spain. There are however still various general elements of Arabic cooking found in dishes, such as sugar, aubergine and saffron. *Zarzuela de Mariscos* is a famous dish from the region; *zarzuela* literally translates as "operetta", indicating "a mess"—in this case "a mess of shellfish" in white wine sauce. Fresh vegetables including garlic, red pepper and artichoke are prominent, along with wheat products, olive oils, legumes, cheese and fish. Dishes fuse sweet and salty, and stews with sauces based on *botifarra*—raw pork sausage—are popular, as are *picada*—ground almonds, hazelnuts, pine nuts, etc.—Wild game even appears on menus during the autumn months. Catalans traditionally celebrate *la Castanyada*, celebrated on November 1st, where they eat *panellets*—small pastries made of pine nuts, almonds and sugar. Barcelona is perhaps the best food city in Catalonia, serving a wide selection of local favourites from the rest of the region, and famed for its monkfish served with toasted garlic.

The Catalan speaking region—Valencia, the Balearic islands and Roussillon—historically incorporated influences from modern Italy. This influence can be traced back by comparing fifteenth century Catalan and Italian recipe books. Catalonia itself was hugely influenced by the 600 year Roman rule of the region that lasted until 476 AD.

The four main distinguishing ingredients of Catalan cooking are *allioli* (garlic and olive oil mayonnaise), *sofregit* (onion, tomato, fried bread and olive oil), *picadia* (pounded garlic, fried bread, oil, nuts, herbs and spices, used as a thickening agent), and *samfaina* (a vegetable sauce, similar to *ratatouille*).

CASTILLA-LEON

Castilla-Leon is the largest region in Spain, and for centuries it relied on *garbanzo* beans or chickpeas for most dishes, which is still the main ingredient of many Castilian stews where it is mixed with cabbage, meat or *morcilla* (blood sausage). Castilla-Leon is also known for its wonderful breads and has a long history of baking, producing round *hogazas* bread—large closed-grain loaves baked in circular ovens. Fine rose wines originate from the Cigales area in the heart of Castilla-Leon.

Morcilla.

CASTILLA-LA MANCHA

A large plain surrounded by mountains on all sides, Castilla-la Mancha was conquered by the Christians from the Muslims in the eleventh century. The Arabic influences are however still felt today through dishes such as *pisto manchego*—a simple combination of red and green peppers, tomatoes, squash, onion and egg—one of the most well-known regional foods. The large plains mean there is a strong history of shepherding.

Workers would be away tending to their flocks for days at a time, so carried a shallow pan called a *gazpachera* so they could prepare dinner. Many of Castilla-la Mancha's traditional dishes originate from the food shepherds ate whilst up in the lonely mountains, such as *manchego* cheese and *migas de Pastor*—which literally means "bread crumbs"—that would be sautéed in the *gazpachera* with garlic, bacon and lard or olive oil.

Manchego cheese.

Left from top: *Asturias; Torta Canarejal;
Garrotxa; Pico de Europa.*
Middle from top: *Al Vino; Manchego.*
Right from top: *Tetilla; Mahon; Villarejo.*

Paella.

VALENCIA

The arrival of the Moors in the eighth century, and subsequent 500 year rule, is still evident across Valencian cuisine and culture. The Moors introduced sugar cane, oranges, almonds, and most importantly, rice, which dominates Valencian menus—especially the famous *paella*, which originates from the region. The coastal areas enjoy fish and seafood, whilst game, lamb and kid goat are more common inland in the mountain areas. The province of Alicante is famous for its sweet desserts, such as *fondillón*, which has a very high alcohol content, and its *paella* made with chicken and rabbit, rather than the traditional seafoods.

Various hanging chilli peppers and jars of Moorish spices.

EXTREMADURA

Extremadura has a diverse countryside of dry plains, pastures, mountains, marshes and meadows, with each terrain producing different products and livestock that influence local cuisine. A key component of cooking is the Iberian pig, which is covered with paprika, and makes a delicious ham. Historically, the Christians, Jews and Muslims lived together in the region, and each religion has left an indelible mark on Extremaduran cuisine. The Arab *ſinabi* is a precursor to *caldereta* or meat stew, and the Jewish *adefina* a precursor to both *olla* and *puchero* stews, all still popular meals in the region. One of the best-loved cheeses in Spain, *torta del caſar*, is from Extremadura.

Olla stew.

MADRID

As Spain's capital city, Madrid does not so much
have a definitive cuisine of its own but rather is an
amalgamation of various cooking practices from
throughout Spain. Absorbing some of the most delicious
menus from across the country, Madrid blends different
traditions to create its own culinary delights. The most
famous dish is probably *Cocido Madrileño*, made with
chick peas and vegetables, followed by the *torrigas*
dessert—similar to bread and butter pudding—a
favourite in spring time, especially around Holy Week.
The people of Madrid also love their fish, and the city
is home to the second largest fish market in the world—
after Tokyo—and despite Madrid's geographical
positioning in the heart of Spain, it has been given
the paradoxical nickname of "the best port in Spain",
to reflect the city's great love of fish and seafood.

MURCIA

Murcia is derived from the Latin term for mulberry, and indeed the region of Murcia was once ripe with mulberry trees. The staples of Murcian diet are vegetables from the valley of Rio Segura, and seafood from the Mediterranean. Signature dishes include *zarangollo*, a combination of *ratatouille* and omelette that is made from tomatoes, onions and most importantly courgettes; and *huevas de mújol*, a type of caviar that is taken from grey mullets reared in salt lagoons in Mar Menor.

Courgette, for *Zarangello*.

ANDALUSIA

Andalusia—the home of *tapas*—represents the food of southern Spain, and its dishes reflect the warmer climate. *Gazpacho*, a key dish, is a chilled soup made with tomatoes, cucumbers, garlic and vinegar, and its popularity has spread throughout Spain. The benefits from the Andalusian coast are felt in various fried fish dishes, like *Málaga-el Boquerón*—fresh baby anchovies; and the region's hot climate is used to grow tropical fruits in valleys across Granada and Almeria. Moorish influences can still be tasted in many desserts flavoured with aniseed, cinnamon, almonds and honey. *Sangria*, wine and citrus juice, is drank to help cool down on summer days. Sherry is produced in Jerez in the province of Cádiz, and is a Protected Denomination of Origin, meaning that all wine labelled as sherry has to come from the Sherry Triangle in Jerez.

Seville, the capital of Andalusia, is famous for its oranges.

BALEARIC ISLANDS

The Balearic Islands are known for their love of seafood, and their cuisine is often regarded as being an extension of Catalonian and Valencian menus. Aubergines are popular in Minorca and are a versatile vegetable, served fried, grilled, baked with meat or fish, and even with honey as a dessert. Lobsters from waters between Minorca and Majorca have a reputation for being the tastiest and are served as *caldereta de langosta*, a lobster stew that is considered a delicacy and is a favourite of King Juan Carlos I. On Ibiza the *guisat de peix* is a signature traditional fish stew—made with potatoes, garlic, and a mixture of ray fish, sword fish and lobster, along with other seafood. There are many widely drunk wines from the islands, such as offerings from vineyards in Pla i Llevant and Felanitx in Mallorca. The British Fleet was stationed on the islands for 150 years, and brought with them gin, clover and cows which now produce milk that is used to make *mahón* cheese.

LA RIOJA

A strong agricultural background has given La Rioja a variety of high quality vegetables and pulses, including peppers, garlic, onions, artichoke, asparagus, lettuce, chard, borage, and more. Pig and lamb are both eaten in vast quantities by Riojans; sweet black pudding and *chorizo* are just two examples of the uses of these meats in the mountain regions. Riojan style potatoes are popular throughout Spain, and are typically prepped with *chorizo* or sometimes spare ribs. La Rioja is, of course, most famous for its Denomination of Origin high quality wines, especially reds. The three main wine producing regions are Rioja Alta, which produces wines with an unripe fruit flavour suited to a lighter palette; Rioja Alavesa, where the wines are fuller bodied with high acidity levels; and Rioja Baja, which makes deeply coloured wines with high alcohol content, which are generally used as blending components with wine from the other regions.

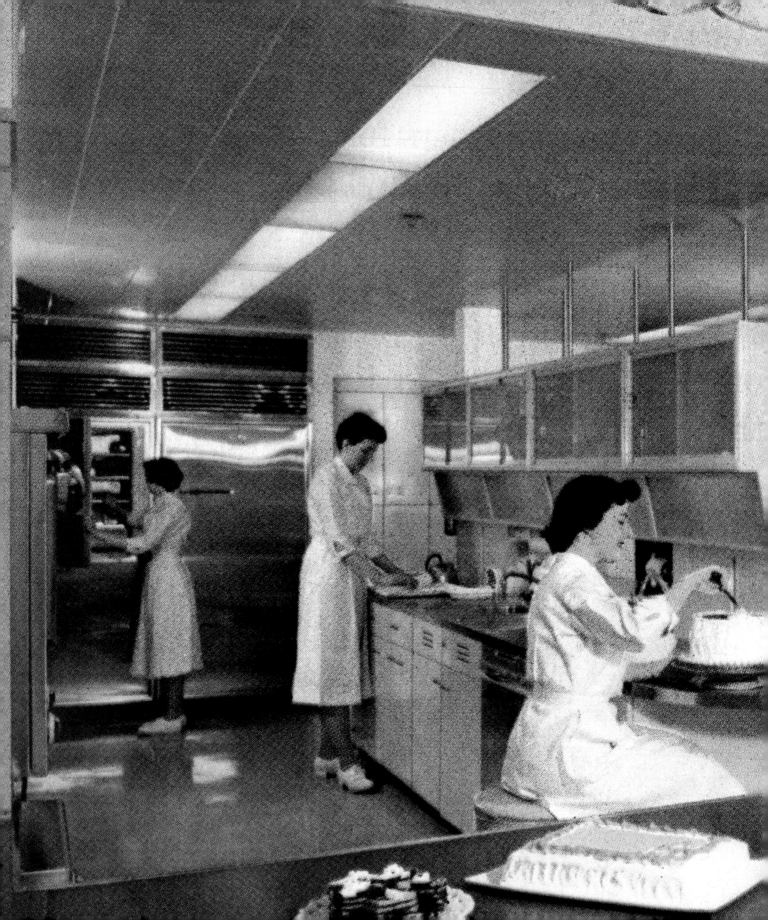

Previous pages: The Betty Crocker test kitchens in Golden Valley.

Opposite: "America's first choice in pies"—lemon meringue pie, apple pie and cherry pie, from the first edition of *Betty Crocker's New Picture Cook Book*.

Right: Amelia Simmons' *American Cookery*, 1796.

EARLY COOKERY BOOKS

The first cookery book to be published in America was Eliza Smith's *The Compleat Housewife*. This important book had been in circulation for several years in England, and had been reprinted several times by the time it reached America, where it was published by William Parks in Williamsburg, Virginia and were very well received.

AMELIA SIMMONS

Following her predecessors in England, Amelia Simmons was required to pay for her own book to be published. In 1796, she published her work with the rather lengthy and descriptive title: *American Cookery; The Art of Dressing Viands, Fish, Poultry and Vegetables, and the best Modes of making Pastes, Puffs, Pies, Tarts, Puddings, Custards and Preserves, and all Kinds of Cakes, from the Imperial Plumb to the Plain Cake*. She included a foreword that explained that she had geared the book to other Americans, and stated that her book used language, recipes and ingredients that only another American would understand. Although much of her work actually plagiarised recipes from English cookery books, she made some effort to allow for varying availability of ingredients. Her book includes a number of recipes substituting English treacle and oatmeal for American molasses and cornmeal, which came to be known as the "Johnny Cake" or "Hoe Cake", a baked flatbread popular with pioneer American communities. She also suggested recipes involving blueberries and turkey, ingredients which at the time were only widely available in America, and her book contains early recipes for apple pie and the first recipe for the traditional Thanksgiving dessert, pumpkin pie.

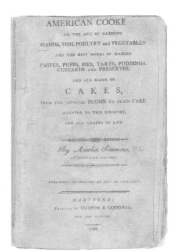

"There is no American food. The fact that we don't have a cuisine is a measure of our ethnic heterogeneity", asserts anthropologist Sidney Mintz. While America is strongly influenced by the cultures and races from which its peoples and their ancestors originate, the criterion of American cuisine is often debated. Adapted from different cultures with varying regional traditions, the term "melting pot" is often relied upon as a catch-all characterisation. Arguably, it is precisely the fusion of influences from around the world that comprises America's national identity. Certain dishes such as apple pie, hot dogs and pizza have inevitably become quintessential American icons. Embedded in that distinction is the "Americanisation" of the original dishes by the way of extra ingredients, enhancements, and a vast variety of deviations.

Apple pie has probably retained more of its original recipe than other Americanised dishes closely resembling its early English equivalent. The American apple pie emerged in the seventeenth century, although its direct influence dates back to fifteenth century England. Recipes from English cookery books as from early as the seventeenth century found their way into the American colonies in the eighteenth century and became well established. Amelia Simmons' seminal *American Cookery* book of 1796 includes early recipes for the dish.

Typically, the dish consists of uncooked apples, sugar and sweet spices, encased in pastry and then baked. In the early twentieth century the dessert became commercialised following the opening of Mrs Smith's Pies, which mass-produced and marketed frozen pies. Today the company is still one of America's largest frozen pie distributors.

• AMERICAN COOKERY •

OR THE ART OF DRESSING VIANDS, FISH, POULTRY AND VEGETABLES,
AND THE BEST MODES OF MAKING PASTES, PUFFS, PIES, TARTS, PUDDINGS,
CUSTARDS AND PRESERVES, AND ALL KINDS OF CAKES, FROM THE IMPERIAL
PLUMB TO PLAIN CAKE. ADAPTED TO THIS COUNTRY,
AND ALL GRADES OF LIFE

AMELIA SIMMONS, *AN AMERICAN ORPHAN*, 1796

TO STUFF A TURKEY

Grate a wheat loaf, one quarter of a pound butter, one quarter of a pound salt pork, finely chopped, two eggs, a little sweet marjoram, summer savory, parsley and sage, pepper and salt (if the pork be not sufficient), fill the bird and sew up. The same will answer for all Wild Fowl. Water Fowls require onions. The same ingredients stuff a leg of Veal, fresh Pork, or a loin of Veal.

TO STUFF AND ROAST A TURKEY, OR FOWL

One pound soft wheat bread, three ounces beef suet, three eggs, a little sweet thyme, sweet marjoram, pepper and salt, and some add a gill of wine; fill the bird therewith and sew up, hang down to a steady solid fire, basting frequently with salt and water, and roast until a steam emits from the breast, put one third of a pound of butter into the gravy, dust flour over the bird and baste with the gravy; serve up with boiled onions and cranberry sauce, mangoes, pickles or celery.

Others omit the sweet herbs, and add parsley done with potatoes. Boil and mash three pints potatoes, wet them with butter, add sweet herbs, pepper, salt, fill and roast as above.

TO PICKLE OR MAKE MANGOES OF MELONS

Take green melons, as many as you please, and make a brine strong enough to bear an egg; then pour it boiling hot on the melons, keeping them down under the brine; let them stand five or six days; then take them out, slit them down on one side, take out all the seeds, scrape them well in the inside, and wash them clean with cold water; then take a clove of a garlick, a little ginger and nutmeg sliced, and a little whole pepper; put all these proportionably into the melons, filling them up with mustard seeds; then lay them in an earthern pot with the slit upwards, and take one part of mustard and two parts of vinegar, enough to cover them, pouring it upon them scalding hot, and keep them close slopped.

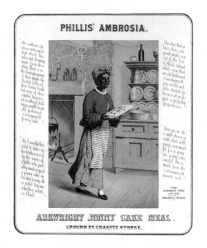

JOHNNY CAKE, OR HOE CAKE

Scald one pint of milk and put to three pints of Indian meal, and a half pint of flour—bake before the fire. Or scald with milk two thirds of the Indian meal, or wet two thirds with boiling water, add salt, molasses and shortening, work up with cold water pretty stiff, and bake as above.

INDIAN SLAPJACK

One quart of milk, one pint of Indian meal, four eggs, four spoons of flour, a little salt, beat together, baked on griddles, or fry in a dry pan, or baked in a pan which has been rub'd with suet, lard or butter.

MOLASSES GINGERBREAD

One tablespoon of cinnamon, some coriander or allspice, put to four teaspoons pearl ash, dissolved in half pint water, four pound flour, one quart molasses, four ounces butter, (if in summer rub in the butter, if in winter, warm the butter and molasses and pour to the spiced flour), knead well 'till stiff, the more the better, the lighter and whiter it will be; bake brisk fifteen minutes; don't scorch; before it is put in, wash it with whites and sugar beat together.

Left: The Native American village of Secotan in the late sixteenth century.

Right: A First World War poster encouraging the consumption of corn.

Opposite: Varieties of American squash.

• NATIVE AMERICA •

Despite its heritage, American cuisine is not without its own exclusive origins, traditions and trends. The cuisine and culinary techniques used by the indigenous communities of North America greatly impacted upon the gastronomic history of the country. The meeting of colonial and native populations in the fifteenth century brought about the diffusion of farming techniques and native foods such as blueberries, cranberries, and turkey throughout the country, as well as squash, beans and maize which remain essential staples of the American diet. The latter were traditionally farmed together by Native Americans: complementing each other, the ground-spread of growing squash prevented weeds sprouting, while beans were able to climb up the tall stems of corn.

Both Native American and early colonial populations would have eaten a corn-based porridge, or "samp", to which preserved, salted meats and shellfish were added. Such one-pot dishes were cooked slowly and at length, with new and fresh ingredients added over several days. On the northeast coast, colonists were introduced to maple syrup, the production of which had been practiced by indigenous communities for hundreds of years. Processed by boiled sap on hot rocks under a canopy of branches, it was used as a sweet drink or to add flavour to food. These makeshift shelters were the forerunners of "sugar shacks" or "sap houses" and became meeting places and communal dining areas, a practice which still continues today.

Left: Women cook clams and lobsters on a beach in Maine in the late nineteenth century.

Below: An early advertising label for lobster, including directions for its preparation.

The New England clambake can be traced back to Native Americans from Martha's Vineyard, south of Cape Cod, who perfected this method of cooking far before the colonial influences of the English, French and Spanish reached North America. A typical clambake begins with participants gathering seaweed and several round, medium-sized stones. A fire pit is then prepared, with the stones placed into the flames, burning until the stones are glowing hot. When the fire has burned out, the ashes are swept off the stones and raked to form a cooking bed, whereon a layer of wet seaweed is placed, topped with traditional regional foods such as clams, mussels, quahogs, and lobsters. Side dishes usually include potatoes, corn on the cob, *linquica* sausages, carrots and onions. Alternating layers of seaweed and food are piled on top of each other until the entire mound is covered in sea water-soaked canvas and allowed to steam for several hours.

• THANKSGIVING •

Thanksgiving is a holiday tradition that is unique to Americans, involving the consumption of a turkey as a main course. Closely identifiable with the traditional harvest festival, it can be traced back to celebrations of good yields, although the precise date and nature of the first Thanksgiving is unknown. The commonly acknowledged link between Thanksgiving celebrations and Pilgrim America did not in fact appear until the mid-1800s, when a letter written by Edward Winslow was published. Winslow made reference to a three-day celebratory feast following a good crop, to which both Puritan and Native American people contributed foodstuffs and ate communally.

Today's traditional Thanksgiving meal, which falls on the last Thursday of November and unofficially kicks off the Christmas season, is accompanied by side dishes including stuffing, cranberries, and pumpkin pie.

A *Harper's Bazar* Thanksgiving advertisement, 1894.

Food for health, 1936.
A government promotion in
support of families growing
their own food.

• THE GREAT DEPRESSION •

Within the first three years of the Great Depression of the
1930s, more than eight million people were living on the
streets and relying on handouts from charities for food
and shelter. These handouts often came from grocers shops
that would donate food to churches, where the food was
then prepared and distributed to the needy. It is said that
even the infamous gangster Al Capone sponsored a soup
kitchen during the Depression in an attempt to better his
name. Many of the homeless travelled to the West in the
hope of finding work. This overwhelmed the workforce in
states such as California and led to vast unemployment and
the development of shanty towns. Those who did not live in
cities hunted small animals such as rabbits, which served
as a staple part of their diets. Likewise, many farming
families reported living on biscuits and gravy for days at
a time, or breads that were little more than water mixed
with meal. In some circumstances, people were able to
farm enough food to feed their family potatoes and other
starchy vegetables. However, the southwest of America
suffered a great drought through much of the 1930s known
as the Dust Bowl, which made farming impossible for nearly
a third of the country. Relief finally came when America
entered the Second World War, bringing jobs to the cities
and demand to farms.

d for health

NEW YORK STRIP STEAK 16
RIBEYE STEAK/CAJUN RIBEYE 17
DOUBLE CUT FILET MIGNON 10/10.75
48 OZ. PORTERHOUSE for one 50
SINGLE CUT FILET MIGNON 49
CHICAGO STYLE BONE-IN RIBEYE STEAK 40/41
DOMESTIC DOUBLE RIB LAMB CHOPS 44
SESAME ENCRUSTED YELLOWFIN TUNA 100
COLOSSAL SHRIMP ALEXANDER 39
JUMBO LUMP CRAB CAKES 50
LIVE MAINE LOBSTER 40
AUSTRALIAN LOBSTER TAILS 34
POTATOES 36
SAUTEED WILD MUSHROOMS 45
ASPARAGUS/CREAMED SPINACH Market
STEAMED FRESH BROCCOLI 43/56
SAUTEED FRESH SPINACH AND MUSHROOMS 85-95
SOUFFLES for two 10.5
MORTON'S LEGENDARY HOT CHOCOLATE CAKE 10.75/11
9
85
16
13

• THE CHICAGO ABATTOIRS •

Chicago was the centre of meatpacking from the 1880s through to the 1920s. During the American Civil War, the city was situated on key railway lines and was therefore able to provide meat to both the Midwest and the East Coast. The butchering industry constituted a great portion of the district's business during the period. Processing plants were opened that relied on new technology for packing meats and maximising profits on the animals, allowing the meat to be cooled or steamed, the hooves and bones to be used for gelatin and glue, and the fat used for soap. Chicago meatpackers also developed methods of canning meat in order to preserve it, and an influential worker named Gustavus Swift introduced an ingenious method of transporting beef in ice-chilled railway cars. The United States government regulated the location of the meatpacking district, forcing the plants to remain on the outskirts of town, as well as monitoring the quality of meat that was to be sold to the public. The Chicago meatpacking district continued to be the country's central abattoir until the 1950s when it could no longer keep up with the new markets that were emerging elsewhere in the United States, such as in New York City.

Right: 500 Bakers recruitment poster for the First World War, 1917.

Opposite: Display of home-preserved food including yellow squash, collard greens and beetroot. During the Second World War Americans were encouraged to store their food in this way.

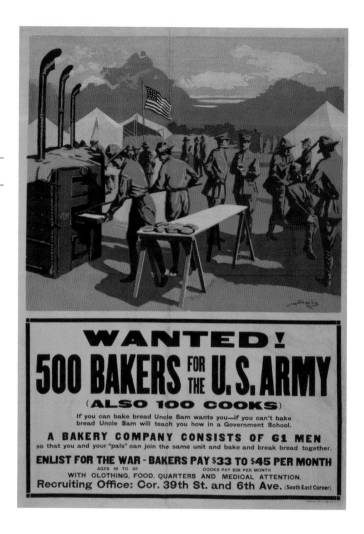

• WARTIME AMERICA •

When the United States entered the First World War, the government quickly instituted campaigns and distribution controls upon food in the country. Just as Allied countries in Europe were in great need of food products, Herbert C Hoover—who would later go on to be President—and the United States Food Administration initiated food preservation campaigns, encouraging Americans to reduce waste, reduce consumption of foods useful to troops such as wheat, and to increase the output of homegrown or farmed produce. Citizens were encouraged to preserve foods at home, particularly vegetables, which many began to grow on what became called "liberty gardens"—small, disused areas of land that could be converted to agricultural plots. Sugar rationing was introduced in 1918, and as a result molasses and syrup became increasingly popular as substitutes. It was during this time that soy products first found their way onto many American dinner tables; pamphlets promoting this foodstuff suggested useful recipes for substituting protein with soy-based meat loaf, and wheat with soy loaves. As a result, the period saw a healthier level of nutrition for many Americans, as vegetable and whole-wheat food intake increased, and the use of sugar, lard and butter decreased. Sales of substitute food products soared, such as Crisco, a vegetable-based shortening that replaced lard.

When rationing became compulsory during the Second World War, advertisements, posters and campaigns were released promoting the idea that restrictions on availability of basic goods was integral to the success of the war. They also reminded the public that while they were going without certain foods at home, many young men were risking their lives across the globe, ensuring public compliance in the face of severe shortages.

The familiar Lincoln-esque face with white beard, stern expression, and stars-and-stripes hat was most famously used by the Office of War Information in an attempt to recruit for the United States armed services. However, the image was widespread across most other departments of the US government. The Department of Agriculture featured Uncle Sam, armed with a hoe and standing in a ploughed field (overleaf), promoting gardening as a means to free up the availability of vegetables to feed soldiers.

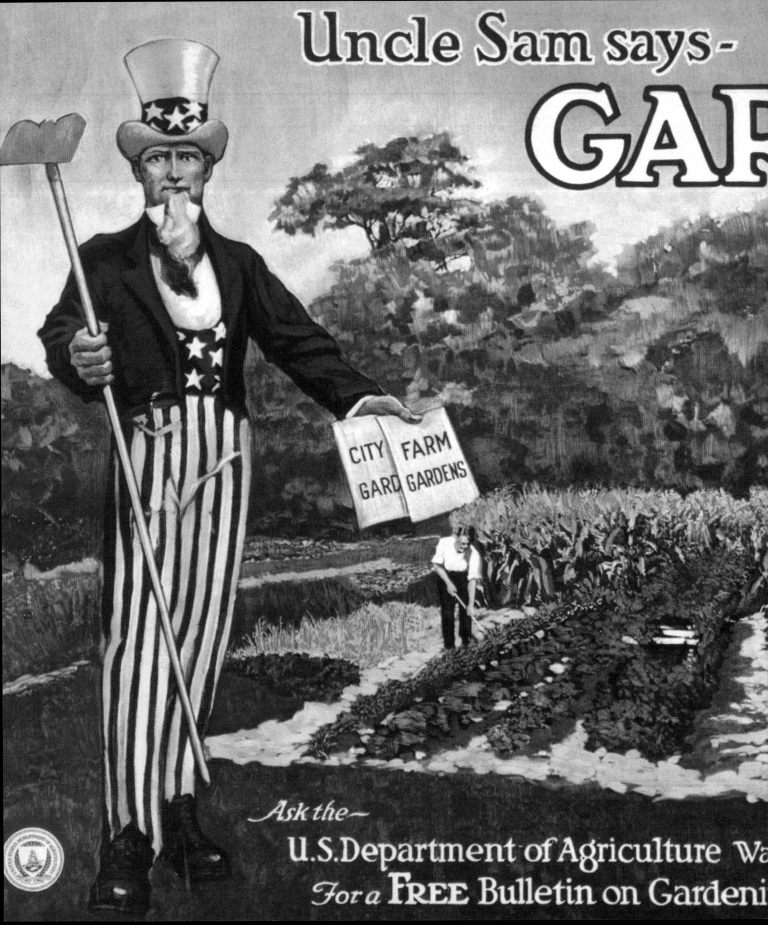

DEN
To Cut Food Costs

gton, D.C.
—It's food for thought

Uncle Sam says "garden to cut food costs", 1917.

• HOW NOT TO BOIL AN EGG •

MFK FISHER, *HOW TO COOK A WOLF*

Probably one of the most private things in the world is an egg until it is broken.

Until then, you would think its secrets are its own, hidden behind the impassive beautiful curvings of its shell, white or brown or speckled. It emerges full-formed, almost painlessly [The *egg* may not be bothered, but nine years and two daughters after writing this I wonder somewhat more about the *hen*. I wrote, perhaps, too glibly] from the hen. It lies without thought in the straw, and unless there is a thunderstorm or a sharp rise in temperature it stays fresh enough to please the human palate for several days.

In spite of the complete impersonality of its shell, however, some things about an egg can be guessed. People who know how can decide several rather surprising facts about it by holding it before a strong light, and even a zany will tell you that if it is none too fresh it will stand up and perhaps bob a little in a bowl of water.

The best thing to do with aged eggs is not to buy them; they are fit for nothing, and a poor economy. If you find your self the owner of a few, change your merchant with no more ado.

Hens, as long as they can find enough to eat, go right along at their chosen profession whether the country is at war or not, but; unfortunately the product of all their industry is so delicate and perishable that when most of the fast trucks of the land are being used to shift soldiers here and there, the price of eggs goes much too high for comfort, whether or not the supply is good... and so does the cost as well as the procurability of their feed.

During the last war housewives used to buy several dozen eggs when they were cheapest, and cover them in a crock with a singularly unpleasant stuff called water glass.

I can remember going down to the cellar and fishing around in the stonejar for two eggs for a cake the cook was making: the jellied chemical made a sucking noise as I spooned out the thickly coated hideous stuff, and I felt squeamish and afraid, alone there in the cool dark room. I decided then, and I still hold to it, that I would rather eat a good fresh egg only occasionally than have a whole cellarful of these dishonest old ones, which in spite of being "almost as good as new" would not make omelets, even, but had to be used in cakes and cookies.

Of course, the finest way to know that the egg you plan to eat is a fresh one is to own the hen that makes it. This scheme has many drawbacks, and I for one, as a person who has never felt any bond of sympathy between myself and a chicken (their heads are too small, somehow, for their stupid, scratching, omnivorous bodies), have always been content to let someone else tend to the henhouse, even if I had to buy the product at much more than it would cost me to own one myself.

Eggs are a good investment now and then, expensive or not, and unless you are told otherwise by your doctor, or hate them in any form, they should be eaten in place of meat occasionally. The old-fashioned idea that they are "invalid food," something light and inconsequential, is fairly well proved foolish by the fact that two eggs are fully as nutritious as a juicy beefsteak... and ten times as hard to digest unless they are cooked with great wisdom.

Probably the wisest way to treat an egg is not to cook it at all. An accomplished barfly will prove to you that a Prairie Oyster is one of the quickest pickups known to man, and whether you are hungover or merely tired, a raw egg beaten with a little milk or sherry can make you feel much more able to cope with yourself, and shortly too. [My children react happily to an egg yolk spread on dark bread and then well sprinkled with brown sugar, for a potent snack.]

A biochemist once told me that every minute an egg is cooked makes it take three hours longer to digest. The thought of a stomach pumping and grinding and laboring for some nine hours over an average three-minute egg is a wearisome one, if true, and makes memories of picnics and their accompanying deviled eggs seem actively haunting.

The simplest way to eat an egg, if you refuse to swallow it raw, even in its fanciest high-tasting disguises, is to boil it. Rather it is *not* to boil it, for no more erroneous phrase ever existed than "to boil an egg."

There are several ways *not* to boil an egg so that it will be tender, thoroughly cooked, and yet almost as easily digested as if it were raw.

One fairly good one is to drop the egg gently into simmering water, first running cold water over it so that it will not crack, and then let it stand there in the gentle heat for whatever time you wish. It will cook just as fast as if the water were hopping about in great bubbles, and it will be a better-treated egg, once opened.

Another way, which I think is the best one, is to cover the egg with cold water in a little pan. Heat it briskly, and as soon as it begins to bubble, the egg is done. It will be tenderer than when started in hot water, which of course makes the part nearest the shell cook immediately, instead of heating the whole thing gently.

I have never yet seen an egg crack when started in cool water, but some people automatically make a pinhole in every egg they boil, to prevent possible leaks, lesions, and losses.

(If you still want hard-boiled eggs, after pondering the number of hours, or days, it would take to digest them according to the biochemist, start them in cold water, turn the heat off as soon as it begins to bubble, and let them stand in it until it is cold. They will be tender, and comparatively free from nightmares.) [This is not as good a system as it is cracked up to be, to make a timid little pun. More often than not, I have found since I so optimistically wrote of it, the eggs do not peel properly. Half of the white comes off with the shell. Ho hum.]

If you think eggs boiled in their shells are fit food for the nursery, and refuse to admit any potential blessing in one delicately prepared, neatly spooned from its shell into a cup, sagely seasoned with salt and fresh-ground black pepper and a sizeable dollop of butter, all to be eaten with hot toast, then it is definitely not your dish. Instead, try heating a shallow skillet or fire-proof dish, skirling a lump of butter [preferably waiting in the bottom, to absorb good melting heat from the egg...] or bacon grease or decent oil [This must have been a wartime aberration. Just lately I fired a cook who fried eggs in my best olive oil. The eggs, the oil, the whole house, and finally the cook took on an unbearable *slipperiness*] in it until it looks very hot, and breaking a fresh egg or two into it. Then... and this is the trick... turn off the heat at once, cover the pan tightly, and wait for about three minutes. The result will be tender and firm, and very good indeed with toast and coffee, or with a salad and white wine for supper.

This method, of course, is a compromise. It is not a fried egg, strictly speaking, and yet it is as near to making *good* fried egg as I have ever got.

I can make amazingly *bad* fried eggs, and in spite of what people tell me about this method and that, I continue to make amazingly bad fried eggs: tough, with edges like some kind of dirty starched lace, and a taste part sulphur and part singed newspaper. The best way to find a trustworthy method, I think, is to ask almost anyone but me. Or look in a cookbook. Or experiment.

There are as many different theories about making an omelet as there are people who like them, but in general, there are two main schools: the French, which uses eggs hardly stirred together, and the puffy or *souflé*, which beats the white and yellow parts of the eggs separately, and then mixes them.

Then, of course, there is the Italian *frittata* school, which mixes all kinds of cooked cooled vegetables with eggs and merges them into a sort of pie; and a very good school that is.

Moreover, there is the Oriental school, best exemplified by what is usually called *foo yeung* in chop-suey parlors and is a kind of pancake of egg and bean-sprouts.

To cap the whole thing, there is the school that has its own dependable and usually very simple method of putting eggs in a pan and having them come out as intended. Brillat-Savarin called them *oeujs brouillis* and I call them scrambled eggs.

The best definition of a perfect French omelet is given, perhaps unwittingly, in Escofficr's American translation of his *Guide Culinaire*: "Scrambled eggs enclosed in a coating of coagulated egg." This phrase in itself is none too appetizing, it seems to me, but it must do for want of a better man to say it. [This is said much more simply in its own language: *une omelette baveuse.*]

A French omelet worthy of the man, if not the definition, can be made, the second time at least if the first

time it turns into a stiff ugly curd, by following these directions:

BASIC FRENCH OMELET

6 eggs
salt and pepper
3 tablespoons butter (good oil if absolutely necessary)

Be sure that the frying pan (8 or 10 inches) is smooth on the inside. Heat the butter in it until if gives off a nutty smell but does not brown. ("This will not only lend an exquisite taste", Escoffier says, "but the degree of heat reached in order to produce the aroma will be found to ensure the perfect setting of the eggs.") Roll the pan to cover the sides with butter.

Beat eggs lightly with a fork, add seasoning, and pour into pan. As soon as the edges are set, run a spatula under the center so that all the un-cooked part will run under the cooked. [By now I know, fatalistically, that if I am using a pan I know, and if I have properly rolled the precise amount of sweet butter around that pan, and if the stars, winds, and general emotional climates are in both conjunction and harmony, I can make a perfect omelet without ever touching a spatula to it. Such occasions are historical, as well as accidental.] Do this once or twice, never leaving it to its own devices. When it is daintily browned on the bottom and creamy on top, fold it in the middle (or roll if you are a master), slide it onto a dish, and serve speedily.

Chopped herbs, cheese, mushrooms, and almost anything else may be added at your discretion, either at the first in the stirred eggs or when it is ready to fold. [Delicate creamed fowl or fish, generous in proportion to the size of each omelet, can be folded in, or new peas or asparagus tips, lightly cooked in butter.]

BETTY CROCKER

The Washburn Crosby Company first invented Betty Crocker in 1921 purely to use as a name to personalise their correspondence with consumers, choosing "Betty" because they thought it sounded friendly and "Crocker" because it was the surname of the company director. The face of Betty Crocker was subsequently created by a worker at the company using the facial characteristics of several other employees. Likewise, Betty Crocker's signature was that of one of the women in the company who gained the honour after a contest.

So influential was the concept of Betty Crocker that in 1945 she was declared the second most popular American woman, behind Eleanor Roosevelt, in *Fortune* magazine. She appeared in the first colour advertisement on American television channel CBS, played by Adelaide Hawley Cumming, and even had her own programme until 1964. Betty Crocker's cookery books are still available.

The signature of Betty Crocker has stayed the same since it was first designed in 1921, but the image of her face has undergone many changes. Most recently the face of Betty Crocker, according to the corporation itself, was created by combining 75 women of various ages and ethnicities to reflect a more 'authentic' image of the American homemaker.

Left: Cover of *Betty Crocker's Picture Cook Book*.

Right: Festive fluffy frostings; twin angel cake, clown cake and pink mountain frosting.

Opposite: The changing face of Betty Crocker throughout the decades, from 1936–1996.

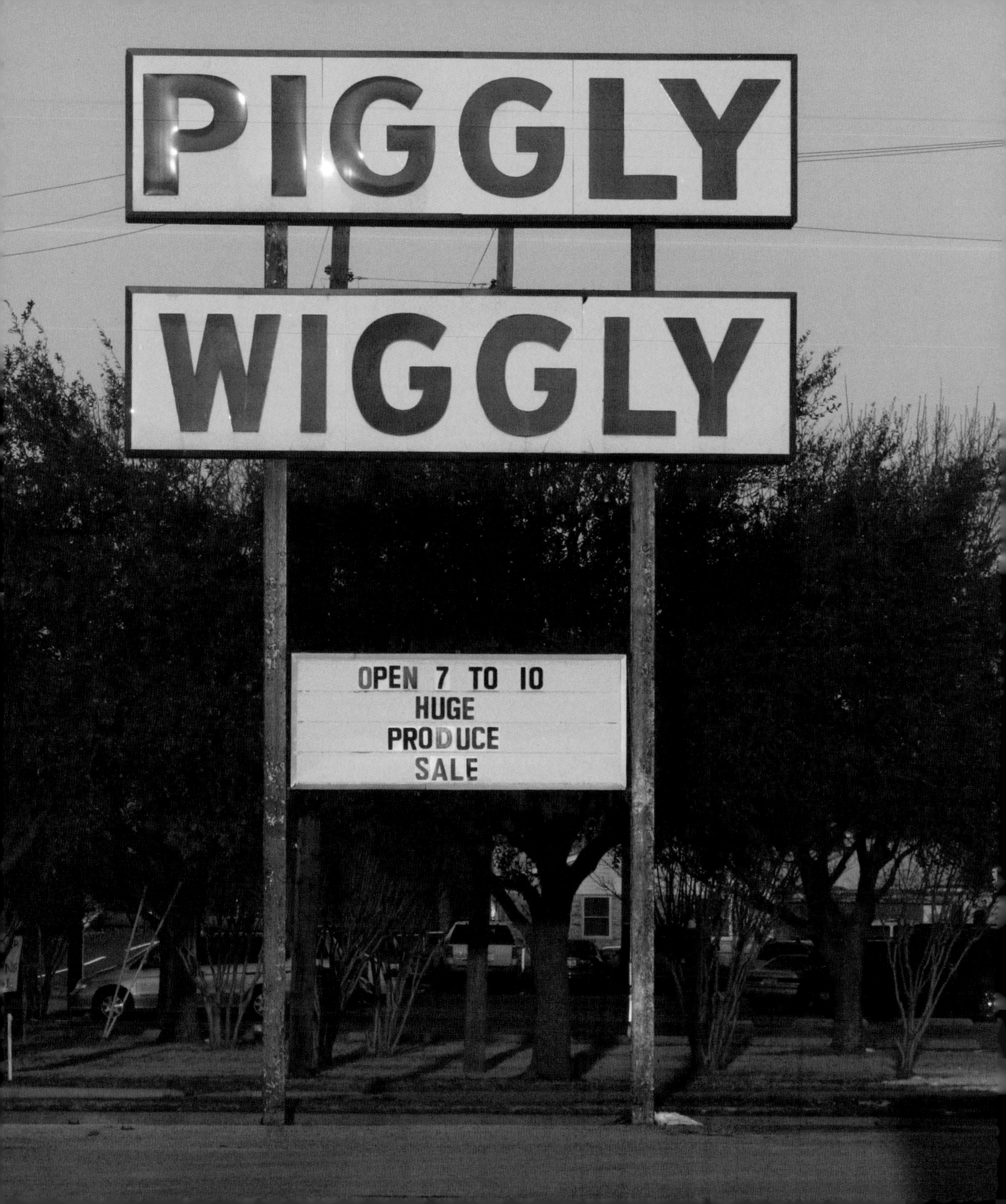
PIGGLY
WIGGLY
OPEN 7 TO 10
HUGE
PRODUCE
SALE

Opposite: An original Piggly Wiggly
sign in Denton, Texas.

Right: Retro Kellogg's Corn Flakes
packaging.

Far right: Betty Crocker carrot cake mix.

• CONVENIENCE FOOD •

Piggly Wiggly was the first modern self-service supermarket.
In 1916, Clarence Saunders opened the first Piggly Wiggly
store in Memphis, Tennessee; customers would enter through
a turnstile and walk up and down four aisles until they reached
the check-out registers. Although taken for granted today, at the
time this was a completely innovative idea and revolutionised
the way consumers shopped. The shop was divided and
organised into departments and included 605 different goods
in its range. This was to kick-start aggressive advertising in
the commercial food industry as sellers relied for the first
time on product and brand recognition. At Piggly Wiggly,
cashiers wore uniforms for the first time, and low prices for
bulk-buying were offered. In 1917, Saunders patented his self-
service shopping idea, and began to franchise other grocers
to operate under his method. Today there are hundreds of
supermarkets across America operating under the Piggly
Wiggly name, each independently owned.

Breakfast cereal first emerged in 1863 when vegetarian
James Caleb Jackson created granula (or granola), a cereal
that needed to be soaked overnight in milk. But this was
not a popular choice and did not catch on. The idea went
into hibernation until 1877 when John Harvey Kellogg,
an operator at the Battle Creek Sanitarium in Michigan,
created a biscuit of wheat, oat and cornmeal to help his
patients with bowel problems. When he left out the rolled-
out dough overnight, it cracked and became flakey. This
was later recreated with corn and became the popular
Kellogg's Corn Flakes. In 1897, John Kellogg was not the
only inhabitant of Battle Creek Sanitarium to contribute
to the early conception of breakfast cereal. Charles William
Post created Grape Nuts, which proved very popular and
still exist today, their curious name not deriving from
grape ingredients but from the natural sugary taste of
the cereal.

In the 1930s, puffed and sugary cereals were introduced
to the market and mascots added to entice children. Although
traditional cereals such as the corn flake are still popular,
many others have been criticised for their deceptively
high sugar content. It has been alleged that there is more
nutritional value to a cardboard box than a bowl of corn
flakes, an idea popularised by an unpublished experiment at
Ann Arbor University in the 1960s, which found that lab rats
fed on a diet of generic corn flakes died earlier than similar
rats fed on the box in which the flakes were packaged.

Left and opposite: A Green Giant sign and retro advertisement.

Overleaf: Two retro advertisements from the original maker of the TV Dinner, Swanson.

General Mills, the largest supplier of frozen vegetables in America, created the Jolly Green Giant, famous for his deep laugh in television advertisements, in order to promote their pea range. First appearing in 1928, the Green Giant caught on and in 1973 was joined by a youthful *protégé*, Little Green Sprout.

The character of the Giant seemed to capture people's imaginations. In 1978, the town of Blue Earth in Minnesota erected a 17 metre high statue of the Jolly Green Giant to mark the east and west sections of Interstate 90. It remains there and still attracts thousands of visitors every year. Michael Jackson owned a large-scale statue of the Giant, and even the artist Andy Warhol spoke of his affection for the food mascot in an interview recorded at Gristedes supermarket in New York City. The Jolly Green Giant continues to be an effective advertising tool in the twenty-first century.

Convenience or fast foods are typified by minimal preparation and ease of portability. Pre-prepared meals, canned drinks, pre-packaged puddings and tinned soups all fit under this category. These foods are heavily criticised as being a culprit for obesity and malnutrition because they are high in salt and fat and largely omit fresh fruit and vegetables, and essential daily vitamins and minerals. Nevertheless, the fast food industry thrives on busy Americans who simply do not have the time to sit down to a proper meal.

The TV Dinner, that most characteristic culinary invention of 1950s America, was introduced to the market by the Swanson food company in 1954. The original frozen dinner consisted of turkey with cornbread gravy, peas and sweet potatoes, each compartmentalised in a foil tray. Already marketing frozen foods, Swanson's primary product was turkey, and a glut of unsold birds reared for Thanksgiving in 1952, combined with knowledge of ready-prepared meals for aeroplane flights, inspired this invention. As Gerry Thomas, the Swanson employee credited with inventing the TV Dinner noted, the reference to television in the product's name ensured its success; a contemporary food product to accompany the most contemporary form of entertainment. The meals simply required re-heating, and were marketed as a means for women to feed their families quickly and well. The original turkey dinner was soon followed by others such as fried chicken, steak and fish fillets, and paved the way for the development of frozen, ready-made and microwaveable meals across the world.

THE *Orchid* OF THE PEA FAMILY

The orchid and the Green Giant Pea.
Both have been reared for a high moment.
The orchid is bred to bloom in sheer
breath-snatching beauty.

The Green Giant Pea is bred to taste like
the sweetest morsel that ever grew.

It is a secret breed produced after years of
scientific research.

It took fifteen years to develop the seed
for this year's Green Giant Brand Peas.
They are picked at the moment of perfect
flavor and popped in a can for you when
bursting with garden beauty (actually less
than three hours from field to can).

At last canned peas with
individuality. As tender as
those little French fellows
but big enough to get your
teeth into them, which
makes them a new gourmet
delicacy among the most
particular young hostesses.
A top-bloom flavor and

tenderness and a rare bouquet which come from per-
fect breeding and perfect
picking time. Packed from
secret breed (Minnesota
Valley No. S537).

P. S.—Try Green Giant
Brand Peas on children
who don't like vegetables.

**DON'T SAY "PEAS"—
SAY "GREEN GIANT BRAND PEAS"**
Identify them by the Green Giant
on the label. Other Green Giant
Products: Del Maiz Niblets Corn,
Del Maiz Cream Style Corn and
Niblet-ears Corn. Packed exclu-
sively by Minnesota Valley Can-
ning Co., Le Sueur, Minn. and Fine
Foods of Canada, Ltd.,Toronto,Ont.

"GREEN GIANT" T. M. REG. U. S. PAT. OFF.

GREEN GIANT PEAS

Swanson Night

A family get-together, a good meaty meal (like this tender pork that's all loin) and time to enjoy both.

"O.K. gang . . . pork and apple slices coming up!"

SWANSON FROZEN LOIN OF PORK DINNER

- Tender pork loin slices.
- Apple slices in natural juices.
- French fries so light and crispy it's hard to believe.
- Plus a special serving of tender sweet peas in seasoned butter sauce.

Have a Swanson Night soon!

Trust Swanson

2 New Swanson TV Dinners!

Brand

New! Chopped Sirloin Beef

Lots of tender beef in Swanson's delectable new TV Brand Chopped Sirloin Beef Dinner! Generous portions of chopped beef from selected sirloin. Superbly seasoned and cooked just right by Swanson chefs to seal in all its juicy goodness. With savory brown gravy, sweet green peas and golden French fries. Just heat 25 minutes, and enjoy. It's another genuine Swanson TV Dinner!

New! Meat Loaf

Plenty of juicy meat loaf in this exciting new TV Brand Dinner from Swanson! Seasoned to a turn, and cooked the careful Swanson way. Served with the richest red tomato sauce, garden-good peas with butter, and buttered mashed potatoes made fluffy with milk. All piping-ready in 25 minutes. Genuine Swanson TV Meat Loaf Dinner—have it soon!

QUICK FROZEN BY SWANSON

New Packages!

Look for bright **new packages** like these on all **Swanson TV** Dinners. Be sure to try Chicken, Turkey, Beef and Filet of Haddock Dinners, too.

SWANSON

TV. Dinners

MADE ONLY BY *Campbell* SOUP COMPANY

Get one FREE!

Here's all you do:

1 Buy two Swanson TV Brand Dinners, at least one of which must be either of the *new* Dinners (Meat Loaf or Chopped Sirloin Beef).

2 Send the two outside wrappers from both **TV Dinner** packages with your name and address and tell us the price you paid for *one* new Meat Loaf or Chopped Sirloin Beef Dinner to: Free Dinner, P.O. Box 84-C, Mt. Vernon 10, N.Y. Swanson will send you the purchase price you paid for the new Dinner. Hurry! Offer good for limited time only. Limit—**one refund per family.**

"TV" AND "TV DINNER" ARE REGISTERED TRADEMARKS

• HOT DOGS •

DACHSUNDS, DOG WAGONS AND OTHER IMPORTANT ELEMENTS OF HOT DOG HISTORY
NATIONAL HOT DOG AND SAUSAGE COUNCIL
AMERICAN MEAT INSTITUTE

Sausage is one of the oldest forms of processed food, having been mentioned in Homer's *Odyssey* as far back as the ninth century BC.

Frankfurt-am-Main, Germany, is traditionally credited with originating the frankfurter. However, this claim is disputed by those who assert that the popular sausage—known as a "dachshund" or "littledog" sausage—was created in the late 1600s by Johann Georghehner, a butcher, living in Coburg, Germany. According to this report, Georghehner later traveled to Frankfurt to promote his new product.

In 1987, the city of Frankfurt celebrated the 500th birthday of the hot dog in that city. It's said that the frankfurter was developed there in 1487, five years before Christopher Columbus set sail for the new world. The people of Vienna (Wien), Austria, point to the term "wiener" to prove their claim as the birthplace of the hot dog.

As it turns out, it is likely that the North American hot dog comes from a widespread common European sausage brought here by butchers of several nationalities. Also in doubt is who first served the dachshund sausage with a roll. One report says a German immigrant sold them, along with milk rolls and sauerkraut, from a push cart in New York City's Bowery during the 1860s. In 1871, Charles Feltman, a German butcher opened up the first Coney Island hot dog stand selling 3,684 dachshund sausages in a milk roll during his first year in business.

The year, 1893, was an important date in hot dog history. In Chicago that year, the Colombian Exposition brought hordes of visitors who consumed large quantities of sausages sold by vendors. People liked this food that was easy to eat, convenient and inexpensive. Hot dog historian Bruce Kraig, PhD., retired professor emeritus at Roosevelt University, says the Germans always ate the dachshund sausages with bread. Since the sausage culture is German, it is likely that Germans introduced the practice of eating the dachshund sausages, which we today know as the hot dog, nestled in a bun.

Also in 1893, sausages became the standard fare at baseball parks. This tradition is believed to have been started by a St Louis bar owner, Chris Von de Ahe, a German immigrant who also owned the St Louis Browns major league baseball team.

Many hot dog historians chafe at the suggestion that today's hot dog on a bun was introduced during the St Louis "Louisiana Purchase Exposition" in 1904 by Bavarian concessionaire, Anton Feuchtwanger. As the story goes, he loaned white gloves to his patrons to hold his piping hot sausages and as most of the gloves were not returned, the supply began running low. He reportedly asked his brother-in-law, a baker, for help. The baker improvised long soft rolls that fit the meat—thus inventing the hot dog bun. Kraig says everyone wants to claim the hot dog bun as their own invention, but the most likely scenario is the practice was handed down by German immigrants and gradually became widespread in American culture.

Another story that riles serious hot dog historians is how term "hot dog" came about. Some say the word was coined in 1901 at the New York Polo Grounds on a cold April day. Vendors were hawking hot dogs from portable hot water tanks shouting "They're red hot! Get your dachshund sausages while they're red hot!" A *New York Journal* sports cartoonist, Tad Dorgan, observed the scene and hastily drew a cartoon of barking dachshund sausages nestled warmly in rolls. Not sure how to spell

American actor and comedian Jerry
Lewis tucks into hot dogs.

"dachshund" he simply wrote "hot
dog!" The cartoon is said to have been
a sensation, thus coining the term "hot
dog". However, historians have been
unable to find this cartoon, despite
Dorgan's enormous body of work and
his popularity.

Kraig, and other culinary historians, point
to college magazines where the word "hot
dog" began appearing in the 1890s. The
term was current at Yale in the fall of
1894, when "dog wagons" sold hot dogs
at the dorms. The name was a sarcastic
comment on the provenance of the meat.
References to dachshund sausages and
ultimately hot dogs can be traced to
German immigrants in the 1800s. These
immigrants brought not only sausages
to America, but dachshund dogs. The
name most likely began as a joke about
the Germans' small, long, thin dogs. In
fact, even Germans called the frankfurter
a "little-dog" or "dachshund" sausage,
thus linking the word "dog" to their
popular concoction.

• HOT DOG ETIQUETTE •

EVERYDAY GUIDANCE FOR EATING AMERICA'S SACRED FOOD, NATIONAL HOT DOG AND SAUSAGE COUNCIL, AMERICAN MEAT INSTITUTE

DON'T...
Put hot dog toppings between the hot dog and the bun. Always "dress the dog", not the bun.

Condiments should be applied in the following order: wet condiments like mustard and chili are applied first, followed by chunky condiments like relish, onions and sauerkraut, followed by shredded cheese, followed by spices, like celery salt or pepper.

DO...
Serve sesame seed, poppy seed and plain buns with hot dogs. Sun-dried tomato buns or basil buns are considered gauche with franks.

DON'T...
Use a cloth napkin to wipe your mouth when eating a hot dog. Paper is always preferable.

DO...
Eat hot dogs on buns with your hands. Utensils should not touch hot dogs on buns.

DO...
Use paper plates to serve hot dogs. Every day dishes are acceptable; china is a no-no.

DON'T...
Take more than five bites to finish a hot dog. For foot-long wiener, seven bites are acceptable.

DON'T...
Leave bits of bun on your plate. Eat it all.

DON'T...
Fresh herbs on the same plate with hot dogs over-do the presentation

DON'T...
Use ketchup on your hot dog after the age of 18. Mustard, relish, onions, cheese and chili are acceptable.

DO...
Condiments remaining on the fingers after eating a hot dog should be licked away, not washed.

DO...
Use multi-colored toothpicks to serve cocktail wieners. Cocktail forks are in poor taste.

DON'T...
Send a thank you note following a hot dog barbecue. It would not be in keeping with the unpretentious nature of hot dogs.

DON'T...
Bring wine to a hot dog barbecue. Beer, soda, lemonade and iced tea are preferable.

DON'T...
Ever think there is a wrong time to serve hot dogs.

Above and opposite: A New York and Chicago style hot dog.

HOT DOGS

Americans eat an unestimatable number of hot dogs each year. In restaurants and at street carts, ballparks and backyard barbeques—hot dogs are everywhere! But depending on where you purchase your hot dog, your toppings may differ radically. Here's our short guide on what to expect when you buy your hot dog away from home.

NEW YORK CITY

New Yorkers eat more hot dogs than any other group in the country. From downtown Manhattan to Coney Island, when you buy your hot dog in the Big Apple, it will come served with steamed onions and a pale, deli-style yellow mustard.

CHICAGO

The possible antithesis to New York dogs, Chicago dogs are layered with yellow mustard, dark green relish, chopped raw onion, tomato slices and topped with a dash of celery salt and served in a poppy seed bun.

ATLANTA AND THE SOUTH

Buying a hot dog at Turner Field, home of the Atlanta Braves, or else where in Atlanta and the south, you'll end up with your dog "dragged through the garden" and topped with coleslaw.

KANSAS CITY

Get the mints out—you'll need them when you order up a hot dog in KC as it is served with sauerkraut and melted Swiss cheese on a sesame seed bun.

BASEBALL STADIUMS

Turner Field isn't the only place to get a hot dog styled to local preferences, here are some others to check out:

THE ROCKIE DOG

Served at Coors Field, the home of the Colorado Rockies—is a footlong dog with grilled peppers, kraut and onions.

THE FENWAY FRANK

Served at none other than Fenway Park—is the only dog to eat while watching the Red Sox. Its boiled and grilled and served in a New England style bun with mustard and relish.

THE TEXAS DOG

Chili, cheese and jalapenos make this the favoured item at Minute Maid Park in Houston.

OTHER REGIONAL PREFERENCES

Midwesterners eat more pork and beef hot dogs than any other region of the country.

Westerners eat more poultry hot dogs than any other region of the country, however, southerns are a close second.

Easterns prefer all-beef hot dogs and consumer more than any other region of the country.

Text reproduced courtesy of the National Hot Dog and Sausage Council, American Meat Institute.

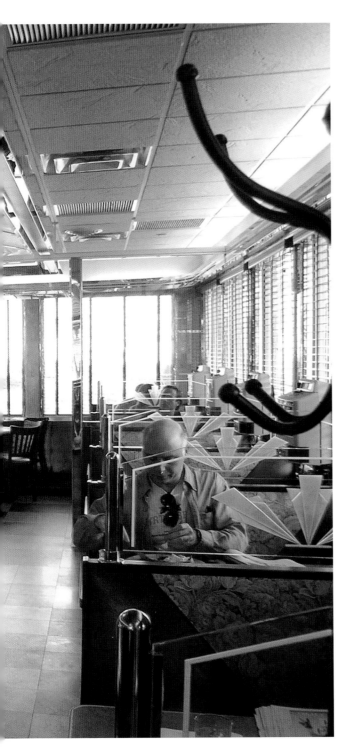

A classic American diner.

• FAST FOOD •

The American diner, thought of as a quintessentially American phenomenon, started life in Providence, Rhode Island in 1872, in the form of a horse-drawn wagon owned by a man named Walter Scott. He served sandwiches, coffee and other simple foods to employees of the *Providence Journal* from his booth outside its offices. Over the next two decades, mass-produced portable lunch wagons proliferated, and were followed in the early twentieth century by prefabricated, stationary eateries: the first true 'diners'.

Diners are known for their vast and diverse menus including 'comfort'-style food such as stews, freshly-baked fruit pies, hamburgers, hot fresh coffee, and full American breakfasts including pancakes, eggs, and French toast. Staying open late—sometimes 24 hours a day, seven days a week—the affordable and mostly family-run diner became extremely popular with Americans of all walks of life. The iconic architecture and interiors associated with American diners originated in the 1940s with the introduction of stainless steel to prefabricated construction, and then in the 1950s with the addition of Formica. Clean, smooth tiled, enameled and laminated surfaces characterised these buildings, and the long, dominating serving counter has remained a key aspect of diner design.

Below: An early McDonalds' restaurant.

Opposite: Every kids' favourite, the Happy Meal, complete with Ronald McDonald plastic toy.

In 1940, the first McDonald's restaurant existed as a drive-in hamburger bar in San Bernardino, California, off the famous Route 66 highway. The idea was to provide a speedy service with no waitresses or dine-in tables. The restaurant served a limited menu of hamburgers, chips, milkshakes and carbonated drinks. The creators, brothers Richard and Maurice McDonald, chose a cartoon man with a burger as a head, known as Speedee, as the restaurant's icon, representing the company's ethos by which food was cooked, packaged, and served with utmost assembly-line efficiency.

In 1954, a man named Ray Kroc arrived at the San Bernardino restaurant, which had bought a number of his Multimixer milkshake-making appliances. Kroc initiated an agreement with the McDonald brothers whereby he could franchise their brand across the whole country. By the 1960s, there were over 100 McDonalds franchises, all attracted by Kroc's marketing ingenuity; by the 1980s it was added to the 30-company Dow Jones Industrial Average. While still focused on hamburgers and milkshakes, McDonald's now also includes in its menu breakfast, salads, sandwich wraps, and fruit.

The success of Ray Kroc's chain—he bought the McDonald brothers out in 1961—inspired a new range of fast food franchises across America. Today the chain operates at over 31,000 worldwide with over 1.5 million employees, and is the largest chain of restaurants in the world.

CANDY, CAKES, SWEETS AND TREATS—AMERICAN JUNK FOOD CLASSICS

Both savoury and sweet, the spectrum of American junk food is wide. Containing artificial flavours, colourings and additives that the average consumer cannot even pronounce, never mind identify, junk food is the number one culprit of heart disease and obesity in America.

For those with a sweet tooth, popular classic indulgences include: Oreo cookies, Tootsie Rolls, Milk Duds, Junior Mints, Krispy Kreme donuts, M&M's, Hershey's chocolate, Skittles and Ben & Jerry's Ice Cream.

For those with a hankering for salty snacks there are the following 'classic' savoury treats: Slim Jim Beef Jerky, Doritoes, Lays, Wise and Ruffles brand potato chips, Cheetos, Fritos corn chips, Cheesz-it, fish fingers, Tater tots, potato skins topped with "the works", Goldfish snack crackers, Ritz crackers, and Orville Redenbacher, Jolly Time and Jiffy Pop popcorn, all of which can be washed down with a nice cold Coca-Cola, or Budweiser Beer.

And as if the lure was not tempting enough, some classics, such as Aunt Jemima Buttermilk Pancakes, Kraft Macaroni and Cheese, Campbell's soup, bagels, pizza, corn dogs, Sloppy Joes, Animal Crackers, candy apples, cotton candy, Twinkies, Jell-O, Kool-Aid and Cracker Jacks have become staples as American comfort food, as well as being strongly associated with American cultural nostalgia.

Opposite and left: Classic American treats—Oreos and Krispy Kremes.

Right: Ben & Jerry's ice cream.

Above: Frontispiece to Charles
Ranhofer's *The Epicurian*, 1894.

Opposite: Banquet in honour
of Frederick A Cook at the
Waldorf-Astoria, 1909.

THE EPICUREAN

Following a distinguished career,
Charles Ranhofer wrote *The
Epicurean* in 1894. Described by *The
New York Times* as "one of the most
complete treatises of the kind ever
published", it detailed his belief in the
equal importance of both preparation
and presentation. It is still held
in high regard and considered an
invaluable indication of high-class
dining in America's Gilded Age.

• FINE DINING •

Charles Ranhofer was born in France but moved to New York
to be the chef to the Russian consul. In 1862 he was hired by
Delmonico's restaurant, where he stayed until 1896. In the
period during which Ranhofer was head chef, the restaurant
came to be considered the finest of its kind in the country, and
its reputation has not waned since. Under Ranhofer's control,
Delmonico's served a fine-dining menu combining traditional
American ingredients with the *haute cuisine* influences of
classic French gastronomy. Delmonico's carried several dishes
on its menu that Ranhofer created himself, including Lobster
Paul Bert, Lobster Newberg and Baked Alaska. His dishes
tended to be named after well-known people, in particular
Delmonico's famous visitors. He also believed that soups
signified a benchmark of restaurant quality, ensuring that he
made them himself, and brought only the freshest seasonal
ingredients to the table.

A Park Avenue landmark, the Waldorf-Astoria was formed
when two neighbouring hotels owned by feuding cousins, the
Waldorf and the Astoria, came together in 1931. The 47-storey
building is renowned for its many famous residents, who
have included Herbert Hoover and Marilyn Monroe, and
for its many restaurants, bars and lounges. They include a
Japanese restaurant, an American brasserie, a steakhouse,
and a small restaurant that pays homage to the history of the
hotel. The Sunday brunch is a particularly celebrated Waldorf-
Astoria meal that continues to incorporate traditional dishes
from the hotel's earliest days. Typically, it consists of an
extravagant spread including dishes such as a carving station
of roast lamb, roast pork, and beef Wellington, luxury seafood
such as lobster, peeled king prawns and king crab, and the
hotel's signature Eggs Benedict.

Right: The Gold Room, at Brennan's restaurant in New Orleans.

Opposite: Salads being served at Galatoires restaurant.

Brennan's restaurant was founded in 1846 by Owen Edward Brennan and has been a staple of New Orleans' epicurean culture since, as well as a leader in imaginative cookery countrywide. Many now famous dishes were created there, including the famous Bananas Foster, made from a sumptuous mixture of alcohol, butter, spices and banana. The restaurant is also known for its wine cellar that boasts over 35,000 bottles. The world renowned status of the restaurant also stemmed from the fact that they only use the freshest ingredients available, as well as the elegant atmosphere in which the customers dine. A patio with

magnolias, foliage and trickling fountain set the scene for their traditional French Creole cuisine.

Galatoire's was founded in 1905. The traditional cuisine comes from family recipes brought over by French founder Jean Galatoire. Still family-owned, the restaurant maintains its authenticity. Until recently there was a strict 'no reservations' rule that forced queues to snake down Bourbon Street most nights of the week. The address certainly helped the restaurant secure its place among the best, as did its renowned Louisiana Creole cooking and consistently elegant service.

• WHAT I BELIEVE ABOUT COOKING •

ALICE WATERS, EXCERPT FROM CHEZ PANISSE MENU COOKBOOK

My approach to cooking is not radical or unconventional. It may seem so because we as a nation are so removed from any real involvement with the food we buy, cook, and consume. We have become alienated by frozen and hygienically sealed packages. Food should be experienced through the senses. What could be more voluptuous than a perfect unblemished apple right off the tree or more appealing than a briny fish straight from the sea? It is a fundamental fact that no cook, however creative and capable, can produce a dish of a quality higher than that of the raw ingredients.

Finding the best food sometimes seems complicated, but there is nothing very mysterious about it, nor is it something only restaurants can do. You only need to open your eyes. When we began our search for the best tasting foods, even here amid the abundance of California, our choices were limited. However, within a short time, an assortment of people began to show up at our kitchen door. Neighbours brought us bunches of radishes, sorrel and herbs from their backyards. A few eccentric foragers would arrive from time to time with baskets of chanterelles and morels, buckets of Pacific mussels, blackberries from the hills, and fish just hours out of the sea. All these beautiful foods were here, just waiting to be discovered. If possible, plant a garden yourself, and above all, patronise your local farmers market. There is no better place to find the best produce of the season—and usually at a good price, too. Always explore your garden and go to the market before your decide what to cook. Plan your menu around what you find there. Select produce that looks freshly harvested and at its peak—food that looks *alive*.

When I cook, I usually stand at my kitchen table. I may pick a bunch of thyme and lay it on the table; then I wander about the kitchen gathering up all the fresh ingredients I can find. I look at each foodstuff carefully, examining it with a critical eye and concentrating in such a way that I begin to make associations. While this method may appear chaotic to others, I do think best while holding a tomato or a leg of lamb. Sometimes I wander through the garden looking for something appealing, absorbing the bouquet of the earth and the scent of the fresh herbs. Sometimes I butterfly my way through cookbooks, quickly flipping the pages and absorbing a myriad of ideas about a particular food or concept. You can use these recipes and adapt them to your regional ingredients. Flexibility is an essential component of good cooking. In the early stages of my culinary pursuits, I cooked as I had seen cooking done in France. I copied some of the more traditional cooks, and I stayed within the bounds they had laid out so carefully because I didn't yet trust myself. I found that with time and experience, their fundamental principles had become a part of my nature, and I began to understand why they had done certain things in a particular way. It was then that I could begin to develop a different and more personal style based on the ingredients available to me here in California.

We all cook differently. My style of cooking involves combining ingredients that harmonise because of their quality, freshness, aroma and flavor. But learn to trust your own instincts and don't be fooled into believing that all the "gourmet" equipment and utensils are vital. To begin with, the terms "gourmet" or "gourmet cooking" have all the wrong associations for me: they somehow seem to imply that one is more interested in the gleaming copper pans than in what one is cooking, and certainly more impressed by them than the food itself. Strangely, some of the best times to cook are those occasions when you are faced with virtually nothing in terms of equipment—you must make do, improvise, and focus primarily on the food itself. So you may gather rosemary branches from the yard and use them to skewer the meat before you put in on to the charcoal grill. If you do, you will have learned something fundamental about food, unrestricted and unhampered by equipment.

When people come to the restaurant, I want to insist that they eat in a certain way, try new things, and take time with the food. I opened a restaurant so that everybody could come and eat. Remember that the final goal is to nourish and nurture those who gather at your table. And it is there, at the table, that I have found the greatest satisfaction and sense of accomplishment.

Text from Alice Waters *The Chez Pannisse Menu Cookbook*. © Alice Waters

JAMES BEARD

James Beard wrote some 22 books, including his classic *American Cookery*, during his 82 years. He is credited with beginning a revolution in American cuisine, not least because of his infectious writing style and sensual description of ingredients and the processes of cooking. More than a simple series of instructions, his books introduced the reader to the appreciation of each ingredient. His first book was *Hors d'Oeuvre and Canapés*, a compilation of his own recipes that he used when catering for cocktail parties. Although he cooked in a time when to cook seriously meant adhering to the French style, he showed the country that America, too, had a cuisine that could be as serious and as elegant as that across the Atlantic.

JULIA CHILD

Julia Child was one of the most famous and successful figures in twentieth century American cookery and food culture. In 1961 and 1970, she published her seminal *Mastering the Art of French Cooking*, a two-volume opus written in collaboration with Simone Beck and Louisette Bertholle. Earlier in her career she had studied in Paris at the renowned Le Cordon Bleu cooking school. It was during this period that she met Beck and Bertholle, with whom she began to teach cooking under the name *L'École des Trois Gourmandes* (*The School of the Three Gourmands*). When *Mastering the Art of French Cooking* was published it was an immediate success, and Child's specialism in French cookery generated great interest amongst its American audience, bringing classic French cookery to the mainstream. In 1963, she made her television cookery debut on her programme *The French Chef*, which continued to air for ten years. Child's television appearances cemented her position as a favourite in American culture, and became known for her catch phrase, "This is Julia Child, *bon appétit!*" Child published several other books and presented numerous programmes; in 2000 she was awarded the *Légion d'honneur* by the French government, and in 2003 was decorated with the Presidential Medal of Freedom in the United States.

Right: James Beard and Julia Child laugh together whilst cleaning a large fish on the TV show *Revolutionary Recipes*.

Opposite: Paul Prudhomme.

PAUL PRUDHOMME

It is probably chef Paul Prudhomme who made Cajun food popular throughout America and celebrated its Louisianan origins. In 1979, he and his wife opened a restaurant in the popular French district of New Orleans where they served red fish with Cajun seasoning. This dish, which had a reputation for being food for the poor, became very popular. He then went on to create and market seasoning for meat, vegetables and poultry.

Left: Martha Steward in her kitchen.
Right: Wolfgang Puck's *lacquered* duck.
Opposite: Wolfgang Puck.

MARTHA STEWART

Celebrity chef, Martha Stewart is as well known for her cooking, homemaking, and social etiquette as she is for her successful—and sometimes highly controversial—business ventures. Stewart has managed to penetrate a variety of media, such as television, magazines, book publishing, radio, internet and merchandising—and not least news broadcasts in 2004 following her conviction and prison sentence regarding a stock market scandal, further contributing to her status as a household name that Americans will not soon forget.

However, the scandal did not keep Stewart down. She is still as successful as ever. Her company, Martha Stewart Living Omnimedia Inc has recently agreed to collaborate with Gallo wine and fellow celebrity chef Emeril Lagasse. Stewart's recipes are classic, wholesome and "all American".

WOLFGANG PUCK

Austrian-born chef Wolfgang Puck began his culinary career cooking with his mother at home before moving to France to apprentice at several restaurants including the noted Maxim's Paris. Having moved to America aged 24, he became head chef at the fashionable Hollywood restaurant Ma Maison, and in 1981 published his first cookery book,

Modern French Cooking for the American Kitchen. One of America's most famous celebrity chefs, Puck's own culinary empire has expanded enormously, with restaurants, bistros and own-brand produce sold all over the world. In the 1980s, American chefs began to develop what has become known as "California Cuisine", characterised by an embracing of

the global influences upon American culinary traditions and the use of organic and high-quality ingredients. Amongst these chefs was Wolfgang Puck, whose Chinois restaurant can be seen as part of the Californian 'fusion' sensibility, innovatively blending Chinese and French-style cooking.

WYLIE DUFRESNE

Wylie Dufresne has been awarded a Michelin star for three consecutive years for his Manhattan-based restaurant wd-50, named after his initials and the building number in which it is located. Dufresne is known for championing a playful, innovative approach to cooking that attempts to use knowledge of the chemical processes involved in preparing food in order to perfect it. Dufresne's cuisine is primarily American with a creative twist as his signature dishes, Pickled Beef Tongue with Fried Mayonnaise and Carrot-Coconut Sunnyside-Up, suggest. No stranger to celebrity, Dufresne has appeared on the television programmes *Iron Chef America* and *Top Chef*, as both contestant and as judge. His restaurant wd-50 was ranked fourth in a list of New York's finest restaurants in *The New York Times* in 2006.

Left and right: Turbot, barbecued lentils, cauliflower and persimmon; Pistachio ice cream, pineapple and pandan, both from Wylie Dufresne's restaurant wd-50.

THOMAS KELLER

Thomas Keller is one of two chefs in the world with two restaurants each with three Michelin stars. He discovered his love for cooking while working at a yacht club, and developed a particular talent for *hollandaise* sauce. Without formal training, he apprenticed at various restaurants where he learned the fundamentals of cookery, and then honed his craft under various Michelin-starred chefs. Finally, in 1987, he opened his first restaurant, Rakel in New York, which specialised in a refined take on French cuisine. Catering to Wall Street traders with expensive tastes, it relied on the strength of stock market trading to keep its business buoyant, and predictably hit trouble as shares fell at the end of the decade. Keller, unwilling to change his cooking to cater for budget tastes, split with his partner at Rakel. Some years later, in 1994, Keller re-emerged with a restaurant in an old steam laundry in California. Named The French Laundry, it flourished and achieved critical success, and was soon coupled with another nearby restaurant, Bouchon. Keller finally returned to New York in 2004 to open Per Se. Built from scratch, it was an immediate and overwhelming success and, like The French Laundry that preceded it, earned him three Michelin stars.

Oysters and pearls by Thomas Keller.

Dried corn.

·EUROPEAN·
INFLUENCES

In the southern states of America, barbecue initially revolved around the cooking of pork, a low-maintenance food source for early American settlers during the nineteenth century. Prior to the American Civil War, southerners consumed more pork than they did any other animal, with every part of the pig eaten or stored—including knuckles, feet and internal organs. The effort involved in capturing and cooking wild hogs became recognised as a marked occasion, such that pig slaughtering became a festive celebration. These feasts, or "pig-pickin's", were the precursors of the modern barbecues prevalent across America.

Traditionally, among southern states, each locale has its own variety of barbecue, with particular methods and typical flavour combinations: in Eastern North Carolina, for example, barbecued food is typified by a vinegar-based sauce, whereas the centre of the state generally uses ketchup in addition. South Carolina is the only state which encompasses all four varieties of barbecue sauce types: mustard-based, vinegar-based, light tomato-based and heavy tomato-based. Texas is often most associated with the American barbecue,

and itself has four main regional variations in flavour and method. An example is the Central Texas Barbecue, influenced by the German and Czech immigrants who settled there in the mid-nineteenth century, who would smoke leftover cuts of meat over a high heat using native woods such as oak or pecan.

Another can be seen along the border between the south Texan Plains and northern Mexico, where barbecue is heavily influenced by Mexican tastes. The birthplace of the Texan ranching tradition, the regions' Mexican farmhands were often partially paid for their work in somewhat undesirable cuts of meat, including the diaphragm—used in fajitas—and cow's head, used in a defining barbecue dish called *baracoa*. The Western part of Texas typically produces a style of method known as "cowboy" barbecue, often cuts of beef cooked over an open pit using direct heat from mesquite wood. Because of the community-oriented nature of the barbecue, the term is often used to refer to a type of gathering across other parts of America, where food is cooked outside over an open grill and is particularly associated with traditional Independence Day celebrations.

Dessert table at a barbeque.

A French market in New Orleans, circa 1900.

FRENCH

Technically, "crab boil" is the seasoning that is used to flavour the water in which shellfish such as crab or crayfish (or "crawfish", to the locals) are boiled. In Louisiana, the term also encompasses any social gathering in which the shellfish are boiled and eaten. The boil typically includes cayenne pepper, hot sauce lemon, bay leaf and a heavy helping of salt, though the recipe can vary widely by region. In 1889, Zatarain's crab boil became available, a commercial crab boil product in concentrated liquid form. It is not uncommon for Louisianans to add extra hot sauce to the mixture to make it more fiery.

The deep south is also well-known for its Creole cuisine, often characterised by its intense spicy flavours and tendency to include seafood. The flavours and influences of the crab boil mirror the cultural make-up of the Creole natives: typically the food is thought to be a mixture of four cuisines from the Native Americans, the French and Spanish colonists, and the Africans who were brought over as slaves.

FRENCH CREOLE

The French market in New Orleans was first established back in 1791 in what is now known as the French quarter of the city. It is the oldest public market in the country and covers five blocks with open-air stalls and shops. Specialities supplied by local farmers include Creole herbs, spices and tomatoes, while well-known restaurants such as the Café du Monde which are clustered around the market, allow visitors to enjoy genuine Louisiana Creole cooking.

Gumbo, a ubiquitous Creole stew.

ITALIAN

Great numbers of Italians emigrated to America in the late nineteenth and early twentieth centuries. Those from rural areas of southern Italy dominated in the movement, and therefore Italian-American cuisine is heavily influenced by southern Italian staples, mostly from Sicily and Naples, such as dry pasta, tomato sauce, and olive oil, while northern influences differ slightly to include rice, butter and fresh pasta. East coast cities, such as New York and Boston boast large Italian-American communities, appropriately named "Little Italy", which is the place to go for the more authentically Italian dishes.

The greatest American influence on Italian food is the abundance of meat, particularly in *bolognaise* sauces, which was most likely not used as widely in Italy due to economics. Another American development is the regional adaptation which transforms simple traditional dishes into indulgent complexities of flavour, for instance, *Rigatoni alla Vodka*, a dish which emerged out of New York in the late 1970s. The *alla vodka* sauce combines, heavy cream, tomato paste and vodka and is usually served with the cured Italian ham *prosciutto* or prawns.

Wine often accompanies Italian-American dishes and Chianti stands out as an affordable favourite amongst diners.

Italian food in America has its own range of convenience and frozen food products as well as fast food chains. Top brands that have withstood the test of time include Ragu brand jarred sauce, Ellio's frozen pizza, and Chef Boyardee canned pasta and meatballs. Equally popular fast food chains which have flourished around the world include Pizza Hut and Domino's Pizza.

On the sweeter side, Italian pastries that have become American favourites include, *zeppole, cannoli, tiramisu,* and *spumoni*. The *zeppole* is usually prepared by frying dough, although it can be baked. Sometimes it will contain a filling of custard of *ricotta* cheese, but traditionally it is a ring of fried dough with no filling sprinkled with white powdered sugar on top. It is commonly accepted that the origins of the *zeppole* lies in Sicily and was initially part of St Joseph's Day, a festival that began in the middle ages to celebrate the end of a draught and is still celebrated annually on 19 March. *Cannolis* are also attributed to the Sicilians, and consist of flaky pastry shells, in the shape of a tube filled with sweetened *ricotta* or *mascarpone* cheeses. There are many variations for the filling; for instance, chocolate chips or sprinkles can be added and sometime vanilla or chocolate flavouring is added to the filling itself, and for that extra indulgence some might enjoy their *cannolis* dipped in chocolate.

Tiramisu originates from either Venice or Sienna, depending on who you ask. It is a layered cake, prepared with lady finger biscuits which are soaked in *espresso* and topped with a layer of light cream consisting of egg yolks, *mascarpone* cheese, sugar, chocolate and Marsala wine or brandy topped with a dusting of cocoa.

Spumoni came to America via Naples and consists of layered flavours of ice cream, usually vanilla, chocolate and strawberry and sometimes contains fruits or nuts in between the layers. The ice cream is usually whipped with cream for a light texture. It is uncommon to find this dessert in Italy today but it is still very popular in Italian communities throughout the United States.

80·2 STREET VENDER, ITALIAN FEAST

Mr. Broadway Kosher Restaurant, New York City.

JEWISH

Between 1830 and the end of the First World War, approximately six million Jewish immigrants from Germany and Eastern Europe immigrated to the United States. Jewish-American food developed, particularly in Cincinnati, Ohio, in the form of American-influenced adaptations such as the substitution of carp with salmon in the cooking of gefilte fish, patties comprising a mixture of ground boneless fish, traditionally made with carp or pike. Jewish grocers and delicatessens developed due to the demand for kosher foods which conform to Jewish religious guidelines.

Street vendors began selling herring and snack foods such as knishes—deep fried, potato pockets with fillings such as sauerkraut or cheese. Mass-production and technological developments in food through the years also brought some of the most famous and successful kosher food products, such as Heinz tomato ketchup, and Crisco vegetable shortening into the market.

Soup with matzah balls.

·ASIAN·
INFLUENCES

San Francisco boasts the largest Japanese-American community, often referred to as "Japantown" or "Little Osaka" equipped with specialty shops, where one can find not only Japanese foodstuffs but Korean and Chinese as well. Japantown is a favourite amongst both tourists and locals for its wide variety of teas and world-renowned sushi.

A selection of Asian and American influenced sushi.

Chinatown, San Francisco, in the nineteenth century.

While most major cities have a Chinese sector, San Francisco's Chinatown, established in the mid-1800s, is the largest of its kind in America. Being one of North America's coastal cities nearest Asia, it acted as a doorway into the country for thousands of Chinese immigrants in the nineteenth century. Chinatowns historically serve both as meeting-places for Chinese communities, but also cater widely to tourists for economic value. The San Francisco Chinatown continues to play host to a great variety of restaurants, from those specifically geared to the American market serving *chop suey* and *chow mein* noodles, to more authentic, home-style restaurants that often specialise in regional varieties of cooking.

Chinois lobster roll by Wolfgang Puck.

"Fusion" cooking—referring to the merging of flavours and techniques from differing world regions—has become a gastronomic methodology particularly characteristic of contemporary American cuisine. The term is particularly used in reference to Asian-inspired cookery, where Asian ingredients may be used to construct 'American' dishes, or traditionally American ingredients are cooked using Asian techniques.

Many Chinese communities formed across the United States in the nineteenth century, as thousands of Chinese arrived in the country. Many Chinese established restaurants and simple eateries, gradually beginning to steer their traditional cuisine towards American tastes. In the twentieth century, many dishes were invented that subsequently became part of the American-Chinese culinary mainstream. These include *chop suey*, chicken with cashew nuts, and the famous fortune cookie. *Chop suey*, a stew-like dish of meat, cabbage, celery and bean sprouts, served with rice, noodles, or even macaroni, can be found on the menus of many Chinese restaurants, despite its obviously American roots.

However, the fusion of cultural cuisines has a long-standing place in the history of cookery, and has often been the starting-point for some of the most innovative and successful dishes and restaurants. Wolfgang Puck, one of America's most famous chefs, has built a career through taking inspiration from Asian food, and serves dishes such salads with chicken flavoured with Chinese-style sauce.

The fortune you seek is in another cookie.

· MEXICAN ·
INFLUENCES

Indigenous foods of pre-Columbian Mexico included *Xocolatl* (chocolate), maize, corn, beans, squash, avocado, *sapote*, chilli peppers, turkey and fish. Meats, such as beef, pork, and chicken, onions, garlic and rice arrived with the Spanish. The western states of California, Arizona, New Mexico and Texas which border Mexico are most heavily influenced by Mexican culture and are certainly the best destinations for authentic Mexican dishes, however, Mexican food is readily available throughout the country.

Americans use more cheese than is commonly used in Mexico as well as putting their own spin on traditionally Mexican dishes, for instance, nachos, which became popular in America. Tex-Mex is one of the more popular variations and is essentially the combination of Mexican, Spanish and American influences.

In the west and southwest states, there is an abundance of independently owned Mexican food shops in addition to the top two fast food chains, Taco Bell and Del Taco.

Packaging for Old El Paso, distributed by Betty Crocker in America.

A selection of Mexican-influenced dishes.

• INDEX •

• S •

• CREDITS •

• INTRODUCTION •

7 Courtesy of Cirio
9 Courtesy of the National Hot Dog Council

• FRANCE •

10-11 Courtesy of denn
20 Courtesy of La Tour d'Argent, Paris
23 Courtesy of Le Grand Véfour
24 Courtesy of DK Images
26 "The Marquis de Sade's Sweet Tooth". Reprinted from Medlar Lucan and Durian's Gray's *The Decadent Cookbook*, 1995, courtesy of Dedalus
35 Courtesy of the Collection of the Foundation of Auguste Escoffier, Villeneuve-Loubet, France (06)
38 "French Culinary and Table Slang". *New Larousse Gastronomique*, Prosper Montagné, 160/1977/1986, courtesy Octopus Publishing Group
40 Courtesy of Restaurant Lasserre
41 Courtesy of Maxim's Paris
42-43 Courtesy of the Maison Troisgros Archives
44 Courtesy of Octopus Publishing Group
45 Courtesy of Paul Bocuse
46-47 Photography by Francis Giacobetti
48 "Nouvelle Cuisine", *Table Talk* by AA Gill and Weidenfeld and Nicolson, an imprint of the Orion Publishing Group, London. Reprinted by kind permission of AA Gill.
50-51 Courtesy of Paul Bocuse
52 All images courtesy of Joël Robuchon
53 All images courtesy of Pierre Gagnaire
57 Courtesy of traveleden
58 Courtesy of Jean Louis Zimmerman
61 Courtesy of alh1
64 Roland Barthes, "Steak and Chips", *Mythologies*, published by Jonathan Cape. Reprinted by permission of the Random House Group Ltd., Hill and Wang and Edition du Seuil.
65 Courtesy of psd
67 Courtesy of star S112
73 Courtesy of Larousse
76 Courtesy of yoppy
77 Courtesy of Stock Food
79 Courtesy of BocaDorade

• ENGLAND •

84 *The Forme of Cury*: reproduced by courtesy of the University Librarian and Director of The John Ryands University Library, The University of Manchester
100-101 Courtesy of The Ritz Hotel London, © The Ritz Hotel, London
108 "Savoury Puddings". *Modern Cookery for Private Families*, Eliza Acton, with an Introduction by Elizabeth Ray, published by Southover Press, 1993, pp. 336-337. Reprinted by permission of Equinox Publishing Ltd.
116 Courtesy of Gordon Joly
117 Courtesy of Pink Fish13
118 Courtesy of Topfoto
119 Courtesy of Geoff Wilkinson/Rex Features
120 Courtesy of Getty Images, photography by Marco Secchi
121 Courtesy of Getty Images, photography by Chris Terry
122-123 Courtesy of Kristen Taylor
125 Courtesy of Toby Barnes
126 "Fish". From 'A La Carte', from *The Enjoyment of Food: The Best of Jane Grigson*. © Sophie Grigson. 1992. Published by Penguin. Courtesy of David Higham Associates
128 Courtesy of EG Focus
130 Courtesy of Richard Moross
132 Courtesy of The Ritz Hotel London, © The Ritz Hotel, London
133 Courtesy of Craig Morey
135 Courtesy of Matt Biddulph
136 Courtesy of Liliana
139 Courtesy of Roland Tanglao
140 Courtesy of Alex Kehr
141 Courtesy of Charles Haynes
142 Courtesy of Tracy N Brandon
143 Courtesy of Beck
145 Courtesy of Erik van der Neut
147 Courtesy of Neal's Yard Dairy, photography by Simon Tobias

• ITALY •

• SPAIN •

• AMERICA •

270-271 From *Betty Crocker's New Picture Cook Book*, first edition, © General Mills Inc., courtesy of General Mills

272 From *Betty Crocker's New Picture Cook Book*, first edition, © General Mills Inc., courtesy of General Mills

276 Right: Courtesy of Library of Congress

277 Courtesy of Shanta

278 Right: Courtesy of Library of Congress

279-287 Courtesy of Library of Congress

288 From 'How Not to Boil and Egg' by MFK Fisher, from *How to Cook a Wolf*, included in *The Art of Eating*, published by Wiley Publishing, Inc. © 1942, 1954, 2004 by MFL Fisher. Reprinted with permission of Lescher and Lescher, Ltd. All rights reserved

292-293 All © General Mills Inc., courtesy of General Mills

294 Courtesy of adonis hunter

295 Left: Courtesy of Kellog Company

296 © General Mills Inc., courtesy of General Mills

297-299 Courtesy of Pinnacle Foods Group LLC

300 "Hot Dogs" and "Hot Dog Etiquette". Text reproduced courtesy of the National Hot Dog and Sausage Council, American Meat Institute

301-303 All images courtesy of the National Hot Dog Council

304-305 Courtesy of gailf548

306-307 All images courtesy of McDonald's Corporation

311 Courtesy of the Library of Congress

312 Courtesy of Louis Sahuc

314 "What I Believe About Cooking". Text from Alice Waters *The Chez Panisse Menu Cookbook*. © Alice Waters

316 Courtesy of Time & Life Pictures and Getty Images

317 Courtesy of Rex Features

318 Left: Courtesy of Getty Images
Right: Courtesy of Johan Ormond

319 Courtesy of Lisa Romerein

320 Top and left: Courtesy of Wylie Dufresne
Right: Courtesy of Joyce George

321 Left: Courtesy of Deborah Jones

322-323 Courtesy of IrisDragon

324 Courtesy of Library of Congress

325 Courtesy of D'Arcy Norman

326 Courtesy of Library of Congress

327 Courtesy of the Southern Foodways Alliance

328 Courtesy of Library of Congress

331 Courtesy of ydhsu

332 Courtesy of syvwich

334 Courtesy of John Ormond

335 Courtesy of orangachang

In-house photography by Katie Fechtmann and Alex Wright

• ACKNOWLEDGEMENTS •

Many thanks to everyone involved in making *A Visual History of Cookery* the vibrant book that it is. Gratitude must first be given to all the contributors, whose eclectic texts give each chapter a thought provoking focal point. Also, special thanks must be given to each of the chefs featured, who readily offered mouth watering material to the book.

Thank you also to the various organisations, groups, businesses and restaurants involved, without whom the book would not be what it is; most notably: the Slow Food Organisation, Neal's Yard Dairy, Betty Crocker, Carluccio and the Renaissance Cookbook and James Prescott for his Le Viandier de Taillevent translation.

And special thanks to all the designers involved in the project: Johanna Bonnevier, Matt Bucknall, Rachel Pfleger, Live Molvaer, Alex Wright, and Katie Fechtmann, the latter of whom must also be thanked for her stylish photography throughout. Also thanks to Rosie French, James Trant, Kate Trant, Elizabeth Waite, Aimee Selby, Sophie Hallam, Phoebe Adler, Tom Howells, Nikos Kotsopoulos, and Stephanie Cottela-Tanner for their various inputs to the book.

Black Dog Publishing Limited
10A Acton Street
London
WC1X 9NG

t. +44 (0)207 713 5097
f. +44 (0)207 713 8682
e. info@blackdogonline.com

All opinions expressed within this publication are those
of the authors and not necessarily of the publisher.

British Library Cataloguing-in-Publication Data.
A CIP record for this book is available from the British Library.

ISBN 978 1 906155 50 6

Every effort has been made to trace the copyright holders,
but if any have been inadvertently overlooked the necessary
arrangements will be made at the first opportunity.

Black Dog Publishing is an environmentally responsible
company. *A Visual History of Cookery* is printed on FSC
accredited paper.

architecture art design
fashion history photography
theory and things

www.blackdogonline.com